Shadowing Ralph Ellison

John S. Wright

Shadowing

Ralph Ellison

University Press of Mississippi / JACKSON

Margaret Walker Alexander Series
in African American Studies

www.upress.state.ms.us

The University Press of Mississippi is a member of the
Association of American University Presses.

∞

Library of Congress Cataloging-in-Publication Data
Wright, John.
    Shadowing Ralph Ellison / John Wright. — 1st ed.
        p. cm. — (Margaret Walker Alexander series in African American studies)
    Includes bibliographical references (p.   ) and index.
    ISBN 1-57806-850-9 (alk. paper)
    1. Ellison, Ralph—Criticism and interpretation. 2. African Americans in literature.
    I. Title. II. Series.
    PS3555.L625Z96 2006
    818'.5409—dc22

                                                                                            2006003519

British Library Cataloging-in-Publication Data available

For Boyd and Mae,

Martha and Wilmette,

Beryl and Lock,

Warren and Katherine,

Fanny and Ralph

Dance and mask collect their greasepaint,

idioms stand on bandstand, in stove-

pipe pants of riverman, gambling shoes,

gold-tooth venom vexing sundown,

the choir at sunrise-service cleansing

a life on a jim crow funeral car.

The first true phrase sings out in barnyard;

the hunt in books for quail.

—MICHAEL S. HARPER

Going to the Territory: Icons of Geography of the Word:
A Meditation on the Life and Times of Ralph Waldo Ellison

Contents

Acknowledgments

Shadowing Ralph Ellison has been harvested from what may be a terminal case of prolonged and aggravated distraction. The book has been gestating over the course of two decades—from its genesis in the pioneering Ralph Ellison Festival that Michael Harper organized at Brown University in 1979, on through a series of literary occasions centered on Ralph Ellison that surfaced intermittently up until his death in 1994, and after. When Professor Harper originally invited me to participate in the Ralph Ellison Festival and to coedit contributions to a resulting publication of poetry, essays, and fiction, I was already embarked on a forbiddingly complex, cross-continental, multicentury research project on post-Enlightenment black intellectual history. In it Ralph Ellison's work itself played only a small part. But the project's framing conceptions had been powerfully shaped by his speculative thinking about the interplay between classical and vernacular culture, the history and sociology of ideas, the environing powers of geography, and the rapidity and omnipresence of technological change. When he and I talked periodically about this loose and baggy monster, he found it fascinating but dangerously ambitious—echoing issues he had himself confronted in the long agons with *Invisible Man* and its unbirthed successor. So, characteristically, he, with Fanny Ellison in chorus, counseled me to let no one distract me from my project. The irony, of course, was that he himself had become my major "distraction" and would continue to be. So over the years, as if I were one of the figments of his frolicking imagination, I have boomeranged back and forth between two irresistible compulsions.

If Michael Harper bears the responsibility and credit for the initial instigation, and Ralph and Fanny Ellison for encouraging me not to be discouraged, then my colleagues at several sites along the way have also been crucial parts of the process. At Carleton College the friends and editorial faculty of the *Carleton Miscellany*—Keith Harrison and Robert Tisdale in particular—lent unstinting support in the course of getting the special Ellison issue, and my title essay along with it, out into the light of day. Across town in Northfield at St. Olaf College, Professors David Vassar Taylor and John Edgar Tidwell patiently entertained my ramblings and kept me moored as much as possible to intellectual terra firma. They have continued to do so, whether near or far, throughout the years. In California's Bay Area, where the editorial work on the festival issue was largely completed and "Shadowing Ellison" composed, Arnold Rampersad, then hard at work on his prizewinning biography of Langston Hughes, advised me knowingly about how to live with my compulsions and distractions. Now, many years later when he has found himself, too, caught up in Ellisonian compulsions, he has generously shared his enormous wisdom once more in leading me out of quandary. Among the original Ralph Ellison Festival participants, Nathan Scott sustained my resolve; Robert Stepto restored my confidence; and John Callahan, as literary executor, has supplied a warm welcome to the Ellison Papers at the Library of Congress. Among my colleagues at the University of Pittsburgh Ellison conference run so ably by Ronald Judy and Jonathan Arac in 2002, Robert O'Meally, Hortense Spillers, and Kenneth Warren shared their rich insights and enthusiasm—and entertained my protracted musings.

At Harvard's W. E. B. DuBois Institute, I sojourned repeatedly, first under Nathan Huggins's solicitous tenure and later on, when Henry Louis Gates, Jr., assumed the mantle of leadership. I found there an almost ideal setting for testing ideas seriously and safely and for forming lasting ties. During my early stints there as a research fellow, staff members Randall Burkett and Richard Newman, both with encyclopedic interests and scholarly skills to match, made themselves pleasurably indispensable. During three years of Rockefeller Foundation support in the early 1990s, the W. E. B. DuBois Institute's Working Group on Black Intellectual History provided one of the most intense and rewarding scholarly experiences of my career. I owe a great debt of gratitude to many of its members and friends: Anthony Appiah, David Blight, Hazel Carby, Trudier Harris, Isaac Julien, Randall Kennedy, Deborah McDowell, William McFeely, Isidore Okpewho,

Robert O'Meally, Amritjit Singh, Wilson Moses, Orlando Patterson, Richard Powell, Jeffrey Stewart, Jerry Watts, Cornel West, and Francile Wilson among them. Similarly, at the Schomburg Center for Research in Black Culture, where I became a scholar in residence, in close proximity to the Ellisons, Director Howard Dodson and Research Director Diana Lachatanere made the environs of the New York Public Library system a genuinely hospitable space for research and spirited exchange. As intellectual guides and guardians for the scholars in residence, Hylan Lewis and Arnold Rampersad, once again, served us with diligence and grace and helped make Harlem seem so very much like home.

Intellectual homes-away-from-home such as these would not have been accessible, however, were it not for the support of regional and national foundations devoted to humanities scholarship and education; and I have been blessed with such support through the years. The National Endowment for the Humanities, the National Research Council Postdoctoral Fellowship Program, and the Bush Foundation Leadership Program all awarded support for my scholarly compulsions and distractions—for which no thanks would be enough. At the University of Minnesota, my primary safehold now for many years, generous leaves while working on this book have been made possible by the College of Liberal Arts Sabbatical Grant Program and, most recently, by the President's Faculty Multicultural Research Awards. Besides such welcome financial sustenance, I have been sustained as well by intellectual sharings with many of my colleagues in the African American & African Studies, American Studies, English, and History Departments and in the MacArthur Program. In fielding the stream of conjecture flowing steadily out of me over the years, however, I am afraid that Professors William Banfield, Lary May, August Nimtz, Alexs Pate, and Rob Silberman have born the greatest burden; and for that I owe them great compensation in one form or another. In fielding my ceaseless stream of challenges to the library sciences, the entire reference staff of Wilson Library deserves recognition and Dennis Lien, that unflappable *enfant terrible* of cyberspace and speculative fiction, immediate knighthood.

Nevertheless, for scholars to connect finally with listeners and readers who are not so close at hand, their work must make its way into print; and to Seetha Srinivasan and Walter Biggins, I am particularly indebted for shepherding this manuscript patiently and caringly to press. Along the way

I have had the great fortune of being invited to contribute portions of this book to published volumes edited by Kimberly Benston, John Callahan, Ronald Judy and Jonathan Arac, Lary May, Robert O'Meally, and Ross Posnock—all scholars of remarkable achievement who have found in Ralph Ellison's creative and critical outpourings, as I have, cause for celebration and close study. In addition to their work, monographs new and not so new by Lawrence Jackson, Alan Nadel, Robert O'Meally, again, Horace Porter, Jerry Watts, and Kenneth Warren—in addition to forthcoming books by Barbara Foley and Arnold Rampersad—bode well for the legacy of Ellison scholarship. Distracted or compelled as the case may be, I look forward to the ongoing feast; and I extend my thanks again to all those who have helped make possible my own contribution to the welcome table. Closest at hand of all, these include the members of my family and the many friends who have kept the faith with me through the years. Most of all, such thanks are due over and over to my incomparably loyal and lovely wife, Serena.

Chronology of Ralph Ellison's Life, Contacts, and of Relevant Events

1913   Ralph Ellison born March 1 in Oklahoma City to Lewis
        Alfred Ellison, an ice and coal dealer, and Ida Millsap,
        a church stewardess.

1916   On July 19, Lewis dies at age 39 after an accident hauling ice.
        Ida now sole support of two sons, Ralph and Herbert (born
        one month before Lewis's death). Ida works as domestic and
        hotel worker.

1919   Ellison family moves into African Methodist Episcopal
        church parsonage, where Ida works as sexton. Ralph
        frequents church library, begins first grade at Frederick
        Douglass School.

1920–24 Ellison family leaves parsonage, lives precariously in rented
        rooms and houses. Ida marries laborer James Ammons, who
        dies a year later. Ralph mows lawns in exchange for trumpet
        lessons from Ludwig Hebestreit, conductor of Oklahoma
        City Orchestra. Inman Page leaves Langston University,
        becomes principal at Douglass school.

1927–30 As member of Zelia Page Breaux's Douglass Junior and
        High School Band, Ellison plays classical trumpet, studies
        symphonic composition, frequents Breaux's Aldridge
        Theater to hear southwestern blues, jazz, and swing by Blue
        Devils, "Hot Lips" Paige, and others. Studies the Harlem

Renaissance in Alain Locke's *The New Negro*. Dreams of becoming a Renaissance man. Reads *Vanity Fair* magazine and becomes aware of Edmund Wilson and cosmopolitan high culture. Builds radio crystal sets with boyhood friend, Hoolie, whose intellectual adventurousness he admires.

1932   Graduates from Douglass High School, achieves first chair as trumpeter in school band.

1933   Wins scholarship to music school at Tuskegee Institute, plans to study with composer William Dawson. Follows trial of the Scottsboro Boys. Hoboes his way by train to Alabama, is rousted from train by armed railroad detectives. Arrives at Tuskegee with two bandaged head wounds that leave visible scars. Does not explain.

1933–34   Faced with indifference from Dawson, studies instead with Hazel Harrison, who becomes mentor. Forms close ties with Morteza Sprague, youthful chair of Tuskegee English Department and a protégé of Alain Locke and Sterling Brown.

1935   Transfers allegiance from music school to English department, discovers T. S. Eliot's *The Waste Land*, begins to write poetry, studies the modernist avant-garde. Tuskegee freshman Albert Murray admires him at a distance. Murray discovers André Malraux as fashionable icon.

1936   Leaves Tuskegee for summer, planning to return for degree; arrives in Harlem on July 4. Meets Alain Locke again, who introduces him to Langston Hughes. Hughes loans him André Malraux's *Man's Fate* and *Days of Wrath*, which lead him to *Man's Hope* two years later, where he discovers Spanish philosopher-novelist Miguel de Unamuno. Studies sculpture with Augusta Savage and Richmond Barthé, works as file clerk and receptionist for psychiatrist Harry Stack Sullivan. Hughes introduces Ellison to leftist literary and cultural circles. Decides not to return to Tuskegee.

1937   Hughes introduces Ellison to Richard Wright, who has moved from Chicago to head Harlem bureau of the Communist Party's *Daily Worker*. As coeditor with

Dorothy West of *New Challenge*, Wright invites Ellison's
first book review; Wright radicalizes Ellison's political and
literary perspectives. Hears Malraux speak in New York on
antifascist fund-raising tour for Spanish Civil War loyalists.
Attends Communist Party-sponsored League of American
Writers Congress, where he hears Kenneth Burke lecture on
"The Rhetoric of Hitler's Battle" and begins studying Burke's
philosophy of literary form and theories of symbolic action.
Mother dies October 16 in Dayton, Ohio. Spends winter
hunting and selling quail for income.

1938   Returns to New York and, with Wright's help, takes job with
Federal Writers Project researching history of blacks in
New York, a job he keeps until 1942. Marries dancer-actress
Rose Poindexter. Works as reviewer for Party-sponsored
New Masses. Declines Party membership but stays a "fellow
traveler."

1939   Publishes first short story, "Slick Gonna Learn," in *Direction*.
Meets C. L. R. James in New York through Wright, discusses
James's Trotskyite views of American culture and of
revolutionary politics.

1940–41   Publishes short stories and reviews in New York magazines.
In May 1940, attends Third National Negro Congress,
a coalition movement he calls "the first real basis for faith
in our revolutionary potentialities" in report for *New Masses*.
Meets poet-scholar Melvin Tolson while Tolson works on
thesis about Harlem Renaissance and shares his attraction
to communist ideals. Reads drafts of Wright's *Native Son*,
hails it in review as "first philosophical novel by an American
Negro." Marriage in dissolution by 1941. Supports A. Philip
Randolph march on Washington movement that spurs
Franklin Delano Roosevelt to desegregate U.S. defense
industries. Reviews "recent Negro fiction" and William
Attaway's *Blood on the Forge* in *New Masses*. Review of
Langston Hughes's autobiography, *The Big Sea*, praises
Hughes but deplores excesses and dependencies of Harlem
Renaissance.

1942   Coedits four issues of *Negro Quarterly* with Angelo Herndon; supports wartime "Double V" campaign and develops cultural analysis increasingly at odds with Stalinist position of *New Masses*. Empathizes with Wright's renouncing Party membership.

1943   Eludes service in Jim Crow U.S. Army by enlisting in integrated Merchant Marines for two years; organizes for National Maritime Union, works as cook. Reviews Bucklin Moon novel "The Darker Brother" in esotericist literary journal *Tomorrow*. Publishes more short stories. Meets Kenneth Burke and establishes friendship. Reports on Harlem riots for the *New York Post*.

1944–45   Publishes "King of the Bingo Game" and "Flying Home," which he regards as first mature achievements in fiction. Meets theater worker and Urban League staffer Fanny McConnell, who shares literary interests. Reviews Wright's *Black Boy* in *Antioch Review*, framing first major statement of an existentialist blues aesthetic. Divorce decree completed. Wins Rosenwald Fellowship to write war novel on black pilot captured in German prisoner of war camp. Returns from war zone in Europe in April 1945. Presents draft of "Twentieth Century Fiction and the Black Mask of Humanity" at Conference of Psychologists and Writers. Goes with Fanny to Vermont farm to recuperate. Meditates on dilemmas of black leadership in war and peace. Reads Lord Raglan's *The Hero* and section of James Joyce's *Ulysses* where pantomime figure declares "I am the boy that can enjoy invisibility." In state of "hyper-receptivity," writes line "I am an invisible man." Kernel of new idea for novel emerges.

1946–52   Marries Fanny McConnell, who gives up her literary career to support his. She supplies main financial support for seven years while he writes *Invisible Man* and tries to supplement income with sales of freelance photography and by building hi-fi amplifiers under tutelage of musician-recording engineer David Sarser. Publishes short story, "Invisible Man," in *Horizon*, which becomes "Battle Royal" chapter of *Invisible*

Man. Anatole Broyard publishes "portraits" of hipsters and "inauthentic Negroes" in *Partisan Review* and *Commentary.* Lionel Trilling collects essays written during the 1940s as *The Liberal Imagination* in 1950, prophesies the "death of the novel." Reinhold Niebuhr's *The Nature and Destiny of Man* and Arthur Schlesinger's *The Vital Center* combine with Trilling's work to define core of the New Liberalism.

1952   *Invisible Man* published by Random House in April, reaches number eight on *New York Times* best-seller list. Theologian literary scholar Nathan Scott publishes *Rehearsals of Discomposure,* a study of alienation and reconciliation in modern literature by Franz Kafka, Ignazio Silone, T. S. Eliot.

1953   *Invisible Man* wins National Book Award on January 27; Ellison meets William Faulkner for the first time that day. James Baldwin publishes first novel, *Go Tell It on the Mountain.* C. L. R. James publishes *Mariner, Renegades, and Castaways,* written at Ellis Island deportation center.

1955–57   Awarded Prix de Rome Fellowship by the American Academy of Arts and Letters; wins a Rockefeller Foundation Award and stays in Rome until 1957. Publishes "Society, Morality, and the Novel" in Granville Hicks's *The Living Novel.* Baldwin publishes *Notes of a Native Son* in 1955. E. Franklin Frazier publishes *Black Bourgeoisie* in 1957.

1958   Begins writing Hickman stories. Lectures on Russian and American literature at Bard College until 1961. Shares house with Saul Bellow. Publishes essay exchange with Stanley Edgar Hyman, "Change the Joke and Slip the Yoke."

1960   Publishes "And Hickman Arrives," first of eight excerpts from novel in progress to be published over next seventeen years. Publishes essay "Stephen Crane and the Mainstream of American Fiction." English translation of Jean Genet's *The Blacks: A Clown Show* is published; New York production begins May 1961, runs for three years of record-breaking performances. Richard Wright dies in Paris.

1961   Accepts appointment to National Association for the Advancement of Colored People Legal Defense Fund

	Committee of 100, endorsing fund-raising for defense of Southern sit-ins, protests, Freedom Rides. Remains on Committee of 100 until 1969.
1962	Visiting Professor of Writing at Rutgers University until 1969. Students include Black Arts literary martyr, Henry Dumas, who plans counternovel, *Visible Man*. Baldwin publishes *The Fire Next Time*.
1963	Publishes excerpt cut from *Invisible Man*, "Out of the Hospital and Under the Bar." Responds to Irving Howe review, "Black Boys and Native Sons," by publishing "The World and the Jug," two-part rejoinder that declares intellectual freedom and defines artistic credo. March on Washington led by Martin Luther King, Jr. W. E. B. DuBois dies in exile in Ghana. LeRoi Jones publishes *Blues People: Negro Music in White America*, theoretical forerunner of Black Arts outlook.
1964	Publishes *Shadow and Act*, collecting two decades of nonfiction prose. LeRoi Jones stages *Dutchman and the Slave*, inaugurating Black Theater movement. *Dutchman* reworks subway motifs from *Invisible Man*. Harsh review of Jones's *Blues People* sparks ongoing animosity.
1965	Becomes member of the National Council of the Arts, forerunner of the National Endowment for the Arts and the National Endowment for the Humanities. *Book Week* poll of leading critics selects *Invisible Man* as best American novel of post–World War II era. Publishes Hickman story, "Juneteenth." Larry Neal publishes *Liberator* series attacking Wright, Baldwin, and Ellison. Malcolm X is assassinated; Alex Haley publishes *The Autobiography of Malcolm X* a few months later.
1966	Named to Carnegie Commission on Educational Television and serves on commission for nine years; witness at Senate subcommittee hearing on urban issues; lectures at Yale University and Library of Congress. Grove Press publishes English edition of Frantz Fanon's *The Wretched of the Earth* with preface by Jean Paul Sartre.

1967   Loses over 350 pages of Hickman manuscript in fire at Massachusetts summer home. Becomes vice president of the National Institute of Arts and Letters. Stokely Carmichael and Charles Hamilton publish *Black Power: The Politics of Liberation in America.* Harold Cruse publishes *The Crisis of the Negro Intellectual,* which defends Ellison against black nationalist and Marxist critiques. Langston Hughes dies.

1968   Publishes "The Myth of the Flawed White Southerner" in James McGregor Burns's *To Heal and Build,* in support of President Lyndon Johnson's civil rights and Great Society domestic programs despite his opposition to Johnson's Vietnam War policy. LeRoi Jones and Larry Neal publish *Black Fire,* manifesto anthology of Black Arts Movement with rejection of *Invisible Man* in afterword by Neal. Julius Lester publishes *Look Out, Whitey! Black Power's Gon' Get Your Mama.* Assassinations of Martin Luther King, Jr., and Robert Kennedy adversely affect Ellison's novel in progress.

1969   Awarded Medal of Freedom, nation's highest civilian honor, by President Johnson at White House. James Alan McPherson publishes short story collection, *Hue and Cry,* with book jacket praise from Ellison for pursuing craftsmanship rather than "publicity-stained" polemics, angering black literary radicals.

1970–79   Appointed Albert Schweitzer Professor of the Humanities, New York University.

1970   Awarded the Chevalier de l'Ordre des Artes et Lettres in New York French consulate by decree of longtime intellectual hero André Malraux, Minister of Cultural Affairs for Charles De Gaulle. Ellison issue of *Black World* publishes Ernest Kaiser denunciation of *Invisible Man* and Larry Neal turnabout defense, "Ellison's Zoot Suit." Toni Morrison publishes first novel, *The Bluest Eye,* which presents womanist revision of Trueblood episode from *Invisible Man.*

1971   Addison Gayle, Jr., publishes *The Black Aesthetic,* critical anthology of Black Arts cultural theories and manifestoes.

1973	Publishes "Cadillac Flambé" excerpt of Hickman manuscript. Tom Wolfe publishes *The New Journalism*, declaring "nonfiction novel" will bring on death of traditional novel. Leon Forrest publishes first novel, *There Is a Tree More Ancient Than Eden*, with preface by Ellison. *Phylon* publishes two-part reassessment of *Invisible Man* and *Shadow and Act*. Cyrus Colter publishes shocking existentialist novel, *The Hippodrome*, with epigraphs from Wright, Sartre, and Genet.
1974	Toni Morrison publishes *The Black Book* as example of new black literary archaeology and communal scrapbook.
1975	Elected to American Academy of Arts and Letters.
1976	Ellison intellectual hero André Malraux dies in France.
1977	Publishes "Backwacking: A Plea to the Senator." Interviewed by Ishmael Reed, Steve Cannon, and Quincy Troupe for *Y'Bird Magazine*, one of the most revealing of all his exchanges.
1978	John Gardner publishes *On Moral Fiction*, kindles debate with William Gass about the art and ethics of the contemporary novel.
1979	Ralph Ellison Festival organized at Brown University by poet Michael S. Harper; Ellison presents "Portrait of Inman Page" and "Going to the Territory," pursues plan to publish second collection of nonfiction prose. Festival proceedings published in special Ellison issue of *Carleton Miscellany* in 1980. *Chant of Saints* anthology published with extended Ellison interview conducted by Harper and Robert Stepto.
1981	John Wideman returns from years of "woodshedding" to begin publishing his Homewood Trilogy—*Damballah*, *Hiding Place*, and *Sent for You Yesterday*—between 1981 and 1983. David Bradley publishes *The Chaneysville Incident*, which critics compare to *Invisible Man*.
1982	Thirtieth Anniversary Edition of *Invisible Man*, with new introduction by Ellison, reframing book's origins and development. Ellison tells *Playboy* interviewer that

invisibility metaphor no longer applies to black America; denounces Reagan administration social policies.

1986   *Going to the Territory* collects nonfiction prose from 1957 to 1986, with previously unpublished major essay, "An Extravagance of Laughter." Charles Johnson publishes *The Sorcerer's Apprentice*. Ishmael Reed publishes *Reckless Eyeballing*. Shirley Anne Williams publishes *Dessa Rose*. Noteworthy reviews published of *Going to the Territory* by white reviewers Richard Farnsworth, Eric Lott, Louis Menand and by black reviewers David Bradley, Cyrus Colter, Leon Forrest, Julius Lester, and John Wideman. Tom Wolfe serializes *The Bonfire of the Vanities* in *Rolling Stone* magazine. Michael Jackson buys ATV Music for $40 million. The *Cosby Show* dominates television sitcom industry. Wole Soyinka accepts Nobel Prize for Literature.

1987   Toni Morrison publishes *Beloved*. Tom Wolfe publishes "Stalking the Billion-Footed Beast: A Literary Manifesto for the New Social Novel" in *Harper's*.

1990   Charles Johnson wins National Book Award for *Middle Passage*, devoting acceptance speech to praise of Ellison and *Invisible Man* as models.

1992   Modern Language Association session, "A Tribute to Ralph Ellison," organized by Michael S. Harper; Ellison unable to attend because of illness.

1994   On April 16, dies in Harlem apartment on Riverside Drive, his home for forty years.

1995   John Callahan, literary executor, publishes *Collected Essays of Ralph Ellison*, with preface by Saul Bellow. Maryemma Graham and Amritjit Singh publish *Conversations with Ralph Ellison*, a compilation of interviews, for University Press of Mississippi series.

1996   Callahan publishes *"Flying Home" and Other Stories*.

1999   Callahan publishes *Juneteenth*, a fragment of unfinished novel, at the request of Fanny Ellison.

2000   Albert Murray and John Callahan publish *Trading Twelves: The Selected Letters of Ralph Ellison and Albert Murray*.

2002   Commemorations of fiftieth anniversary of *Invisible Man* publication. Lawrence Jackson publishes *Ralph Ellison: Emergence of Genius*, a pioneering biography of Ellison's life up to the publication of his first novel in 1952.

2004   PBS *American Masters* series airs Avon Kirkland's documentary film biography, *Ralph Ellison: An American Journey*.

2005   Arnold Rampersad's comprehensive biography in press, with expected release in early 2006.

Shadowing Ralph Ellison

"Tell me, Major, how can one make the best of one's life, in your opinion?"

An ambulance bell, shrilling like a danger-signal, sped past them and receded. Garcia was pondering.

"By converting as wide a range of experience as possible into conscious thought, my friend."

—ANDRÉ MALRAUX, *Man's Hope*

An idea is something solid, fixed, formulated; a thought is fluid, changeable, free. A thought turns into further thought; an idea collides with another idea. A thought might be defined as an idea in action, or an action in the form of idea; an idea is a dogma. Men of ideas, men taken by ideas, rarely think.

—MIGUEL DE UNAMUNO, *The Agony of Christianity*

Whatever the so-called phenomenon of consciousness may be, it occurs in situations marked by conflict. It thus ranges from the simple consciousness of deliberate choice, through an indecisive weighing of all the facts and consequences, to deep conscientiousness at the scrupulous fear that some important aspect of the case has been slighted, and thence to the aggravated crises of conscience. A distinguishing feature of consciousness is likewise a concern with motives. . . . Orientation is thus a bundle of judgments as to how things were, how they are, and how they may be. The act of response, as implicated in the character which an event has for us, shows clearly the integral relationship between our metaphysics and our conduct.

—KENNETH BURKE, *Permanence and Change*

Prologue

ORIENTING METAPHORS FOR
A METAPHYSICAL MANHUNT

In September 1979 poet and scholar Michael S. Harper orchestrated a festival at Brown University to honor Ralph Ellison who, at age sixty-five, had recently retired from his post as New York University's Albert Schweitzer Professor of the Humanities. After more than a decade and a half of intensive service in the public sector on an array of national commissions, committees, and boards—the National Council of the Arts, the Carnegie Commission on Educational Television, the National Institute of Arts and Letters, the John F. Kennedy Center for the Performing Arts, and the Committee of 100 for the National Association for the Advancement of Colored People Legal Defense Fund among them—Ellison intended to focus his energies as fully as possible on the unfinished "Oklahoma novel" he had been wrestling with since the mid-1950s.

Instead of buttressing the worldwide reputation he had established with *Invisible Man*, his book in progress had increasingly become, like the haunting Robert Johnson blues, "a hellhound on his trail"—bedeviled by misfortunes and maledictions of fire and storm. Through a dogged attempt at reconstruction, Ellison had haltingly overcome part of the trauma of losing over 350 pages of the manuscript in a fire at his Massachusetts summer home back in 1967. During the years that followed that conflagration, he had also been trying to steel himself against the storm of rhetoric directed against him and many of his peers after the mid-1960s by a younger generation of black literary radicals inspired by Black Power and the Black Panthers. Fully versed in the secular scriptures transmitted through Frantz Fanon's *Black Skin, White Masks*, Antonio Gramsci's *Prison Notebooks*, and the *Red Book* of Mao Tse-tung, they were full of enthusiasm for the revolutionary examples of Cuba, Algeria, and the "great proletarian cultural revolution" of mid-1960s China. They seemed fully prepared to eliminate all presumed obstacles to a genuine revolutionary black consciousness in art and literature by purging all signs of bourgeois and patriotic influence associated with older generations of unreconstructed "Negro" elders. If they lacked Mao's "iron broom" to sweep away "old ideas, culture, customs, and habits," they experienced no shortage of revolutionary "black fire"; and through the end of the 1970s, at least, *its* conflagrations dominated public perceptions of the generational dialectic at work in African American communities.

A more complex and less romantic set of competing truths were entailed, of course, and the Ralph Ellison Festival reflected them. Although he was poet laureate of the state of Rhode Island and an Ivy League professor, Michael Harper moved in and out of Black Arts Movement circles and had become a core member of the St. Louis–based Black Artists' Group (BAG) that included painter Oliver Jackson, poet Quincy Troupe, playwright-scholar Paul Carter Harrison, and free-jazz musicians Oliver Lake and Julius Hemphill among others. The concept of an "African Continuum" as a field of spiritual forces binding communities of African origin together across time and space—and across generations—was foundational to BAG and to artist collectives like it across the country. While insisting that there was nothing mystical about any of this, that it was part of a psychic survival kit fashioned out of harsh necessity, artists of the African Continuum believed fervently that harmonizing creative visions could develop only out of membership in *whole*, not fragmented or patricidal, communities and out of a reverence for ancestral wisdom and generational continuity. To achieve a sense of rootedness, Toni Morrison argued in similar fashion at the time, black artists must learn again to regard the ancestor "as foundation"—not slavishly, or uncritically, or without a sense of the need for revolutionary change, but always with a sense of each generation's inescapable ancestral ties to the overarching limits and possibilities of the human condition.

In that spirit, the Ellison festival became one of a series of related ceremonial occasions Michael Harper organized to honor valued elders under siege, with efforts on behalf of Robert Hayden and Sterling Brown following soon thereafter.

Accordingly the Ralph Ellison Festival took the form of communal homage to a live ancestor and distinguished elder in a time of trial, an homage that brought together not just writers and professional scholars but singers, painters, musicians, photographers, students, the young and the old. Brown University's first black graduate and class orator, Inman Page, class of 1877, had by wondrous serendipity eventually become Ellison's principal at Frederick Douglass High School in Oklahoma City; and Page's daughter Zelia Breaux had become Ellison's music teacher, mentor, and "second mother." So painter Richard Yarde had been commissioned to render Page's image in oil as a gift for the presentation ceremony at which Ellison delivered his own rollicking "Portrait of Inman Page." Before joining BAG and recording such Africa-conscious free-jazz cosmological meditations as *Dogon A.D.* (1972) and *'Coon Bid'ness* (1972), Texas-born jazz clarinetist and alto saxophonist Julius Hemphill had grown up in the Southwest and Kansas City jazz milieu that Ellison had been weaned on decades ahead of him. So Hemphill composed a musical tribute, "Ralph Ellison's Long Tongue," for the occasion. Photographer Lawrence Sykes, fresh from photographic studies of Old World and New World African cultures in Ghana and Haiti, joyfully created a photomontage poster that fused topographical maps of the Oklahoma Territory with Page's visage, with the Statue of Liberty, the skyline of Manhattan filtered through mazes of electrical transmission poles, and with the central shadowed face of Ellison himself.

Novelists Barry Beckham and Leon Forrest—who were now generational successors to Ellison as storyteller and, in Forrest's case, a rapt disciple—offered commemorative and critical assessments. Yale University professor Robert Stepto, whose groundbreaking theoretical study of African American narrative, *From behind the Veil* (1979), made Ellison's work a hermeneutic pivot, fleshed out new insights about Ellison's paradigmatic creative and critical achievements. John Callahan, who would eventually become executor of the Ellison estate, presented an early installment of a book on "democracy and the pursuit of narrative" that would appear finally as *In the African–American Grain* (1988). Alongside a group of fledgling scholars, poets, and fiction writers who had been invited—myself among them—chair-holding senior scholars and Ellison peers such as R. W. B. Lewis and Nathan A. Scott, the first a longtime ally as well as a central figure in the postwar American Studies movement and the second an old Ellison confrere and the founding father of religious literary studies, were on hand to supply the long view of Ellison's literary legacy. The festival's presiding *genius loci*, Michael Harper, whose singularity as a poet was being forged in no small part then by his powerfully evocative images of kin and kinship, home and family, penned a series of photopoetic memorates—"Hemp," "Nathan's Cadenza," "Stepto's Veil," "Richard Yarde's Blues," and "Secretary"—that gave the ceremonies an ornamental frieze and captured at the same time the character of a family gathering. At the center of it all, Ralph Ellison, with Fanny Ellison close at hand throughout, used his orienting keynote address, "Going to the Territory," to emphasize his own place in the geography of fate as a lucky legatee of all those who had gone before him, making a way out of no way, through the marvels and terrors of the American experience.

The lead chapter in this book, "Dedicated Dreamer, Consecrated Acts: Shadowing Ellison," emerged first in these circumstances as a fragment and evolved into something more ambitious as Professor Harper and I wrestled with the editorial tasks of transforming the festival proceedings into a special Ellison issue of the old *Carleton Miscellany*, one of the last of a species of worthy arts-and-letters journals heading rapidly toward extinction at the time. The small circulation of the *Miscellany* notwithstanding, the finished volume quickly became a collector's item when it appeared. Ralph and Fanny Ellison took great pride in it; and they dispensed box after box of copies to circles of friends and associates, who included such literary luminaries as Kenneth Burke, Joseph Frank, and Irving Howe, to name just three of the most visible. My own role on the *Miscellany* board and as coeditor of the special issue led to a warm personal relationship with the Ellisons, which continued over the next fifteen years and produced a flow of correspondence, mutual gifts, and dinners at their apartment in New York City that cumulatively enriched my understanding of Ralph's life and work, as well as making us both keenly aware of intersecting personal interests and family histories in Oklahoma and Minnesota. My own paternal family had migrated northwestward after the years of Southern Reconstruction, from Kentucky to the fledgling state of Minnesota. There, as the geography of fate again would have it, my grandparents had provided their Bethesda Baptist Church a parsonage for the family of John William Dunjee, the fugitive slave and itinerant Baptist minister whose journalist son, Roscoe Dunjee, and historian-journalist daughter, Drusilla Dunjee Houston, would later become formative influences on young Ralph Ellison after the Dunjees relocated from Minneapolis to Oklahoma City at the turn of the century, where they became pillars of yet another community of strivers. My grandfather, the only son of one of the longest-serving Ninth Cavalry Buffalo Soldiers, had come of age in the Ninth's regimental home at Fort Duchesne, Utah, while his father's troop maneuvered through Arizona, Colorado, the Dakotas, Kansas, Missouri, New Mexico, Texas, Wyoming—as well as Oklahoma—and abroad to Cuba and the Philippines. Since Ellison's own father had also served with the Buffalo Soldier regiments—the Twenty-fifth Infantry in Lewis Ellison's case—in Cuba and the Philippines, the probabilities were high that my forebear and his had served together. In any event, from my earliest encounters with Ellison's *Shadow and Act*, the richly autobiographical portions describing this kinetic frontier milieu and its extensions resonated intensely with me, gave new dimension to my own family traditions, and helped me understand Ellison's essays not as an adjunct to *Invisible Man* but as its creative coequal and intellectual point of origin.

Though Kimberly Benston published a stringently abridged excerpt of this chapter in his pathbreaking critical collection, *Speaking for You: The Vision of Ralph Ellison,* in 1987, "Dedicated Dreamer, Consecrated Acts: Shadowing Ellison" has not been otherwise accessible before now. With a primary focus on the evolving framework of what Ellison insistently referred to as his "conscious thought," it provides the scaffolding for this book's subsequent explorations of Ellison's creative and critical productions. It makes less mysterious, I hope, the eventual appearance of *Invisible Man* as a first novel so masterly that its seemingly unprecedented precociousness continues to baffle many readers—as was revealed again in some of the professional commentary for the recent PBS *American Masters* film *Ralph Ellison: An American Journey.* My approach now as before stakes a claim R. W. B. Lewis also asserted at the original festival, that *Shadow and Act*, not *Invisible Man*, is the closest thing we have to Ellison's real autobiography—an autobiography-in-outline expanded finally by accumulating interviews and the ultimate retrospections of *Going to the Territory*. In a corollary way, my approach to *Invisible Man* treats the novel more as a fictionalized "anti-memoir" akin to André Malraux's conceptualization than as an aesthetically enhanced transcription of Ralph Ellison's documentable lived experience.

This book's concluding chapter, "The Man of Letters and the Unending Conversation," attempts to close the circle around Ellison's creative and critical career by approaching *Going to the Territory*, the final installment of his "conscious thought," in a framework somewhat different from what I employ with *Shadow and Act*. Out of a determination not to ossify and isolate the septuagenarian Ellison of the 1980s as a detached elder statesman and icon en route to a final resting place—a premature "burial" he emphatically abhorred—I have tried to approach his second expository collection not so much as a psychograph of Ellison's final phase of intellectual development, but as a locus of his ongoing engagement of other thinkers, past and present, white and black and other, who were wrestling in sometimes oblique or subterranean ways with Ellison—and he with them—and of the unending crises of art and democracy in what he considered still to be a land most strange. The Ralph Ellison Festival had helped restore Ellison's faith in his ability to engage younger audiences and in the rightness of building his second essay collection around the theme of imaginative freedom—of "going to the territory"—that Bessie Smith had long since given a blues commemoration. So, with the help of organizing tropes imported from Kenneth Burke, I have retraced Ellison's look backwards, through "Society, Morality, and the Novel," to the 1950s' cold war era "quarrel" over the liberal imagination and the "death of the novel," at the same time that I have tried to present him—as he saw himself and *Going to the Territory* in the middle 1980s—as caught still in the existential middle of a new era of culture wars and future shock and the reverberations of Black Art.

I have chosen not to address at any length here the vexed matter of Ellison's unfinished novel and the fragment published as *Juneteenth* (1999) at Fanny Ellison's request and with John Callahan's editorial assistance. Professor Callahan has acknowledged scrupulously that *Juneteenth* is *not* Ralph Ellison's long-awaited second novel but only the most coherent and retrievable extract from the vast novelistic saga he had conceived, labored prolifically over for forty years, released in scattered fragments but had never, to his satisfaction, reduced to "eloquent form." With this delimiting judgment I wholeheartedly agree, even as I eagerly await the publication of a promised scholarly edition of the complete unpublished manuscripts. In the absence of some unforeseen disclosure, Ellison's literary reputation will remain circumscribed by the texts he himself always ushered carefully and consciously into the public record. What remains to tantalize us will generate its own unending conversation.

Shadowing Ralph Ellison has been designed to profile Ellison's intellectual career as novelist, cultural critic, and man of letters. It explores his landmark novel, *Invisible Man* (1952), his two nonfiction collections, and his published interviews, speeches, and correspondence through the aforementioned scaffolding of "conscious thought"—the vitalistic, antimaterialist outlook and orientation inspired by French writer, revolutionist, and philosopher of art André Malraux—which Ellison began erecting in the 1930s in the wake of the waning Harlem Renaissance, and which he first elaborated publicly in the riveting essays and interviews of *Shadow and Act* (1964) and, during his final decade, in the still underexplored second nonfiction collection, *Going to the Territory* (1986).

My title chapter grounds its approach in the rhetoric of motives and theories of symbolic action developed by philosopher-critic Kenneth Burke, which Ellison wholeheartedly absorbed; and it interprets Ellison as conscious thinker in terms of his own jazz-driven improvisational strategic framework—as synthesizer, celebrant, dialectician, and demiurge. Set against the backdrop of the Black Arts insurgency, this first chapter reveals the formative array of philosophical, aesthetic, and vernacular influences behind Ellison's critical and creative development, before and after the canonization of his prizewinning first novel. The second chapter reinterprets *Invisible Man* as a political novel by situating it among the World War II era's jointly emerging sociology of leadership and mythography of hero-worship as they defined, for Ellison, key cultural issues facing the postwar black freedom movement. Building on Ellison's recurrent account of the wartime "psychogenesis" of *Invisible Man*, this chapter reads the novel's militaristic motifs as a ritualistic design of heroic biography and Gestalt psychology. As Ellison conceptualized it, the novel "charts," in terms again of Burke's orienting philosophy of literary form, the progress in "conscious thought" of its protagonist "from purpose to passion to perception" and, in a manner akin to Malraux's novels of contemporary revolution and civil war, the trajectory from political disillusion to artistic transcendence.

The third chapter focuses on the broader meanings of "technique" and "technology" in Ellison's writings, stressing the import of science and invention over narrower aesthetic contexts while probing the influence of cultural critics Edmund Wilson and Lewis Mumford on Ellison's fiction and essays. The fourth chapter, the first extended treatment of *Going to the Territory* and its contextual vortex, is organized in two sections. The first section revisits Ellison's cold war era 1950s critical exchange with Lionel Trilling and the New York Intellectuals in the debate over the "death of the novel," and it brings Ellison's circle of African American critical comrades into clear view also for the first time. The second section situates *Going to the Territory* in the broader cultural milieu and quarrels of the 1980s. It figures Ellison in both subsections as a double for the wily vernacular persona "Mose" that he and Albert Murray referenced reverentially but jokingly during their years of correspondence. By configuring the environing contexts and quarrels as engagements in the kind of "unending conversation" Kenneth Burke hypothesized in *The Philosophy of Literary Form* (1941), this section treats Ellison's second set of nonfiction essays first as a lens for refocusing the "culture wars" swirling through the 1960s, 1970s, and 1980s over the nonfiction novel, the New Social Novel, the Black Aesthetic, and postmodern popular culture. Then, by probing beneath the surface of the major reviews of *Going to the Territory* written by writers outside and inside the African American community, the second section dramatizes the resulting array of "conversations" with Ellison as a measure of his artistic and intellectual impact on his literary rivals and successors.

A short epilogue, "The Last Gestalt: Ellison's Unfinished Business," acknowledges the complex questions surrounding Ellison's posthumous literary legacy by linking the problem of his uncompleted second novel— and the fragment published posthumously as *Juneteenth*—to his own public ruminations on "writer's block" and the shock of unprecedented social change. Returning again to the framework of Gestalt theory that Ellison so often consciously employed, the epilogue links the stylized patterns of subconscious "dreamwork" and "unfinished business" in Ellison's writings to the post-Romantic tradition of existential angst in the arts over the twin demons of artistic ambition and what Honoré de Balzac called the "unknown masterpiece." As a "man of letters," not just a storyteller, Ellison, like Edmund Wilson, Kenneth Burke, and even Lionel Trilling, left marks on our literary landscape both as a novelist of ideas and a critic of culture. Beyond them and all their other literary peers, however, when Modern Library's 1998 panel of scholars and critics created dual lists of the twentieth century's greatest one hundred English-language novels and greatest one hundred works of nonfiction, Ralph Ellison stood in equipoised singularity, four years after his death, as the only writer to appear on both lists. This book explores some of the reasons for this final triumph, the processes of consciousness and conscientious art through which, by analogy with Duke Ellington, Ralph Ellison confronted life as a blue fog one could almost see through and, in an unsentimental mood, made of it a near-tragic, near-comic *transbluency*.

The Big E. is still making up
complexity;
      he can't be stolen
from—his long black tongue
isn't nearly as deadly
      as his memory . . .
The Big E. don't like theft—
he got powerful arms, a scarred
eyelid, and a pocketknife
that has a fast safety and quick release—
it has a double-edge sword,
      it is as black
as gunpowder, as red as a hieroglyphic
rose

—MICHAEL S. HARPER, "Hemp"

Without doubt, even the most engagé writer—and I refer to true artists, not to artists manqués—begin their careers in play and puzzlement, in dreaming over the details of the world in which they become conscious of themselves.

—RALPH ELLISON, "Hidden Name and Complex Fate"

Chapter One

Chapter One

DEDICATED DREAMER, CONSECRATED ACTS:
SHADOWING ELLISON

Nicknaming is a deadly art in black communities, Ralph Ellison taught the world some years ago in a time of trial, a gamely practiced art in a tightly pressed but voluble social world supremely aware of the power of words to mask, to reveal, to assault, or to embrace whatever human beings do and are that warrants being codified. Street-corner raconteurs have made it also an analogical and hyperbolic art, devoted to sizing up the ludicrous and the laudable, to extracting essences. Such masters at "capping" simultaneously wreak havoc and do homage with simple sobriquets. So it suits vernacular tradition that poet Michael Harper's testamental riffs have bestowed "The Big E." on Ellison himself. For such a monicker evokes the muscular skill and grace of some Harlem hoopster or the vital force of some street-life magnifico as an analogue for the creative and exegetical rigor of a major literary intellect. It unmasks the bodacious homeboy in a heady man of words; and it makes a celebration of that coming to terms with articulate elders which the communal will to continuity and memory requires.

A grimmer spectacle, though, hypnotized the public eye during a decade and a half of Black Power and Black Arts through the literary politics which, Ellison himself admitted, turned him for that moment in history into "a hateful straw man" targeted by radical discontent (Ellison, "Study and Experience" 426). His staunchest observers saw in this an unwitting rehearsal of those ancient rituals of sacrifice and exculpation around a scapegoat king that Ellison, ironically, had anatomized nearly two decades earlier in a provocative review essay on the private torments and public fate of fabled, waggishly monickered jazzman Charlie "Yardbird" Parker (S&A 218–27). Little of the orgiastic excesses and frenzied cult worship that ultimately maimed and martyred Bird, however, was to surface in Ralph Ellison's experience as a writer. But in the much publicized images of one of Harlem's literary lions playing scarecrow to an irreverent, besieging throng of the black-plumed disaffected, there was more than a little of the spectacle he had so wryly described of the darktown rebel artist become, in reverse proportion to the intensity of his own creative struggles, a white hero-victim and black reprobate picked clean and picked again—like the eponymous Poor Robin in the old jazzman's ditty—before a culturally disoriented and divided public which had but the dimmest notion of his real significance.

But with the savant's grasp of social ritual—and his entanglement in it—Ellison, unlike Bird, marshaled the fortitude he cites as essential equipment for any vital man or artist and endured patiently the rites of political assault that threatened for a while to reduce the debate on his work and life "to the level of the dirty dozens" (Ellison, "Study" 427). That same fortitude would sustain forty years of battlefield maneuvers in the literary career he long conceived of as "a guerilla action in a larger war, in which I found some of the most treacherous assaults against me committed by those who regarded themselves either as neutrals, as sympathizers, or as disinterested military advisers" (S&A 122).

Ellison traces his schooling in stylish forbearance to the Georgia-born, plantation-bred mother whose frontier odyssey in turn-of-the-century Oklahoma produced, among other things, a son whose passion for reading, dreams of faraway places, and drive to excel she nourished with the rich texture of her own limit-defying personal and political experience and with her counterbalancing "tolerance for the affairs of the world" (Graham and Singh 267–69). He credits, too, more obliquely, the father who named him and then died when he was three—the ex-soldier, construction foreman, and lover of books who bequeathed to his infant son the hidden name and complex fate of a poet and philosopher, which a recalcitrant, music-minded Ralph Waldo Ellison would, through a first unconscious, then mysterious, then consuming process, discipline his life to achieve. And in dedicating the collection of essays which still comprises the most profound statement of the pluralist position in African American letters to one Morteza Sprague, "A Dedicated Dreamer in a Land Most Strange," Ellison acknowledges his indebtedness also to the idealistic black teachers who, by their own example, helped him see that dreamers could function responsibly and durably even in a nightmare world.

That the dreamer's bent might be transformed by literary technique into consecrated acts of staggering power, Ellison claims first to have glimpsed through his Tuskegee confrontation with T. S. Eliot's *The Waste Land* in 1935 (*S&A* 159–60). Decades later, from Eliot's "The Hollow Men," he gleaned a title for the American drama of power and pathos his gathered fugitive essays tried to name:

> *Between the idea*
> *and the reality*
> *Between the motion*
> *and the act*
> *Falls the Shadow.*

To return to *Shadow and Act* now, when many of the specific issues the essays addressed are faint at best in the popular imagination, must be justified by a focus on what it is they hold of enduring relevance and on what—when their chronology is straightened somewhat and the broader context in which they originally appeared sketched out—they can reveal about the movement to maturity of one of the nation's most important literary minds. Despite Ellison's longevity in the public eye, we still know but little about these things.[1] Ralph Ellison's characteristic rhetorical canniness and cultivated complexity in his fiction, essays, and interviews have posed part of the problem. But the larger part derives from readers of *Invisible Man* and *Shadow and Act*, on both sides of the racial divide, who have routinely approached the politics, the art, and the "racial" values these books codify in terms narrower than those Ellison himself proposes.[2] As a consequence the body of "conscious thought" he has erected since the late 1930s has been left in shadow, artificially isolated from its intellectual roots in African American tradition and almost invariably denied a critical context as pluralistic in its techniques and cultural references as Ellison's extraordinary eclecticism demands.[3]

In retrospect the reasons for his essays' ambiguous fate at the hands of the reading public seem clear enough. For the moment in American cultural history between *Shadow and Act*'s hardback and softcover issuances in 1964 and 1966 was a time seized also, and more extravagantly, by the apocalyptic social essays of James Baldwin's *The Fire Next Time* and LeRoi Jones's *Home* and by the dramaturgical insurgencies of the former's *Blues for Mister Charlie* and the latter's *Dutchman and The Slave*. In those years *The Autobiography of Malcolm X* and Claude Brown's *Manchild in the Promised Land* uncloaked scarifying rites of racial passage that seemed attuned to the prophetic insurrectionary mode of Frantz Fanon's newly translated *The Wretched of the Earth*. In close conjunction, a New Breed of black poets led by African-aliased Jones and Don L. Lee (not yet Haki R. Madhubuti) were transmogrifying Langston Hughes's and Sterling Brown's legacy of folk panegyric into incendiary "assassin poems" suffused with the ritual scatology and warrior ethos of urban street gangs.

Entering the literary race war with vocal disdain for the "easy con game" of black separatist militancy and with continuing, if not uncritical, faith in the old black-Jewish-liberal alliance, Ellison's compilation of two decades' literary skirmishes and epiphanies struck establishment reviewers as comparatively calm and meditative. They remarked almost gratefully the aesthetic and integrationist concerns of *Shadow and Act* and its seeming divorce from the politics of protest and revolt. In September 1965 a *New York Herald Tribune Book Week* poll of 200 authors, critics, and editors recognized *Invisible Man* as "the most distinguished single work published in the last twenty years"—an all-American story about the search for self that expanded the 1950s' preoccupations with existentialism, "identity crisis," and introspection. Ellison's work was canonized, in part, as a quiet counterpoint to the discordant literature of Black Power and American Negritude. Since *Invisible Man*'s original appearance, the WASP literary sensibility had almost invariably blunted any wrenching confrontation with Ellison's world by diffusing his novel's specific angers into an abstract statement about Man, at the same time confining the book to the traditional literary ghetto. Initial black critical response, limited largely to the African American press and periodicals, had polarized around the black Left's formulaic allegations of reactionary decadence and the black bourgeoisie's racial uplift preachments against the novel's unseemly emphasis on the "unrepresentative" black lower class. Amidst clamorous disapproval, the steady voices of Langston Hughes and Alain Locke—two "heroic figures" for Ellison since boyhood—had been almost alone in praising his big book in expansive terms (Covo 11–16). So white reviewers largely evaded Ellison's attack on racist ideology and seemed barely able to comprehend the broad implications of the first successful attempt to dramatize, through a single incisive metaphor, the historic panorama of an Afro-American cultural tradition that had been suppressed in the national mind since the Jazz Age. Conversely, black reviewers, bound to the exigencies of political struggle or the defensive imagery of upward mobility, disputed the cloying vision of reality Ellison proposed and the modernist hyperbole with which he conveyed it.

This first phase of glancing encounter with primarily a white audience gave way in the age of Black Power to a frontal collision with radical black scholarship and opinion. Jacqueline Covo's 1974 survey of international reaction to Ellison's writings suggested that, after the publication of *Shadow and Act*, a second phase of Ellison's passage into the heart of the American darkness balanced the continued growth of his literary reputation against the exactions of ideological warfare, with Ellison himself registering the consequent tensions in an increasingly embattled series of interviews in the late 1960s and early '70s.[4] The "blackness" of his fictive vision became more and more suspect; and the black press essentially ignored *Shadow and Act* save for a few superficial or condemnatory notices. By contrast, Ellison's essays were embraced with uncommon attentiveness by white reviewers who nonetheless subordinated his focus on the relationships between newly renamed "Afro-American" culture and "American" national character to their own preoccupation with Ellison's unsparing chastisement of critic Irving Howe in "The World and the Jug." But *Shadow and Act*'s temperate mood and analytic mode apparently undermined an image of Ellison that now took on various denigrified forms: to Reed Whittemore, then, he seemed a "humanist of fairly spacious nineteenth century sort" propounding boyish dreams of possibility (25–26); to the *Nation*'s reviewer he was a dark-skinned Huckleberry Finn somehow untouched by the black angst and activism of the times (De Lissovoy); to Southern Agrarian Robert Penn

Warren he seemed a secular spokesman for Martin Luther King's Christian conception of *agape* (91–96); and to neoconservative Norman Podhoretz he was a "touchy" but happily unaggressive antitype to the black nationalists, stubbornly denying the hard fact that the black world was "graying" even in his own work and that blacks, like Jews, must ratify that homogenization as the price of relative acceptance and safety in America ("Melting" 1+). Even the more knowing assessments by literary allies and clairvoyants seemed unable to place Ellison as intellectual in an Afro-American context or to locate him in the larger world of ideas with his "Negroness" intact.

Correlatively, Ellison's refusal to discard "Negroness" for "blackness" at a time when nationalist fervor made these terms antonymic offered one more pretext for the assaults on Ellison's world that multiplied from outside the academy as a wave of new black journals and magazines formed during the height of the nationalist movements and as older black periodicals yielded to the growing resistance against integrationism. With the spirit of LeRoi Jones's "Black Dada Nihilismus" presiding, two of the architects of the new Black Arts—Hoyt Fuller of *Negro Digest*, soon to be retitled *Black World*, and Larry Neal, arts editor of *Liberator*—shepherded a campaign against Ellison's alleged acts of artistic and political betrayal. Beginning in 1965 with a chastening review of *Shadow and Act*, *Black World* arraigned Ellison for "his above-it-all pose relative to the racial conflict," for his public criticism of radical black writers' technical deficiencies, and for his seemingly imperturbable optimism about the course of American democracy (Fuller 51–52). The campaign reached fever pitch late in the decade after Ellison's unflinching book-jacket counterthrust (on James Alan McPherson's quiet, workmanlike short story collection *Hue and Cry*) against the "obscenely second-rate" and "dead, publicity-stained" literature which, he felt, had come increasingly, lamentably, "to stand for what is called 'black writing'" (Ellison, Blurb).

Defending that writing with apostolic fervor, Larry Neal, whose manifestoes did more to define the emergent Black Arts Movement than any other force save his cohort LeRoi Jones, had unleashed a series of essays in *Liberator* in 1965 and 1966 outlining "The Black Writer's Role," which garroted Richard Wright, Ralph Ellison, and James Baldwin in succession with the sinuous thesis that "the Black writer's problem really grows out of a confusion about function, rather than a confusion about form." Recasting Wright's diagnosis from the 1930s, Neal insisted that Western bourgeois assumptions about the uses of art, and a "narcissistic preoccupation with individual suffering and estrangement," had left black writers alienated from their folk tradition and oriented more toward entertaining whites than attending, "priest-like," the spiritual needs and social objectives of blacks (Neal, "Black Writer's Role" 9). Ralph Ellison, aloof but technically skilled, immersed in the African American folk mythos but politically disengaged and read more by whites than blacks, posed a special problem. He was, Neal presumed, "a divided man," a walking repository of black vernacular lore, idioms, and blues whose critical ideas, on the other hand, derived from white writers. Instead of attempting to escape from black culture, though, Ellison was in fact a vague kind of "cultural nationalist" striving to apotheosize it—but one whose commitment to his communal tradition and his craft nonetheless left him detached from black audiences, movements, and institutions. The artist's responsibility to unify his art and ethics was the real issue, Neal announced; and he resurrected the more demonstrably radical Ellison of the 1940s *Negro Quarterly* to chide the now "silent and disillusioned" man, who, he charged, no longer had any intention of helping black leaders understand and canalize the repressed social energy and incipient forms of action revealed in black myths, symbols, and folklore (Neal, "Black Writer's Role" 10–11).

Remonstrances notwithstanding, the New Breed reaction to Ellison disclosed ambivalence more than antipathy, as the afterword to Neal and Jones's movement anthology, *Black Fire* (1968), revealed in acknowledging *Invisible Man* to be undeniably "a profound piece of writing" but one that nevertheless had "little bearing on the world as the New Breed sees it" (Neal 652). Furthermore, if Neal mourned Ellison in the *Liberator* series as another vital black mind "lost in the graveyard that is America" ("Black Writer's Role" 11), in *Black World*'s special issue on Ellison in 1970, the Black Arts Movement's prime manifestant so reversed his perspective on Ellison as to lead a vigorous defense against the studied invective of Ernest Kaiser's leftist anti-Ellison crusade in the same issue (Neal, "Ellison's Zoot Suit" 58–79). The recantation had been sparked by Neal's plunge into black political history and by a careful culling of Ellison's "mean but eloquently controlled" rebuttal to Irving Howe's radical prescriptions and literary black-baiting in

The New Leader. A look back at Wright's and Ellison's own left-wing travail in the 1940s, augmented by Harold Cruse's trenchant historical anatomy of Marxist machinations in *The Crisis of the Negro Intellectual* (1967), resolved the most pressing questions about the "function" of black literary libera-tionists and convinced Neal that even black neo-Marxian thought generated miasmic oversimplifications about African American life that weakened the movement and black art.

Clearly, the social realism and formulaic stridency that many of Ellison's critical antagonists espoused did not allow for the free play of fantasy and myth that Ellison had attempted, nor for the intellectually independent black political theory that he and Angelo Herndon tried to fashion in the short-lived, Party-sponsored *Negro Quarterly* during the 1940s. Always resistant to regimentation, Ellison's early elevation of style over ideology as a cultural force, his "nascent, loosely structured form of black nationalism," and his counter-Marxian gropings for an indigenous cultural theory rooted in African American imperatives, made Ellison's work highly relevant to the contemporary search for new systems of social organization and creative values, and revealed a complexly dimensioned vision "not that far removed from the ideas of some of the best Black writ-ers and intellectuals working today" (Neal, "Ellison's Zoot Suit" 63). Indeed, in approaching African American life through a psychology of survival and transcendence rather than a psychology of oppression, it was really Ralph Ellison more than Richard Wright, Neal implied, who had provided the cultural blueprint for the new black literary radicals—with a positive ver-sion of black lifestyles as profoundly human and spiritually sustaining and with a theory of black "cultural compulsives" that turned Marxian class analysis on its head and made such political meanings as are concealed in the psychic geometries of hipster zoot suits and ghetto choreography the cultural keys to a strategy of liberation. Concomitantly, Ellison had con-fronted many of the conceptual problems that now faced the Black Arts Movement; and his foray for answers into the murky world of mythology and folklore had yielded an unparalleled sensitivity to the blues, ballads, spirituals, dances, idioms, and heroic archetypes which could genuinely constitute a revolutionary aesthetic. It was in Ellison, Neal surmised, that one could find that "black aesthetic" at its best and find at the same time in *Invisible Man* one of the world's most successful "political" novels—the confusion had risen from not realizing that Ellison's politics are "ritualis-tic" rather than secular (Neal, "Ellison's Zoot Suit" 79).

In a concerted rapprochement that even paused to mediate the con-troversy raised by Ellison's harsh review of LeRoi Jones's procrustean *Blues People*, Neal retained only one "fundamental difference" with the older man: while a zoot-suit-like appropriation of white, Western aesthetic ideas did not mean that Ellison had become a white man, his insistent location of his philosophical and literary sensibility in the West had perhaps unin-tentionally fashioned that zoot suit into a straitjacket for younger black writers. Irretrievably disparate and distant to Wright, Ellison, and Baldwin, the non-Western world now offered a vitalizing avenue of cultural inquiry to a later African American generation brought by simultaneous intercon-tinental political resurgences, by the rise of diasporic festivals, by media magic and modern transport, into closer cultural colloquy with the exco-lonial writers of Africa and the Third World, who had now become liter-ary as well as political movers and shakers of the modern mind. Art *was* more psychically powerful than secular politics, Neal finally concurred, and through it black people, as Ellison suggested, could dominate Western culture or be dominated by it. But the conglomerate of knowledge, East and West, was the proper source of a liberating black vision, and the role of synthesizer the proper aesthetic stance in a world where, alone, no Western or Eastern ethos disclosed the means of humankind's spiritual emancipa-tion (Neal, "Ellison's Zoot Suit" 77–78).

Though Neal's essay had appeared amidst the continuing ideological onslaught that Ellison later admitted he "mentally walked 'away from,'" it signaled a growing sophistication among the New Breed literary radicals and a fuller comprehension of Ellison's whole corpus of work. The "trials of the word" had not ended for him, however, as became clear in 1973 in a lengthy bipartite tract in *Phylon*—the long-lived Atlanta journal of race and culture founded by W. E. B. DuBois in the 1930s—which attempted to reassess *Invisible Man*, as well as the world of Ellison's essays, by exten-sion, "within the framework of an American society which has experienced a radical alteration in black consciousness during the past twenty years" (Walling 120–21). Ostensibly a vindication of Ellison's fictive vision, the *Phylon* essays exercised themselves to show how the very structure and con-trolling metaphors of *Invisible Man*, the optimistic Emersonian humanism of *Shadow and Act*, and Ellison's own public career as speaker and cultural committeeman, had set the man and his work "running against the grain" of an ascendant concept of Negritude and a strategy of cultural decolonization whose antipathetic pressures had reduced Ellison "to a position of isolation" (Walling 125, 127). Taking the spirit of activism and racial self-pride in DuBois's turn-of-the-century classic *The Souls of Black Folk* as a reference point, the *Phylon* reevaluation lauded the enduring humanist values of Ellison's work but corroborated the charge that *Invisible Man*'s strategy of artistic amalgamation and its apparent disavowal of any form of direct protest showed "tendencies, toward passive acquiescence and unworthy self-suppression" which linked it in spirit with Harriet Beecher Stowe's *Uncle Tom's Cabin* and which, in "any reasonably thorough analysis," would spark in the hypothetical black man on the street "a sense of instinctive resentment" (Walling 133).

Thoroughness, however, was hardly the leading attribute of analyses that read simple accommodationism into Ellison's jazz-derived concept of cultural synthesis as a subversive strategy of empowerment. For passivity was repudiated nowhere more emphatically than in Ellison's besieged novel, which hypothesized not a mythic sickness unto death or dissimulation but a myth of rebirth effectively articulated by an originally ineffective activist hero, whose being buffeted into hibernation finally transforms him "from ranter to writer" and prepares him for a more socially responsible form of overt action than he has previously been capable of. He is a hero who, despite all his "sad, lost period" of misguided political enthusiasms, still believes "in nothing if not action," who has been a rabble rouser "and perhaps shall be again," and who has stopped smoking reefer, for instance, precisely because the drug inhibits action (*IM* 10–11). The irony Jacqueline Covo noted in Invisible Man's career—that a book which had become a modern classic to American and European readers has been almost smothered in commentary yet largely ignored on its most challenging levels—stands starkest here. Amidst civil disorder and political assassination, amidst black cults and cadres often misled by charismatic impresarios or con men, critical responses remained fettered to radical cliché and academic exegeses of imagery and symbolism that all but ignored *Invisible Man*'s central concern with political power and the problems of black leadership. While scholars explored industriously the novel's affinities with American apocalyptic, prophetic, picaresque, and comic traditions and linked Ellison's essays vaguely to nineteenth-century transcendentalism and the mid-twentieth-century existential temper, such explorations typically discovered blood ties only to traditional Anglo-European models and showed almost no comprehension of Ellison's relation to an African American literary and philosophical tradition with its own syncretic modes and genres.

The critical mind had come to see Ellison's connections to a black folk heritage of blues, jazz, and hyperbolic tales but not to a belletristic tradition of cosmopolitan humanist activism that extended from Benjamin Banneker, Frederick Douglass, Martin Delany, and Alexander Crummell to W. E. B. DuBois, James Weldon Johnson, Alain Locke, Sterling Brown, Langston Hughes, and Richard Wright. Essays on Ellison as "brown-skinned aristocrat" (Kostelanetz, "Ralph Ellison" 56–77) and on his uses of the imagination (Bone 86–111) discussed his devotion to elegant and eloquent style and his ideas on literature, music, politics, and culture as if they embodied an idiosyncratic ethos without demonstrable antecedents. In fact, Ellison's achievement, only now being fully recognized, is that of codifying, refining, and extending for creative use a body of African American thought on expressive character, on art and freedom, on democracy and the folk tradition, on pluralism and the national culture, which had been elaborated in detail in the first half of the twentieth century by DuBois, Johnson, Locke and a legion of street-corner intellectuals and Talented Tenth "race men."

If almost no one seemed able to come fully to terms with Ellison's world of flux and contrariety and riddling codes of conduct, dissipating political tensions after the mid-1970s permitted the freer dialogue that made fragments, at least, of Ellison's cultural thought a source of ethnomusicological and folkloric insights for a new generation of scholars reinterpreting America's pluralistic popular culture. Elements of his aesthetic furnished literary techniques and theories for black literary figures such as Leon Forrest, Michael Harper, Charles Johnson, George Kent, James McPherson, Toni Morrison, Albert Murray, Ishmael Reed, Nathan Scott, Stanley Crouch, and Robert Stepto. However, though Stanley Edgar Hyman had acknowledged Ellison the profoundest cultural critic that we have, and though sociologists deemed him one of the few humanists at ease in the world of social theory, his meditations on subcultural autonomies and interdependencies, on the psychohistory of American race rituals, and on the vernacular process have no more penetrated the formulas of social diagnosticians and prognosticators than the sardonic, heavy-headed "mugging" that opens *Invisible Man* penetrated the awareness of its white near-victim. Before his death in 1994, the scholarly combine, while beginning to explore Ellison's "ancestral" ties to black literary traditions, had yet to see his career as a whole, to link his early fiction and political thinking to his mature work. And led by the rhetoric of denunciation of Imamu Amiri Baraka né LeRoi Jones, the Black Arts neo-Marxian resurgence, reluctantly fading from popular memory, continues to inhibit dogmatically attempts to identify the patterns of continuity beneath the surface clichés about the political and generational animosities between Ellison and the Black Arts writers. So, Ellison's critique of Baraka's cultural hypotheses in *Blues People* continues to be submitted as evidence of the two writers' alien sensibilities, to the utter neglect of such confraternity as might be implied, for example, by Baraka's taking his most celebrated step toward a 1960s revolutionary black theater—*Dutchman*—through what is in part a dramaturgical elaboration of Ellison's originary image of his naive narrator seated on a subway train plunging underground into Harlem while "across the aisle a young platinum blond nibbled at a red Delicious apple as station lights rippled past behind her" (*IM* 190): that portent in *Invisible Man* of subsequent entanglements in the labyrinthine psychosexual motives of pale bohemian sibyls which Baraka turned into transfixing Black Arts theater.

Tangled just as undiscerningly in the superficialities of radical chic, fragmenting glosses of Ellison's essays and literary exchanges have persisted in focusing, out of context, on his declarations as a writer that political programs and ideologies are secondary to style and that he is concerned more with art than with injustice. Couched in the full contour of Ellison's thinking, however, these priorities reflect no overweening aestheticism but rather an unswerving belief in the supreme moral force of the imagination and in the utility of approaching life's enduring problems through literary modes of perceiving and of investing meaning. Viewed in terms of the enduring tragic and comic aspects of the human condition, political parties and programs *are* transitory, pragmatic, and ameliorative agencies "guided not by humanism so much as by the expediencies of power" (*S&A* 296). Indeed, Ellison's professed subordination of human wrongs to aesthetic imperatives follows tactically from his belief that "it is a matter of outrageous irony, perhaps, but in literature the great social clashes of history no less than the painful experience of the individual are secondary to the meaning which they take on through the skill, the talent, the imagination and personal vision of the writer who transforms them into art. Here they are reduced to more manageable proportions; here they are imbued with humane values; here injustice and catastrophe become less important in themselves than what the writer makes of them" (S&A 148–49).

Clearly Ellison came close to accepting what Richard Wright projected as an essentially hierophantic role devolving upon black writers: in the face of a decaying folk religion and a debilitated bourgeois leadership, they were being called, Wright had proclaimed, to "do no less than create values by which their race is to struggle, live, and die," to "furnish moral sanctions for action," to "create the myths and symbols that inspire a faith in life" (R. Wright, "Blueprint" 11). Rooted more deeply in communal traditions, however, Ellison leaned away from Wright's Nietzschean autogeny and toward the conservation, more than the creation, of value. His detractors have read acquiescence, disillusionment, or desperate optimism into his fiction and essays—and a corollary defection from the struggle for freedom—because they cannot comprehend, or partisanly deny, that his commitment to preserving attitudes toward life which are sometimes stoic, sometimes quietist, is no more a code of resignation than are his allusively omnipresent blues. Like the blues, which the Black Arts radicals frequently repudiated, but which Ellison used paradigmatically as an instrument of heightened consciousness, writing for him became a way of confronting the jagged pain and pleasure of black lives and of "seeing that it be not in vain," a way of striking through the masks of power and illusion that make remediable human problems seem insoluble and the insoluble seem unbearable.

As such, despite all Ellison's derogations of the world of secular politics, the central drama of his work is the unraveling imaginative confrontation with the chimeric forms of power and of freedom. Drawn initially into writing, he has told us, by the desire to understand "the aesthetic nature of literary power" and the devices through which literature commands the mind and emotions, he found himself, "like a sleepwalker searching for some important object," seized with a sense of mission to preserve in art, as codified in African American experience, "those human values which can endure by confronting change" (S&A 35, 39–40). The essays and interviews of *Shadow and Act* are his witness to a shift of role and strategy in a continuing quest for power and possibility. They chronicle his "slow precarious growth of consciousness" and, he wrote, the related effort "to confront, to peer into, the shadow of my past and to remind myself of the complex resources for imaginative creation that are my heritage" (S&A xix). From the early, doctrinaire jottings in his collected and uncollected articles, reviews, and short fiction, through the proliferating series of interviews, speeches, and profiles that marked the anxious watch for his second novel, Ellison continued formulating his own "program" for a black literary initiative and enlisted himself "for the duration" in what he agreed with Wright was the pivotal political battle of American culture—the struggle between black folk and white over the very nature of reality. Contrary to Wright's spartan ideological perception, however, for Ellison this was not the unrelievedly grim and morally unambiguous confrontation of a group and its allies challenging the defenders of an existing horror but rather a tragicomic battle royal the painful joke of which squares off two interbred, interdependent peoples, each of whom knows *its* experience is the real American experience, knows the other group knows as much, and cannot understand why they will not admit it.

From Ellison's effort to carry on the combat, what has emerged in the course of forty-odd years of writing is a dynamic but self-consistent body of "conscious thought"—referencing André Malraux's eclectic, iconoclastic, antisystematizing, experiential ideal—devoted to transforming the themes, the enigmas, the contradictions of character and culture that are native to the African American predicament into literary capital. The DuBoisian echoes of Ellison's opening paragraphs in *Shadow and Act*—the Icarian image of himself "with these thin essays for wings, . . . launched full flight into the dark" where "beyond the veil of consciousness" he seeks to function responsibly, "to range widely and, sometimes, even to soar" (S&A ix, xi)—mark the visionary and poetic mode in Ellison's essays that, though more muted than in DuBois and largely unremarked by critics, yet signals a shared thrust beyond the attractive but reductive materialism of Marxian political theory and conventional social science to a more humane and liberating vision animated both by a revitalized humanism and by the cultural ethos and spiritual strivings of black folk.

This liberating vision in Ellison's work reveals at least four major organizing impulses—or "motives," in Kenneth Burke's terms—four intermingled disciplining strategies for divining order in the experience he knows and for converting that experience into potent symbolic action: the *syncretic* impulse in his "passion to link together all I loved within the Negro community and all those things I felt in the world which lay beyond" (*S&A* 31); the *celebratory* impulse to explore "the full range of American Negro humanity"and to affirm the attitudes and values which gives African American life "its sense of wholeness and which render it bearable and human, and when measured by our own terms, desirable" (*S&A* xviii, 36); the *dialectical* impulse behind his "ceaseless questioning of those formulas through which historians, politicians, sociologists, and an older generation of Negro leaders and writers—those of the so-called 'Negro Renaissance'— had evolved to describe [his] group's identity, its predicament, its fate and its relation to the larger society and the culture which we share" (*S&A* xvii); and finally the *demiurgic* impulse to seek cultural power and personal freedom through art, to propose "an idea of human versatility and possibility which went against the barbs or over the palings of almost every fence which those who controlled social and political power had erected to restrict our roles in the life of the country," and so to dominate reality by a willed projection of cultural personality nourished on the highly developed African American ability to abstract desirable qualities even from enemies and on the "yearning to make any- and everything of quality Negro American, to appropriate it, possess it, re-create it in our own group and individual images" (*S&A* xii, xiv).

The literary imagination, as a comprehensive way of perceiving and controlling, as "a form of energy through which experience is transformed into consciousness" (Ellison, "Ralph Ellison" 22), became Ellison's agency for guiding these impulses and for answering the questions "Who am I, what am I, how did I come to be? What shall I make of the life around me, what celebrate, what reject, how confront the snarl of good and evil which is inevitable? What does American society mean when regarded out of my own eyes, when informed by my own sense of the past and viewed by my own complex sense of the present?" (*S&A* xix). From his vantage point in culture, regional geography, and the social hierarchy, and out of his commitment to a fulsome neo-Cartesian doubting of all negative definitions imposed on him by others, Ralph Ellison tests and sifts and remolds the prevailing concepts of man, of culture, of the national experience, of high art and popular traditions, of the links between art and freedom, in order to fashion a credo capable of comprehending that experience in all its mystery, contradiction, and plurality. The syncretic, the celebratory, the dialectical, and the demiurgic impulses that shape his critical vision and "conscious thought" mediate the tensions between the concepts he confronts and the experience he knows in the same way that technique—ever the key to creative freedom for Ellison—mediates the tension between human desire and human ability.

Ellison's syncretic drive to combine, reconcile, and reintegrate competing cultural realities is amply evident throughout his work, but nowhere more suggestively than in his theories of African American and American character, and nowhere more unexpectedly than in his resurrection of Renaissance Man. In order to reveal the truths of his own experience and those around him, Ellison quite early discovered the need for a concept of man and a concept of culture that could illuminate that blind spot of irrationality Americans called "the Negro problem," that site in psychic geography where he saw theologians and humanists and social scientists alike stumble and "where Marx cries out for Freud and Freud for Marx" (*S&A* 297). Gunnar Myrdal's 1943 proclamations in *An American Dilemma* notwithstanding, African American culture and personality were not simply a product of social pathology, Ellison argued in his then unpublished review; and black folk had not lived and developed for over three hundred years simply by reacting "to more primary pressures from the side of the dominant white majority." African Americans were more than creatures of white men. They had "helped create themselves out of what they found around them," had, just as men had made a life in caves and upon cliffs, "made a life upon the horns of the white man's dilemma," a life whose enforced distance and exclusion from white patterns had created the objectivity and countervalues that enabled black folk to consciously reject or accept the allegedly "higher values" of the dominant group according to their own subjective design for the good life (*S&A* 301–2). Written as Ellison struggled to incorporate his subjectivist cultural theories into a Marxian sociology, this review, declined publication by the academic journal that commissioned it, unveiled a startlingly avant-garde conception of minority group culture as evolving from voluntaristic and interactive processes with the dominant society, regardless of the imbalance of power. It rejected the rigid environmentalism and social Darwinism of the Robert Park school of race relations theory and clarified the political role played by social science itself in the maintenance of racial oppression.

Most of the detractors and many of the liberal defenders of black America—like Myrdal—had forgotten, Ellison emphasized in his paean two years later to Richard Wright's *Black Boy*, "that human life possesses an innate dignity and mankind an innate sense of nobility, that all men possess the tendency to dream and the compulsion to make their dreams reality, that the need to be ever dissatisfied and the urge ever to seek satisfaction is implicit in the human organism, and that all men are the victims of the goading, tormenting, commanding, and informing activity of that imperious process known as the Mind—the Mind . . . armed with its inexhaustible questions" (*S&A* 92). The creative significance of the life black Americans had made upon the horns of the white man's dilemma could not be comprehended by the anthropology of Franz Boas, Ruth Benedict, and Melville Herskovits, by the sociological postulates of Myrdal and even E. Franklin Frazier—whose ideas Ellison often improvised upon—nor by the romantic mystique of the New Negro Movement. "Man," as Ellison abstracted his model of prototypic humanity from the concrete whirl of black migration and from urbanization, from depression and disillusion, from folk endurance, folk imagination, folk transcendence, was not the creature of fixed, innate feelings and intellect the interpreters of "Negro life" described. The human creature Ellison hypothesized was rather a multivariant plurality of essences and expressions, solitary and self-reliant in "a world so fluid and shifting that often within the mind the real and the unreal merge, and the marvelous beckons from behind the same sordid reality that denies it existence" (*S&A* 284). Through the agency of their own symbolistic imaginations, black Americans had steered a course through the three-dimensional reality of racial oppression, revolutionary technological modernity, and the encapsulating American national experience, with cultural consequences Ellison tried to make comprehensible by progressively fusing, over the course of two decades, the existential concepts newly ascendant in the radical thought of the 1940s, the wide-ranging speculative insights of Kenneth Burke, and his own extrapolations from the African American folk ethos.

As he acknowledged in a 1977 interview with Ishmael Reed and others, the apprenticeship in literature which enabled him to accomplish this took place in the Harlem of the 1940s amidst the complex crosscurrents of the waning Negro Renaissance, the Federal Writers Project milieu, and the Stalinist-Trotskyite radical Left. Besides "the living presence of Langston Hughes, Claude McKay, Countee Cullen, Sterling Brown, and Alain Locke" and the powerful intellectual influence of Marxian political theory and Freudian psychology, his efforts "to make connections" between his own background and the larger world of ideas drew most extensively on the fiction and criticism of French writer-revolutionary André Malraux, to which he was initially led by Hughes and through which he became aware of Soren Kierkegaard and Miguel de Unamuno and a body of ideas that revealed to him the existential elements in African American spirituals, folk tales, and blues (Ellison, "Essential Ellison" 132–34). In Malraux, Ellison discovered an adoptive literary "ancestor" who combined in a single powerful personality the revolutionary artist, the hypnotic political "rabble-rouser," the philosopher of art, the man of action, and the novelistic historian of cultural conflict and political crisis. In *Man's Fate* (1935), *Days of Wrath* (1936), and *Man's Hope* (1938)—the novels Ellison most often alludes to—Malraux had fashioned artistic answers to human problems Ellison confronted in their American racial incarnation. Malraux had managed, in recreating novelistically the fervor and tension of the Chinese Revolution, the Nazi concentration camps, and the Spanish Civil War, to dramatize empathically the collision of diverse cultures, moral systems, national and social types, while discovering in partisan struggle the possibility of human brotherhood and in the act of "imposing the personality upon the external world" humanity's one and only chance of escaping, if imperfectly, from the emptiness and despair of modern life. Malraux's concept of fiction as transposed memoir and as a means of expressing the tragic in human life, his belief in transcendence of the human condition through immersive action and through art, and his antideterminist view of history as a dialectical progression of events willed by the human self reinforced Ellison's aesthetic and philosophical inclinations and enlarged his sense of the possibilities in the fictional material around him in African American life (Graham and Singh 278).

Miguel de Unamuno, the Spanish philosopher and novelist whom Ellison first discovered as a character in Malraux's *Man's Hope* and whose book *The Tragic Sense of Life* he later pored over with Richard Wright, had become a *cause celebre* for the American liberal intelligentsia after Unamuno's defiance of Spain's Rivera dictatorship and his subsequent exile made him an international symbol of the artist-philosopher grappling with the political anxieties of the age. Lauded in America in the 1930s for his prototypical "Spanishness" and for his "ideophobic" rebellion against Western rationalism, Unamuno had a special relevance for Ellison and Wright over later existentialists such as Jean-Paul Sartre and Albert Camus precisely because of those facets of his thought which made him to many at home in Spain not so much a symbol of the Spanish spirit as of the subversion of Spanish tradition. For the image in the eyes of the outside world of Unamuno as Spain's "native son" was, as Ellison and Wright could understand from their own vantage point in black America, highly ironic. Born into the belabored Basque minority, his first novel an inspired reaction against the Carlist bombardment of his home city, Bilbao, Miguel de Unamuno had internalized and projected Spain's seemingly permanent state of civil war. Torn by a philosophical attraction to Kierkegaard and the modern Protestant theologians on the one hand and, on the other, by his spiritual roots in Catholic culture and pagan Spain, he saw himself, like Spain, as tragically divided; and he dramatized obsessively in his novels the theme of the fratricidal Cain complex and group hatreds he considered to be the national disease. A critic of Spanish machismo and the code of honor, Unamuno had turned violently against European traditions, had emphasized the unique Spanish cultural legacy of a history shared intimately with Jews and Moors and, taking pride in Spain's African ancestry, had prophesied further Africanization as the key to Spain's and Europe's regenesis (del Rio 11–35).

Unamuno's existential humanism, which Ellison and Wright absorbed without the religious framework, portrayed the human condition as a dramatic *agon*, a tragic wrestling with uncertainty en route to a meaningless death. Unamuno's prototypic "man of flesh and bone," a spiritual forebear of Ellison's Invisible Man, fights against destiny with no hope of victory but nevertheless "quixotically" in order to dramatize, at least, the injustice of life's inescapable agony. As Ellison's own fictive "man of flesh and bone, fiber and liquids" would later conclude in his heroic image of jazzman Louis Armstrong quixotically trumpeting a lyrical defiance to the world, "humanity is won by continuing to play in the face of certain defeat." Unamuno's tragic vision, in delineating a code of conduct akin to Ernest Hemingway's canonical "grace under pressure" but immersed instead in a communal ethos, unveiled to Ellison the possibility of understanding the attitudes in the blues tradition, whose literary value Langston Hughes and Sterling Brown had helped him appreciate, not as something quaint, folksy, melancholic, fatalistic, and formless, but as magisterial, tragicomic, transcendental, and spiritually disciplined. The blues, as Ellison subsequently reconceived them, were actually "an impulse to keep the painful details and episodes of a brutal experience alive in one's aching consciousness, to finger its jagged grain, and to transcend it, not by the consolation of philosophy but by squeezing from it a near-tragic, near-comic lyricism" (S&A 90). Codified from long experience at the edge of an existential abyss, their emotive power lay in the fact that "they at once express both the agony of life and the possibility of conquering it through sheer toughness of spirit" (S&A 104). Much more than a laconic wail of the dispossessed, they were not "low-down" and peripheral to the American experience but, indeed, a gauge of the democratic experiment and the very closest Americans had come to embracing the tragic. Modally, they were an art of ambiguity and assertion capable of making the details of sex "convey meanings which touch upon the metaphysical"; and they were the only native art in the United States "which constantly reminds us of our limitations while encouraging us to see how far we can go" (S&A 239).

In a 1973 interview with novelist John Hersey, Ellison reiterated his nondogmatic view of the existential qualities inherent in black life, emphasizing the ambiguity of African American social status—kept violently below the threshold of American social hierarchy "in a way that neither our Christianity nor our belief in the principles of the Constitution could change"—while being at the same time "existentially right in the middle of the social drama." In the face of a society that spent great rhetorical and political energy "proving to itself that we were not human and that we had no sense of the refinement of human values," black Americans were forced, in order to survive psychically, Ellison insisted, to rely upon their own resources and sense of life, were forced to define and act out their own idea of the heights and depths of the human condition. They had developed an existential outlook, Ellison maintained, "because human beings cannot live in a situation where violence can be visited upon them without any concern for justice—and in many cases without possibility of redress—without developing a very intense sense of the precariousness of all human life, not to mention the frailty and arbitrariness of human institutions" (*S&A* 280).

The culture and identity black Americans had improvised out of ambiguity embodied an *agon* but not a state of irremediable agony, as Ellison had explained in a long, reiterably eloquent passage a decade earlier in the exchange with Irving Howe. "Negroness," he maintained, resided in nothing so simple as skin color or victimhood but in a willed existential affirmation of self as against all outside pressures:

> Being a Negro American has to do with the memory of slavery and the hope of emancipation and the betrayal by allies and the revenge and contempt inflicted by our former masters after the Reconstruction, and the myths, both Northern and Southern, which are propagated in justification of that betrayal. It involves, too, a special attitude toward the waves of immigrants who have come later and passed us by. It has to do with a special perspective on the national ideals and the national conduct, and with a tragicomic attitude toward the universe. It has to do with special emotions evoked by the details of cities and country-sides, with forms of labor and with forms of pleasure; with sex and with love, with food and with drink, with machines and with animals; with climates and with dwellings, with places of worship and places of entertainment; with garments and dreams and idioms of speech; with manners and customs, with religion and art, with life styles and hoping, and with the special sense of predicament and fate which gives direction and resonance to the Freedom Movement. It involves a rugged initiation into the mysteries and rites of color which makes it possible for Negro Americans to suffer the injustice which race and color are used to excuse without losing sight of either the humanity of those who inflict that injustice or the motives, rational and irrational, out of which they act. It imposes the uneasy burden and occasional joy of a complex double vision, a fluid ambivalent response to men and events which represents, at its finest, a profoundly civilized adjustment to the cost of being human in this modern world. (*S&A* 136–37)

The conceptual keys for distilling fragmentary patterns of sense, memory, imagination, and rite into this careful codification of African

American ethos and worldview Ellison had discovered, in part, in the philosophic criticism of Kenneth Burke. Decades ahead of the anthropologists who have turned to Ernst Cassirer and to Burke for a semiotic concept of culture, Ralph Ellison appropriated the theories of symbolic action (after first hearing Burke's critique of Adolf Hitler's *Mein Kampf* in 1937) because he perceived that to approach African American culture simply as patterned behavior or as a model in the mind, or even as a mixture of the two, failed to divulge the true import of a way of life whose profound, inescapable material constraints and compensatorily muscular subjective structures implied human beings who defined themselves, and dealt with the existential dilemmas of living, through the medium of symbolic actions (*S&A* 148). Neither material reflex or disengaged ideation, symbolic action gave ritual form to the attitudes Homo sapiens worked out, in solitude or in concert, for coping with real situations. Though we hardly recognized it, much of human "reality" consisted of such systems of gyroscopic meanings. For human beings, as Burke conceived them, were quintessentially symbol-making, self-fabricating beings who struggled compulsively for order amidst the clutter of self-propagated signs and metaphors that constitute human culture. Humanity's cultural creations—myths, religion, folklore, music, dance, visual art, science, and literature—were all symbolic "equipments for living," stylized strategies for naming or prescribing attitudes toward recurring human problems. The pattern of black life, especially, as Burke pictured it, embodied a "complex, subtle, and gratifying" symbolicity that, under intense pressure, mediated aesthetically between the beleaguered life of the body and the processes of spiritual gratification (Burke, *Philosophy of Literary Form* 361–68).

As Ellison employed it, such a view finally made visible and dynamic black cultural patterns that had been shrouded by the concept of race, or else misinterpreted mechanistically as impassive artifacts, traits, and survivals. Ellison saw "Negro" or "Afro-American" life as vitalistically expressed "in a body of folklore, in the musical forms of the spirituals, jazz, and the blues; in an idiomatic version of American speech . . .; a cuisine; a body of dance forms and even a dramaturgy which is generally unrecognized as such because still tied to the more folkish Negro churches" (*S&A* 254). But the culture itself consisted of actions, symbolic actions, that were no less real for often being checked, diverted, or concealed. Again, this accolade to Richard Wright's blues-toned autobiography, even as it marked the maturation of Ellison's prose style and offered penetrating literary insights, also provoked a cultural redefinition and a new awareness of covert black symbol systems. Besides presenting the now classic definition of the blues as a complex, cathartic symbolic strategy, Ellison attempted to describe in "Richard Wright's Blues" how, crucial for self-definition, black Americans always had had a margin of freedom to choose the cultural means and ends with which they would confront the destiny white oppression had prepared for them.

That the resultant symbolic maneuvering might distort the "inner world" or be maladaptive was evident to Ellison in the "homeopathic" intrafamilial violence and "pre-individualistic" values Southern black communities employed, in the face of organized terrorism, to deflect the individual will from dangerous self-assertion (S&A 94–96). Symbolic deflection was evident also in the deceptively "physical" character of black expressive culture, where music and dance were frenziedly erotic; religious ceremony violently ecstatic; speech propulsively rhythmical, gestural, and imagistic. But this symbolistic sensuousness, Ellison admonished, did not "mean" the simple spontaneity of primitives and peasants that whites often interpreted it to be. For Afro-American life existed "in the seething vortex of those tensions generated by the most industrialized of Western nations"; and the physicality offered as evidence of the black man's primitive simplicity was "actually the form of his complexity" (S&A 99–100). In response to social conditions that drove the self in turns from comatose to hysterical states, black dance, for instance, had become the symbolic strategy for creating an alternative form of consciousness that was a kind of reverse cataleptic trance: "Instead of his consciousness being lucid to the reality around it while the body is rigid, here it is the body which is alert, reacting to pressures which the constricting forces of Jim Crow block off from the transforming, concept-creating activity of the brain. The 'eroticism' of Negro expression springs from much the same conflict as that displayed in the violent gesturing of a man who attempts to express a complicated concept with a limited vocabulary; thwarted ideational energy is converted into unsatisfactory pantomime and his words are overburdened with meanings they cannot convey" (S&A 99–100). Ideas and concepts which the intellect could not or dare not formulate, Ellison hypothesized, were literally being, in Burke's terms, "danced out," albeit unsatisfactorily. And because the defensive character of black life transmuted the human "will toward organization" into a "will to camouflage, to dissimulate," the public meanings symbolized in such cultural forms were so distorted "as to render their recognition as difficult as finding a wounded quail against the brown and yellow leaves of a Mississippi thicket" (S&A 99–100). Deciphering the covert symbolic meanings of African American culture required the methodology of a quail hunt, then, Ellison hinted metaphorically, and hunters sympathetic enough with the quarry to be able to ask themselves, and to answer, the question "Where would I hide if I were a wounded quail?"

That this mode of cultural inquiry would be neither an inspiriting jaunt or a pilgrimage for wound-worshippers Ellison made clear in another essay unpublished before *Shadow and Act* and written in 1948 while he was hard at work on *Invisible Man.* "Harlem Is Nowhere" presented his existentialist reading of African American culture at its bleakest and most nearly deterministic, although this meditation on a visit to the psychiatric clinic for Harlem's underprivileged that he and Richard Wright had helped found acknowledged both the "mark of oppression" and the possibility of transcendence for men and women who had momentarily become confused before chaos. Sanity, more than simple physical survival, was the object of human action here; and the field for symbolic maneuver had shifted from the feudal darkness of Wright's Southern nightmare world to a garish Northern, urban surreality whose wastage, grotesqueries, and masquerades diverted the major energy of the imagination from creating an orienting art to overcoming the frustrations of discrimination and to locating an alienated self in "a labyrinthine existence among streets that explode monotonously skyward with the spires and crosses of churches, and clutter under foot with garbage and decay" (S&A 283). The Harlem Ellison portrayed here was not the New Negro mecca and culture capital it had been to James Weldon Johnson and Alain Locke in the 1920s but instead a wasteland ruin, "the scene and symbol of the Negro's perpetual alienation in the land of his birth" and a site where symbolic possibilities proliferated even as personality became more fragmented. Here the traditional symbolic linkages between black culture and personality had been disrupted so that the symbology of transcendence was that by which the talented grandchildren of peasants who believed in magic and possessed no written literature had come to master technology and "examine their lives through the eyes of Freud and Marx, Kierkegaard and Kafka, Malraux and Sartre" (S&A 284). The symbology of prophylaxis was that word-magic through which songs like the "Blow Top Blues" and vernacular expressions like "frantic," "buggy," and "mad" were conjured to neutralize the states they named: Harlemites answered the greeting, "How are you?" with a formulaic "I'm nowhere, man" that ritually objectified their feelings of homelessness and facelessness and their status as "displaced persons" (S&A 287).

To Ellison's dissecting eye, the supports of Southern black rationality—the protective peasant cynicism, the sense of rootedness, the authoritative religion, the gyroscopic folklore—had been largely surrendered and not replaced through migration northward: as "the near themeless technical virtuosity of bebop" did not replace the lyrical, ritual elements of folk jazz. So black Americans had lost many of the symbolic bulwarks they had placed between themselves and the threat of chaos. The patients at the Lafargue clinic had succumbed to "irrational, incalculable forces that hover about the edges of human life like cosmic destruction lurking within an atomic stockpile" (S&A 285–86). So for them the last-ditch symbology of survival was the white man's frustrated psychic science, deflected from the treatment of a sick social order and incapable of dispelling the unreality that haunted Harlem but modestly attuned to helping bewildered black patients understand themselves and their environment enough to "reforge the will to endure in a hostile world" (S&A 289).

Against the backdrop of this tragic adaptation of symbolic action to social pathology, the concept of Renaissance Man that Ellison reclaimed from his boyhood for *Shadow and Act* by his own admission "seems a most unlikely and even comic concept to introduce" (x). But he did so, and with a straight face, because, as taken over and transformed by his "wild free outlaw tribe" of Oklahoma boys, Renaissance Man became a potent symbol of that cultural playing with possibility and that syncretic and potentially subversive processing of dream and reality which Ellison believed to be the saving dynamic of African American culture. Transmitted originally "from some book or from some idealistic Negro teacher, some dreamer" and suggesting a surreptitious sociology of ideas that intellectual historians have only begun to contemplate, Renaissance Man as elaborated by Ellison's youthful cohort functioned as a projective father-surrogate for boys who, like Ellison himself, were often fatherless (*S&A* xi, xiii). It offered, he reflected, a way to fuse symbolically the black middle-class faith in education and the idea of self-cultivation with a notion of aristocratic elegance that was fervently populist and full of roguish style. A strategic antidote to self-hate and defensiveness, Renaissance Man formulated an ideal image of intellectual competence and verve which was neither foppish nor effete. It encouraged self-discipline and expansive growth. Moreover, it "violated all ideas of social hierarchy and order and all accepted conceptions of the hero handed down by cultural, religious, and racist tradition": "Gamblers and scholars, jazz musicians and scientists, Negro cowboys and soldiers from the Spanish-American and First World Wars, movie stars and stunt men, figures from the Italian Renaissance and literature, both classical and popular, were combined with the special virtues of some local bootlegger, the eloquence of some Negro preacher, the strength and grace of some local athlete, the ruthlessness of some businessman-physician, the elegance in dress and manners of some headwaiter or hotel doorman" (*S&A* xiii).

This was no anachronistic nineteenth-century humanism preserved in the Oklahoma black community through cultural lag. Renaissance Man in Ellison's "ragtime" version presented a thoroughly modern and palpably black distillation of an enduring human ideal—adaptive, humane, creative, moral, refined, and heroic. Embodying an implicit critique of the pillars of white society, whom from the confines of their segregated community Ellison's band understandably saw as "crooks, clowns, or hypocrites," this Renaissance Man functioned as a counterimage to the failed "humanities" imaged in such literary types as Melville's Ahab and Conrad's Kurtz. As a cultural archetype it projected the humanist as self-redemptive outsider and outlaw who, like the jazzmen on whom he is so heavily modeled, is "less torn and damaged by the moral compromises and insincerities which have so sickened the life of our country" (*S&A* xii). That this was the heroic ideal of black boys who lived so much in their imaginations and to whom the cost of realizing such an ideal in action could barely be grasped is simply more testimony to Ellison of the vital social role of the imagination. For Renaissance Man was this ideal synthesized in childhood fantasy, he recalled, that later served "to mock and caution" him when Marxist political theory and the communist ideal claimed his attentions (*S&A* xv).

It guided his subsequent apprenticeship as a writer. Moreover, in the remarkable accomplishments of his boyhood comrades despite all racial obstacles, it revealed, as he discovered on periodic returns to Oklahoma City, the reverse potentiality for symbolic action to be converted into lived experience (Anderson, "Profiles" 55+). Nor was this Renaissance ideal devoid of public and political meanings, for a prideful Oklahoma teacher had taught young Ralph Ellison black American history and introduced him, through Alain Locke's volume *The New Negro*, to the major figures of what seemed a glorious racial awakening in Harlem (*S&A* 161)—so that his boyhood "dream of possibility" took place precisely amidst that racial "coming-of-age" called the Negro Renaissance, whose expansive exhortations to humanistic self-mastery and nationalistic black pride wedded culture and commitment, elegance and militancy, fused Renaissance Man with Race Man in the "conscious" intellectual leadership of W. E. B. DuBois, James Weldon Johnson, Alain Locke, and Paul Robeson.

The relation of this syncretic conception of communal style and ideal character to Ellison's encompassing view of the national culture is clear enough: Renaissance Man is an analogue, a metaphor for the broader cultural processes and national character as historically evolved. Ellison's theories of American national culture cast aside completely "the sterile concept of race" (while conceding that the relations between culture and biology remain "mysterious") and carefully distinguish the forms of the nation's inner "spiritual" life, as projected in the imagination, from the forms of material compulsion. Like American literary nationalists from Ralph Waldo Emerson onward, Ellison's is the "organic" theory, Herderian in origin, that national culture is, or ought to be, a crystallization in language, music, dance, architecture, art, and literature of the character of the people as a whole and the contours of the land. The radical heterogeneity of a population compressed together through colonial conquest, slavery, and immigration, and through the democratic principles that rationalized revolution, is the prime support, in Ellison's construct, of the cultural pluralism and egalitarian "folk ideology" which he inherited and extended. His roguish Renaissance Man, though, supplants Emerson's Representative Man as a projection of national possibility. Hence the jazz, folk blues, city/country, cinematic, and vernacular folk/classical amalgam he personifies represents a new pluralism, philosophical and cultural, revived and progressively indigenized by Ellison's syncretic use of the Emerson-Whitman legacy, the theories of Constance Rourke, the literary works of Herman Melville, Mark Twain, and William Faulkner, the critical insights of Kenneth Burke and Stanley Edgar Hyman, and the social thought of W. E. B. DuBois and Alain Locke.

This strain of pluralist social thought in Ellison's speculations about the national culture has its broader antecedents in Thomas Paine's Quakerism and immigrant J. Hector St. John Crèvecoeur's agrarian cultural ecumenism; in Emerson's and Walt Whitman's and Margaret Fuller's transcendentalist advocacy of a "spiritual" fusion of the races; in William James's pluriverse and John Dewey's promulgation of the "Freedom to Be One's Best Self"; in Randolph Bourne's image of a "Trans-National America"; and in the ideas of philosophers Horace Kallen and, again, Alain Locke. Always at war with racism, with nativist xenophobia, and with the anti-amalgamation doctrine of racial purists, pluralist social thought has characteristically been a submerged, antinomian current in our intellectual and imaginative life, championed in its fullest implications mainly by out-groups and radical democrats. For Ellison, the pluralist outlook afforded the only version of the past that could explain the complex present and offered the only prospect for a livable future. To him, the misnamed "Negro problem" has been the most potent symbol of the issues raised in America by the plurality of races and cultures; and the enduring relevance and power for him of the nineteenth-century works of Whitman, Emerson, Henry David Thoreau, Nathaniel Hawthorne, Melville, and Twain is that, for them, he argues, the question of the Negro and other races in the development of an American literature was an "organic" part of the debate (*S&A* 149).

As for the question of slavery—it was not termed a "Negro problem" then, he tells us—it was "a vital issue in the American consciousness, symbolic of the condition of Man, and a valid aspect of the writer's reality" (*S&A* 108). But one of Ellison's most recurrent themes, elaborated earliest and most fully in the 1945 and 1946 essays "Beating That Boy" and "Twentieth Century Fiction and the Black Mask of Humanity," is that the post–Civil War betrayal of the Negro exacerbated in the white American mind an ethical schizophrenia and a guilty need to "force the Negro down into the deeper level of his consciousness" (*S&A* 108). Sterling Brown's scholarship in the late 1930s demonstrated that the American literary imagination had historically been obsessed with the symbolic figure of the Negro—multivariously stereotypic—and Brown had initiated a critical war on literary stereotypy in support of which Ellison, with telling originality, now marshaled the psychoanalytic insights of Freud (Brown, *Negro Poetry and Drama* & *The Negro in American Fiction*). The borders between the white world and the black, Ellison argued, were not spatial or merely social, but psychological and ritual. Racial oppression's social symbiosis had a psychic counterpart which made it "practically impossible for the white American to think of sex, of economics, of crime, his children or womenfolk, or of sweeping socio-political changes, without summoning into consciousness fear-flecked images of black men" (*S&A* 109). The black man in the white mind had become an ambivalently attractive and repulsive image of "the unorganized, irrational forces of American life"; and the black stereotype in literature became part of a ritual of exorcism, sacrifice, and consolation that sublimated white men's guilt, confirmed obversely the "white" identity, and systematically evaded human reality. The American writer, who, Ellison insisted, could be "no freer than the society in which he lives," was inescapably but uncalculatedly tied to the currents of popular belief. In suppressing in the moral imagination, since Reconstruction, the organic national tragedy of race, American writers, with rare exception, routinely evaded their responsibility for the health of democracy. They had "formed the habit of living and thinking in a culture that is opposed to the deep thought and feeling necessary to profound art; hence its avoidance of emotion, its fear of ideas, its obsession with mere physical violence and pain, its overemphasis of understatement, its precise and complex verbal constructions for converting goatsong into carefully modulated squeaks" (S&A 110).

R. W. B. Lewis may have been correct in describing Ellison's countervailingly radical reading of the nineteenth-century classic American writers as the idiosyncratic "critical paraphrase" through which every authentic writer fabricates a new literary tradition for himself (Lewis, "Ellison's Essays" 19–20). Clearly, Ellison retrospectively pushed the ethos of the American Renaissance where many of its authors were loathe indeed to go—past Emerson's professed "instinctive colorphobia," past Whitman's nativist crudities and antimongrelization missives, past Hawthorne's derogation of social reform and Melville's fear of anarchy. Ellison buoyed his sense of being symbolically rooted in an exemplary literary past with Constance Rourke's characterological citings of the cross-racial folk roots of the national culture; and he opposed the monistic, Brahmin reading of American traditions with a view that locates the keys to our creative evolution in the metaphorical power of blackness; in the masquerade of minstrelsy; in the drama of interbreedings, cultural and biological; in the irrepressible interpenetration of ideas across caste and class lines; in the stimulus of cultural conflict and incessant change and rebellion. Ellison's is the almost anarchic, Jamesian philosophy (William's in this instance, brother Henry's elsewhere) of a world still imperfectly unified and perhaps always to remain so: spontaneous, discontinuous, unpredictable, and alive with possibility—a reality analogous to the mind which struggles to navigate it. The wholeness and truth of American experience, to him, "lies in its diversity and swiftness of change," in its "almost magical fluidity and freedom" (S&A 113). His literary apprenticeship gave this puzzling stream of the one-and-the-many a concrete, human form—"the mystery of how each of us despite his origin in diverse regions, with our diverse social, cultural, religious backgrounds, speaking his own diverse idiom of the American language in his own accent, is, nevertheless, American" (S&A 166). The language to resolve the mystery and render this pluralist reality Ellison discovered in the "rich babel" of idiomatic black speech around him—"a language full of imagery and gesture and rhetorical canniness, . . . an alive language swirling with over three hundred years of American living, a mixture of the folk, the Biblical, the scientific and the political. Slangy in one instance, academic in another, loaded poetically with imagery in the next" (S&A 112). The cultural implications of African American idiom extended in Ellison's outlook beyond what the purified sermonic renderings of James Weldon Johnson had suggested, beyond the transcriptive "folksay" of Langston Hughes or the proletarian folk metaphysics of Sterling Brown. What Whitman had left as mere hypothesis—the claim that the representative polyglot language of the new American literature would be found in the mouths of slaves—Ellison made a "conscious" reality.

But Ellison's transforming the nineteenth century's abstract racial romanticism into a modern existential pluralism rooted in Afro-American cultural particularities was no idiosyncrasy. It built carefully, if contentiously, upon the cultural history and theory of distinct "racial gifts" propounded since before the turn of the century by W. E. B. DuBois in *The Conservation of the Races* (1897), *The Souls of Black Folk* (1903), and *The Gift of Black Folk* (1924). And it radicalized and refined the pluralist values and imperatives announced during the New Negro Movement and after by Alain Locke. DuBois's early cultural panorama had incorporated the nineteenth-century phylogenetic notion of discrete, plural, "racial temperaments" and "racial geniuses" and deployed it to confront the arrogantly Anglophile interpretations of American tradition with an image of the ostensibly inferior black man as in fact a consummate cultural creator and the bringer to the nation of largely unacknowledged racial "gifts"—"the gifts of story and song," "the gifts of sweat and brawn," "the gift of the spirit," and the gift of an uncompromised "vision of democracy." DuBois had portrayed his "veiled" black genius as neither alien nor exotic, neither a cultural error nor a liability, but as a venerable cultural insider woven so thoroughly with the very warp and woof of the nation that "dramatically the Negro is the central thread of American history"—America's metaphor (DuBois, *Gift* 65). "The whole story turns on him," DuBois had argued, "whether we think of the dark and flying slave ship in the sixteenth century, the expanding plantations of the seventeenth, the swelling commerce of the eighteenth, or the fight for freedom in the nineteenth. It was the black man that raised a vision of democracy in America such as neither Americans nor Europeans conceived in the eighteenth century and such as they have not even accepted in the twentieth century; and yet such a conception which every clear sighted man knows is true and inevitable" (*Gift* 65). Du Bois prophesied that, as they emerged from behind "the Veil"—the original analytic visual metaphor for racial alienation—double-visioned black writers would eventually turn this story into great art. For even though economic stress and racial persecution forestalled the leisure and poise necessary for stable literary development, "never in the world had a richer mass of material been accumulated by a people than that which the Negroes possess today and are becoming increasingly conscious of"—it awaited only the "artists of technic" whose alchemy would transmute it (*Gift* 169).

As the new social and psychic sciences undermined the notion of innate racial genius, however, DuBois had turned increasingly from mystical racial messianism to Marxian class analysis, so that critic-historian Benjamin Brawley and Rhodes scholar Alain Locke, a Harvard-trained philosopher-aesthetician, then masterminded the cultural interpretation of African American experience. It was Locke, as literary "midwife" of the Negro Renaissance, who in 1925 had spurred the "Younger Generation" to reject the social attitudes which had made the Old Negro "more of a formula than a human being"; and it was Locke who proclaimed philosophically what Ralph Ellison would eventually dramatize in fiction—the necessary turn toward self-understanding of the prototypic "New Negro" leader who spiritually would have to "hurdle several generations of experience at a leap" and consciously transcend the distorted perspective in which, as social bogey and social burden, "his shadow, so to speak, has been more real to him than his personality" (Locke, *New Negro* 3–4).

In promoting this racial awakening Locke had shifted the focus of cultural analysis from the racial mystique to the folk ethos; and he elaborated a doctrine of formal cultural pluralism within the dual context of modern race-relations theory and the new literary regionalism of the 1920s and '30s—both of which, however, tended toward antiquarian views of folk tradition and evolutionary rather than revolutionary social change. Within this frame Locke projected a new model of cultural organicism: the national culture reflected and was evolving toward a heterogeneous, hybrid "confederation of minority traditions," a system not of water-tight compartments, or nations within a nation, but of profoundly interlinked variants of a diffuse cultural composite, so that, Jim Crow notwithstanding, "the cultural products of the Negro [were] distinct hybrids, culturally 'mulatto' generations ahead of the mixed physical condition and ultimate biological destiny, perhaps, of the human stock" (Locke, "Negro Poets" 143; "Negro Contributions" 522–23). By an irony of history, racial oppression had, in spite of its political, economic, and social exactions, "turned out to be a great spiritual discipline and a cultural blessing in disguise," preserving and intensifying black folk values so that they now stood out in the "rather colorless amalgam of the general population" as the "cornerstone spiritually in the making of a distinctive American culture" (Locke, "Negro in American Culture" 525). Locke described his nationally "emblematic" Negro folk culture as an indigenous synthesis, neither atavistically African nor imitatively European but a distinctive new cultural creation. Locke's patrician ambivalence, however, about the world of the folk made it seem paradoxically both antiquated and modern, durable and doomed, appealingly universal but embarrassingly naive, profound but not fully articulate.

Confronting DuBois's and Locke's widely influential interpretations, and with them the problematic creative legacy of the Negro Renaissance, Ralph Ellison struggled toward a philosophy of his own at the beginning of his career by retaining what seemed valuable, reconciling it with his then clear commitment to Marxist theory, and rejecting the rest. Richard Wright's manifesto essay of 1937, "Blueprint for Negro Writing," offered an attractive challenge to young black writers, such as the then twenty-three-year-old New York newcomer from Oklahoma, to help mount what seemed to be the staunchest program for a new synthetic revolutionary literature. It rejected the bourgeois mystique of race for a folk-oriented cultural nationalism that would ideally transcend itself in the wider Marxian social consciousness. It defined a sense of perspective, subject matter, and theme immersed in a holistic group history; and it asserted a thoroughgoing literary professionalism which differentiated itself from "the so-called Harlem school" by its emphasis on the discipline and autonomy of craft and on the need for a rigorous criticism freed from racial defensiveness and self-congratulation. Most important, it elevated art and the writer to the apex of the struggle for freedom and balanced the requirement of an orienting radical "ism" with the call for a literary *vision* that would flesh out "the magic wonder of life" and its "complex simplicity" (R. Wright, "Blueprint" 12).

Wright's ideas and literary achievements gave Ellison an initial point of reference for evaluating the racial tradition in literature and for erecting a controlling vision in accord with his own considered experiences. In his early reviews and essays for the radical press, Ellison attempted, while straining against the limits of communist doctrine, to measure the formulas and handiwork of the Negro Renaissance against Wright's and his own maturing values. Ellison's review of Langston Hughes's autobiography, *The Big Sea*, in 1940, his notice praising the Negro Playwright Company's production that year of *The Big White Fog* (Theodore Ward's gripping drama of a black family pushed by oppression toward the polar millennialisms of the Garveyites and the Communists), and the critical essay he wrote the following summer discussing recent black fiction in the light of *Native Son* present the clearest record of his thinking ("Stormy Weather," "Big White Fog," and "Richard Wright and Recent Negro Fiction," respectively). The New Negro Movement as a whole Ellison denounced as an unqualified failure: he exempted only the work of Langston Hughes. Though the movement had apparently risen out of postwar riots and lynchings which generated a new nationalistic phase in the black masses' struggle toward freedom, it had quickly fallen pray, Ellison declared in strident radical rhetoric, to the perverting bohemianism of world-weary white exoticists, and to the pathetic attempts of a self-serving Negro middle class to "reconcile unreconcilables"—bourgeois passivity with proletarian militancy ("Stormy Weather" 20–21). Brushing aside James Weldon Johnson's and Claude McKay's autobiographical chronicles of the movement as patently unrealistic and self-deceiving, Ellison lauded Hughes's book as the more realistic record of one of the few survivors of the Negro Renaissance who was still a vital writer on a revolutionary path. The source of that vitality, Ellison believed—and here he sounded a theme that would persist in his thinking long after the leftist line had vanished—was Hughes's rootedness in "the crystallized folk experience of the blues, spirituals, and folk tales" and his rejection of the ideological world of the black bourgeoisie ("Stormy Weather" 20). As an account of the personal struggle to achieve that vital consciousness, however, *The Big Sea* was analytically deficient— merely a charming, picaresque narrative of an adventurous life, limited to that superficial level by an understated style which avoided the dramatic deeper meanings of the life it described and which deprived the book of "that unity which is formed by the mind's brooding over experience and transforming it into conscious thought" ("Stormy Weather" 20).

Ellison had come to see the crucial subject of literature to be the drama of mind, fettered by illusion, moving toward freedom through expanding, intensifying, self-consciousness. When he examined current black fiction at the turn of the decade, he noted first, caustically, that the older generation of black writers had produced little fiction since the early 1930s; and he concluded that, while Arna Bontemps, Zora Neale Hurston, and William Attaway had all demonstrated "a slow but steady movement toward reality" at that point, the prime contrast with the "timid," "apologetic" black fiction of the 1920s was the fiction of Richard Wright (Ellison, "Richard Wright" 12). It was in Wright's work that a radical heightening of consciousness was most evident and the whole American caste system most clearly contradicted; for against the odds of inherited privilege and wealth, he had mastered American civilization through the techniques and discipline of his art. Together with Langston Hughes, Wright offered the promise of reorienting a whole narcissistic tradition which had "ignored the existence of Negro folklore and perceived no connection between its efforts and the symbols and images of Negro folk forms." Somehow, it had "avoided psychology" and was "unconscious of politics and most of the deeper problems arising out of the relationship of the Negro group to the American whole." At the same time, it clung to "racial and narrowly nationalistic" protest that was divorced from "the international scheme of things" (Ellison, "Richard Wright" 12–13).

Ellison was actually offering inadvertent support here for Alain Locke's concurrent claim that the new black literary radicalism constituted not so much a countermovement to the Negro Renaissance as a maturation of its ideals. Locke charged that the young writers bred instead by the Depression had systematically ignored or misinterpreted the New Negro credo to justify the strategy and tactics of their own generational rebellion. Indeed, Ellison's critique of the New Negro novel, shorn of the Marxian framework, provided in its implicit countertheory a fairly precise restatement of Locke's own New Negro formulation, which Ellison would transmute into a radical and existential fiction over the course of the next decade. At the time, his short story, "Mister Toussan," which was published in *New Masses* late in the fall of 1941, attempted to chart a concrete course toward that fiction through the use of a revolutionary theme, folk motifs, and the mythic and ritualist mode. When Ellison reviewed William Attaway's powerful new novel of the Great Migration, *Blood on the Forge*, the following month, he felt himself carried one step closer to the prose narrative his own ideas anticipated: here was a novel of black American life which mined a vital body of folk experience through a system of cogent symbols and symbolically variegated attitudes toward life, a novel rich in the poetry of folk speech and the blues ethos, sophisticated in its economic analyses of the movement from medieval to modern America, and stylistically attuned to rendering the effects of technology and shifting social realities on the simultaneously expectant and disillusioned personality. What Attaway's work lacked, as well as Hughes's and even Wright's mind-numbing narratives, which Ellison would have to perfect, was the still unplumbed subjective drama of the processes by which the questing black personality attains a heightened consciousness and the will to endure amidst the flux and force of competing values and changing landscapes (Ellison, "The Great Migration" 23–24).

Wright had fashioned a possible cultural and historical milieu for that drama in the text of his *Twelve Million Black Voices*, published that same fall, which confronted DuBois and Locke and the Talented Tenth reading of the cultural past with a lyrical, Marxian black "folk history" of the complex passage in America from plantation feudalism to urban, technological capitalism—a book Wright intended not only as a distillation of what was "qualitative and abiding" in the experience of the black masses but also as his framework for a planned saga cycle of novels (Fabre 234). But Wright's outlook largely elided or subordinated the questions that increasingly intrigued Ellison. As the 1940s became for American literary intellectuals generally a time for synthesizing a balanced view from the insurgencies and accomplishments of the three previous decades, so Ellison's essays taken together reflect a conscious effort to retain the legacy of DuBois's sweeping insights while separating them rigorously from the race concept, to divine the "technic" for integrating the resources of the black past into a framework of myth and rite, to resolve the cultural paradoxes Locke and the Negro Renaissance left intact, and to incorporate, free of Wright's constraining naturalism, an existentialist reading of the folk tradition.

As his comments later to interviewers make clear, in discussing these technical and conceptual problems with the older generation of black writers, Ellison found them to be essentially intuitive artists, largely inarticulate as literary theorists and technicians—save Langston Hughes and Richard Wright, whom he consciously distinguished from the rest by their more extensive contacts with the larger white literary world ("Essential Ellison" 133). But Hughes had written little fiction that could still interest Ellison; Wright had become less interesting to him as an ideological novelist than Malraux and the nineteenth- and twentieth-century Russian masters; and Ellison turned increasingly to the world of critical scholars for syncretic strategies.

Constance Rourke's regionalist folk criticism, for instance, opened new possibilities for the interpretation of national character through the medium of black folk and popular traditions and suggested techniques for extracting valuable fictional material from the debilitating conventions of minstrelsy, the plantation tradition, and local color. The American folk heritage, Rourke had demonstrated in *The Roots of American Culture* (1942), was primarily abstract and formal rather than naturalistic and informal, a drama of comedy and archetypal character grounded in a ritual, allegorical rendering of a racially intermingled past. In her discussion of the "Traditions for a Negro Literature," Rourke showed that, claims of white provenience notwithstanding and despite systematic distortion, African American dances, jokes, jingles, and songs were the creative source of minstrelsy's ritual forms and that, once stripped of the debasing dialect and pursued to their folk origins, black cultural elements preserved nowhere else save in minstrelsy could furnish a vital tradition of fabling, of protest and rebellion, and of comic and heroic character for contemporary writers. Ellison discovered scholarly grounds for his own intuitions in Rourke's cultural history and in her earlier *American Humor* (1931), which delineated a black comic mode rooted in "cryptic and submerged" revolt and in the triumphant resilience of the folk. Rourke linked American rituals of comic masking to the ambiguities of national identity; and she portrayed the folk mind not as quaint and culturally subordinate but as energetically barbaric, subversively democratic, and a dominant national force in spite of social stricture.

In treating Rourke along with the other major literary thinkers of the era, Stanley Edgar Hyman's *The Armed Vision* (1948), published later in the decade, served the 1940s synthesizers by identifying and dissecting the major critical achievements of the preceding decades and by suggesting the utility of "an integrative frame able to encompass and use the newest advances in all fields of knowledge," a frame such as most readily offered itself in the form of Marxism, or the concept of Organicism (the organic unity of the human personality), or in Kenneth Burke's metaphor of Dramatism (Hyman 387–90). Ellison ultimately absorbed all of these into his creative and critical method, along with the Cambridge School mythic and ritualist approaches that led him, for instance, to link Lord Raglan's and Otto Rank's studies of the myth of the hero with his own consuming interest in the political problems of black leadership—the theoretical genesis of *Invisible Man*. The approach to African American life through myth and ritual offered Ellison a conceptual release from racist intellectual and popular traditions that denied any broad significance to "minority" experience. Moreover, it allowed him to fuse his political, anthropological, psychological, and folkloric insights with classical aesthetic theory to provide a comparatist, pluralist framework grounded in

American historical particularities but bound to what he regarded as timeless human universals. Mythopoetic thought enabled him also to extend the implications of Rourke's characterology and comedic analysis to the sweeping interpretation of the national literary tradition that he attempted in "Twentieth Century Fiction and the Black Mask of Humanity," where he reinvigorated an old DuBoisian trope by projecting American moral life as a ritual drama acted out upon the trussed and prostrate body of giant black Gulliver (S&A 46).

But abstract myth mongering and archetype hunting by themselves have held little creative value for Ellison, as he made clear in "Change the Joke and Slip the Yoke" (1958), his part of the exchange of essays with Hyman on the role of folklore in black American writing. In *The Armed Vision* Hyman had argued that Constance Rourke's achievement was narrowed by a chauvinistic preoccupation with American national character which, in treating black folk tradition for instance, led to her failure to take up what Hyman felt was the basic question—"its complicated relationship to primitive African myth and ritual" (Hyman 121). But Ellison allied himself instead with Rourke's view that the significance of African American folk traditions, as with American folk traditions generally, lies not so much in their origins as in their uses. And he pointed out that Hyman's own preoccupation with archetypal origins led to his failure to distinguish Anglo-Saxon from Afro-American elements in the minstrel tradition, to understand how mythography in America is qualified by the fact that "ours is no archaic society," and to see the incorporation of folklore in modern black writing not as a matter of racial or cultural predisposition but, as Ellison's long labor with *Invisible Man* showed, rather one of hard-won, self-conscious creative techniques (S&A 61–73).

Ellison used folklore in his work, he argued, not because he was black but because other writers had made him conscious of the literary value of his folk inheritance. Yet, though he had learned from Joyce and Eliot and Hemingway to value myth and ritual, they had not taught him *how* to adapt the material confronting him. For the conceptual framework to identify and deploy creatively the ritual forms beneath the social conventions of American life, Ellison feels most indebted to Kenneth Burke's dramatistic method and philosophy of literary form. *Invisible Man*, Ellison repeatedly acknowledged, was "charted" on a lattice of interconnected symbols, ideas, and incidents, in a three-part scheme dictated by Burke's theory that "ritual drama is the hub" of classically unified symbolic action, and its ideal rhythm the protagonist's movement from "purpose to passion to perception" (S&A 177). Burke's Aristotelian conclusions about the overriding psychological importance to the audience of beginnings and endings resonate in Ellison's comments about his epilogue and prologue to the novel and in his discussion of his early narrative struggle "to manipulate the simple structural unities." And Burke's emphasis on the strategic "placing" of a "representative anecdote"—a key narrative metaphor which contains the larger symbolic action in capsule form—seems clearly to have influenced Ellison's deployment of the multivalenced "battle royal" passage that some critics have found so intensely symbolic as to make what follows in *Invisible Man* seem almost anticlimactic.

For a writer so devoted to conscious thought as Ellison, the metaphorical center of Burke's system—the dramatistic pentad of Act, Scene, Agent, Agency, and Purpose—provided a scheme for analyzing the "drama of human relations" dialectically and symmetrically in terms derived from the theories of fiction elaborated in Henry James prefaces, theories Ellison assimilated approvingly early in his literary training. Besides these cues to the rhetoric of fiction Ellison is so mindful of, Burke's basic conceptions— of "literature as equipment for living"; of the symbolic act as "the dancing of an attitude"; of the symbolic process as "the ritualistic naming and changing of identity"; of style as a "strategy" for commanding the army of one's thoughts; of "perspective by incongruity" as a key to creative insight; of jokes and puns as powerful vehicles of illumination; of rituals for initiation, masking, rebirth, purification, and scapegoating as "magical ceremonies"; of the comic as an attitude of ambivalence dialectically fusing transcendental and material motives—all have influences traceable in Ellison's critical and creative writing which this very finite exploration can only suggest.

But more perhaps than discrete concepts, more than giving Ellison a consistent and comprehensive framework for expressing his own ideas, Burke offered what Ellison understood to be a supremely syncretic "intellectual Gestalt"—a willful unification and rectification of all human knowledge capable of illuminating literature and its linkages with life. Burke's infinitely fertile, frequently bewildering attempt to show the integral relationships among a panoply of cultural manifestations that were often considered only in isolation was a compelling analogue for Ellison's own syncretic passion to link the world within the African American community with the world which lay beyond. Moreover, in Burke's reconciliation of contradictory theories in psychology, sociology, linguistics, philosophy, and theology in order to turn them to the concerted illumination of a work of art, Ellison found a metaphor for his own struggle to transform the social sciences, the humanities, history, and political theory into tools for illuminating his "group's identity, its predicament, its fate and its relation to the larger society and the culture which we share." It was the integrative and analytical "play" of Burke's method, then, its ability to reconcile Marx with Freud, the anthropological with the humanistic concept of culture, high art with folk traditions, the sacred with the secular—not simply its eclecticism—that Ellison absorbed and turned to resolving the stubborn paradoxes of African American culture. Ultimately, it was Burke's philosophical pluralism, an analysis as multifaceted as the changing human reality it tried to chart—Man the Declaimer, Man the Artist, Man the Gesturer, Man the Warrior, Man the Actor, Man the Symbol-Maker—that helped guide Ellison's efforts to celebrate the pluralistic character of American life.

What Ellison found, in the face of radical despair, to celebrate in the dream and nightmare of American life is, first of all, the democratic principle that liberty-lauding rebel slave masters birthed in contradiction and which, the invisible Jack-the-Bear tells us, had been "dreamed into being out of the chaos and darkness of the feudal past, [then] violated and compromised to the point of absurdity" (*IM* 433). Beyond this unretractable promise of a future, it is not the material, technological, or institutional achievements of American civilization he exalts—its ordering forces—but rather the qualities that most closely approximate chaos and disorder: the formlessness, the fluidity, the instability, and the diversity of American life—precisely those features that American writers such as Hawthorne and Henry James found cause to lament. Again, this is in Ellison not so much the obsecration of an anarchist, for whom chaos is a subversive god, but the revelation of an *artist* for whom chaos is possibility in life as in literature. For when Ellison turns to explore the broad continuum of black American experience and to affirm its enduring values, it is precisely the ordering, stabilizing, controlling qualities he celebrates most expansively—style, discipline, technique, abstractive and assimilative powers, and will.

This is no contradiction, but rather an Hegelian corollary of Ellison's belief that "the mixture of the marvelous and the terrible is a basic condition of human life" and of the American experience: as in a fairy tale, "here the terrible represents all that hinders, all that opposes human aspiration, and the marvelous represents the triumph of the human spirit over chaos" (S&A 39). As in Marx's Hegelian phenomenology, here those who dominate through force and a contempt for human life exercise a destructive freedom that breeds death and chaos, while the dominated, forced to struggle with the world's intractability, learn its secrets and infuse it with mind. Whether he is describing the intricate vocal pyrotechnics of Mahalia Jackson's priestly art or upholding that "American Negro tradition which teaches one to deflect racial provocation and to master and contain pain," Ellison perceives black folk defining and creating themselves against the background of America's chaotic mixture of the marvelous and the terrible. Though admitting that he "would be hard put to say where the terrible could be localized in our national experience," he sees "in so much of American life which lies beyond the Negro community the very essence of the terrible" (S&A 39).

This is hardly the unqualified optimism often attributed to Ellison's outlook, hardly the nonpartisan relativism that the crusading New Liberal imagination embraced as differentiating him from Baldwin and Baraka and other black artists whose allegedly "arrogant" assertions of black moral and cultural superiority are allegedly inimical to the pluralist ideal. For Ellison does believe, qualifiedly, in the moral and cultural superiority of the oppressed—in a complex cultural "secret" wherein "the weak do something to correct the wrongs of the strong" (Ellison, "Alain Locke Symposium" 27). Concomitantly, he conceives of pluralism not as a passive idealism but, like his ideal prose, as "confronting the inequalities and brutalities of our society forthrightly, yet thrusting forth its images of hope, human fraternity and individual self-realization" (S&A 113). As an artist and revisionary humanist, Ellison rejected the idea that novels are either "weapons" or public relations vehicles for the view that "true novels, even when most pessimistic and bitter, arise out of an impulse to celebrate human life and therefore are ritualistic and ceremonial at their core" (121). The riddle posed him by the dual commitment to the black struggle for human freedom and to the celebration of human fraternity-in-difference was What values conditioned by oppression but opposed to it can be celebrated both by those who oppress and those who are oppressed?

His answer was to assert, first, that the condition of oppression is not the whole, or even the most salient, feature of African American experience; and insofar as it *is* salient, oppression has not "caused" but only occasioned or constrained the nature of the cultural forms black people willed into being. Their attitudes toward their "condition," he emphasizes in "The World and the Jug," and the strategies they styled for resolving or escaping or surviving it could no more be caused by oppression than their will and their imagination were caused by it: "For even as his life toughens the Negro, even as it brutalizes him, sensitizes him, dulls him, goads him to anger, moves him to irony, sometimes fracturing and sometimes affirming his hopes; even as it shapes his attitudes toward family, sex, love, religion; even as it modulates his humor, tempers his joy, it conditions him to deal with his life and with himself. He must live it and try consciously to grasp its complexity until he can change it; must live it as he changes it." Rather than the product of unmediated victimage, "he is a product of the interaction between his racial predicament, his individual will, and the broader American cultural freedom in which he finds his ambiguous existence. Thus, he, too, in a limited way, is his own creation" (S&A 119–20).

Because the struggle to destroy those limits takes place within the context of a life that has to be lived—and might be lost—during the process of ever-contested change, it is crucial, Ellison argues, to celebrate values of endurance and transcendence as well as those of revolt, to recognize that black people's "resistance to provocation, their coolness under pressure, their sense of timing and their tenacious hold on the ideal of their ultimate freedom are indispensable values in the struggle" and at least as characteristic as the rebelliousness militant ideology glorifies single-mindedly (S&A 121). As such, by encompassing life's inevitable flux and agon, the strategic values of endurance, fortitude, and forbearance are not a skin to be shed but a vital legacy to be preserved, by all human beings, in a violent and divided plural society where change and struggle are pervasive and survival always at issue.

The pluralist society Ellison celebrates, then, is no utopian construct predicated on the elimination of group conflict and the achievement of absolute democracy but rather a living, evolving, *improvised* social order struggling toward stability, coping and sometimes failing to cope with the fact of its radical heterogeneity—through the principles of democratic process on the one hand and the hard realities of a racial and cultural "Battle Royal" on the other. In the wake of the Negro Renaissance, Alain Locke, who in Ellison's eyes stood always for the "conscious approach to American culture" (Ellison, "Alain Locke Symposium" 20), had elaborated, in a series of philosophical essays written between 1935 and 1944, his own theory for reintegrating into a cultural pluralist ideal the problematic facts of social diversity. Locke proposed to make the historically subordinate goal of "unity through diversity" the active social philosophy of American democracy. He claimed that it was, after all, our values and value systems that have divided us "apart from and in many cases over and above our material issues of rivalry and conflict." Locke insisted that "ideological peace" could be achieved between America's contending ethnic cultures only through the pervasive diffusion of a relativistic perspective which might discover among the competing values some "harmony in contrariety, some commonality in divergence" (Locke, "Pluralism and Intellectual Democracy" 196–209; "Cultural Relativism and Ideological Peace" 609–18; "Pluralism and Ideological Peace" 63–69).

As Ellison acknowledged in a 1974 commemorative symposium at Harvard, for him "Locke was to act as a guide" in assessing the pluralistic condition of American culture and projecting an end to ethnic antagonisms ("Alain Locke Symposium" 20). Ellison's lasting conviction, however, was to be the tougher, more pragmatic view that conflict is inevitable but potentially creative as well as destructive; that, because "the basic unity of human experience" moderates social fragmentation and assures us some organic possibility of identifying with those of other backgrounds, a proud assertion of cultural personality rather than a relativistic weakening of cultural loyalties is the richest form of cultural reciprocity; and that the principles of constitutional democracy—when used strategically even by democracy's victims—are the most effective mediators of conflict. In "The World and the Jug," after chiding assimilated Jewish intellectuals for writing guiltily as though Jews were responsible for slavery and segregation,

Ellison suggests that "passing for white" through a facile identification with the power elite is where their real guilt lies and that, in the interest of historical and social clarity and in order to understand the specific political and cultural boons flowing from the Jewish presence the positive distinctions between whites and Jews should be maintained (*S&A* 132). To deny or fail to make such distinctions, he asserts, "could be offensive, embarrassing, unjust or even dangerous." He conceives the danger to be, in part, the possible loss of the balancing forces that plural perspectives on reality provide: "[I]t is to forget," he warns very soon after in "Hidden Name and Complex Fate," "that the small share of reality which each of our diverse groups is able to snatch from the whirling chaos of history belongs not to the group alone, but to all of us. It is a property and a witness which can be ignored only to the danger of the entire nation" (*S&A* 167). Similarly, bound together in conflict and interdependence, no group within the United States, he contends, "achieves anything without asserting its claims against the counterclaims of other groups. . . . As Americans we have accepted this conscious and ceaseless struggle as a condition of our freedom" (*S&A* 262). Ellison's often reiterated term for this process, wherever it operates in private or public life, is "antagonistic cooperation"—a dramatistic and oxymoronic naming of social ambiguity rooted in Ellison's fertile strategy of infusing aesthetic concepts into social analysis, a strategy designed to yield "close readings" of the textured psychic, cultural, and political meanings in American social chaos, by turning such subtle tools as poet-critic William Empson's sevenfold concept of poetic ambiguity into an exegetical instrument able to encompass intricacy, tragedy, dramatic irony, and progressive disorder in social spheres of buried meanings and tense contradiction.

With all its encoded ambiguities, Ellison's celebration of the one-and-the-many in American culture, then, is ultimately a *dialectical* pluralism, one which envisions America's unprecedentedly polyglot and inescapably agonistic "culture of cultures" moving from lesser to greater forms of freedom only through an historical process of unending struggle. The peculiarities of American history have made this developing social synthesis as mysterious and unpredictable as the forms of our emblematic vernacular traditions. Here, ethnicity rather than class has been the fundamental schism dividing humanity against itself—though that fact, too, is being slowly reversed by change. And the guiding teleology in the nation's arduous evolution is, in Ellison's terms, the common search for "that condition of man's being at home in the world, which is called love, and which we term democracy" (*S&A* 114). "The diversity of American life," he reasons, "is often painful, frequently burdensome and always a source of conflict, but in it lies our fate and our hope" (133).

The "tragic optimism" this blues-tinged credo reveals is necessarily contingent on Ellison's faith in the broadly regenerative social potential of African American values and operates in accord with how he views "the marvelous and the terrible" distributed through American life. The wisdom distilled from three centuries of unique American experience has an ineluctable role to play in the conquest of American reality and in the expansion of American freedom that Ellison sees, like the conquest of the frontier, as a necessarily cooperative and competitive venture in which no single group has a premium on truth. The tribal achievement African American values represent, he suggests, is part of an inadvertent and mysterious division of cultural labors amongst the nation's tense tribal confederation—and all the more significant for that. Most of Ellison's observers, of course, have acknowledged what Ellison has made explicit—that he locates this achievement, first, in music; that his own "basic sense of artistic form" is musical (Graham and Singh 275); and that his love for the blues and jazz, on the one hand, and the European classics, on the other, weaves a complex design through the fabric of his literary ideas and social philosophy. But only glancing attention has been paid to the larger political and cultural meanings conveyed in his celebration of African American musical creativity. It is clear enough that jazz and the blues offer Ellison a model of technical excellence, discipline, tradition, and creative ethos; clear also that he sees a potential rectification of social democracy in the forms of black folk music. But it has been less apparent that jazz, in particular, *as a form of consciousness* provides him a living metaphor for both the vernacular process he idealizes as the cutting edge of cultural democracy in America and for the dynamics of the Freedom Movement whose secular politics embody black hopes and hold the shape of future freedoms for the entire nation.

About the potency of the black achievement in sound, Ellison is unequivocal: "the most authoritative rendering of America in music is that of American Negroes," he argues; and he theorizes that "it would be impossible to pinpoint the time when they were not shaping . . . the mainstream of American music" (*S&A* 248). The source of this specialized authority in sound, he stresses in his provocative review of LeRoi Jones's *Blues People*, is not "racial genius" but, first, cultural inheritance—"it was the African's origin in cultures in which art was highly functional which gave him an edge in shaping the music and dance of this nation"—and, second, social constraint: "art—the blues, the spiritual, the jazz, the dance—was what we had in place of freedom" (247–48). Elsewhere, Ellison often argues that the creative edge came also from the "freedom of experimentation" open to those who, at the bottom of the social hierarchy, could be innovative and daring because the strictures of "good taste" and aristocratic tradition were not imposed on them save in ridicule (Ellison, "Alain Locke Symposium" 21; "Study and Experience" 431). The main agency of black musical achievement, though, in his view, is what he calls "the vernacular process"—that diffusive, adaptive, assimilative, unsuppressible flow of ideas, styles, images, attitudes, and techniques across all lines of caste, class, region, or color: "In the United States," he insists, "when traditions are juxtaposed they tend, regardless of what we do to prevent it, irresistibly to merge" (Ellison, *GTT* 22–26). As Ellison describes it, the random and the regularized contacts between the disparate social segments of our hierarchically shifting society make this process inevitable on the interpersonal level; and the magic of human symbol systems makes it accessible to all but the most solitary victims of the most absolute repression.

The vernacular process is the basis of the American revolutionary tradition, Ellison believes (*GTT* 23), as he believes it was the vernacular process which enabled slave musicians to realize themselves in music, as men and women, by appropriating any and all sound within hearing and then, impervious to the censure and ridicule of their masters, transmuting it into self-expression so aesthetically appealing as to fashion for themselves the ironic triumph "of enslaved and politically weak men successfully imposing their values upon a powerful society through song and dance" (*S&A* 249). Accordingly, in Ellison's recollections in *Shadow and Act* of his Oklahoma boyhood, it was the vernacular process exemplified in jazz that best represented a profound regional amalgam that was simultaneously confusing, liberating, tense, and omnipresent: "Culturally everything was mixed, you see, and beyond all question of conscious choices there was a level where you were claimed by emotion and movement and moods which you couldn't put into words" (*S&A* 30). Operating below the level of conscious culture, the vernacular process infiltrated churches, schoolyards, barbershops, drugstores, poolrooms, and street corners. Through jazz, Ellison suggests, it became an unavoidable "third institution," complementing the churches and schools into whose official attitudes its eclecticism and unfettered imaginativeness did not fit (*S&A* 30). More than any other cultural force, the vernacular is Ellison's model of uncensored Mind freely acting—transcending time, space, geography, and social structure and offering in its fragmentary, chaotic simultaneity a populist, pluralist traditional reservoir of the cultural unconscious to supplant T. S. Eliot's repressive neoclassical tradition of the consciously supereminent.

"Consider," Ellison notes in his essay on the Charlie Parker legend, "that at least as early as T. S. Eliot's creation of a new aesthetic for poetry through the artful juxtapositioning of earlier styles, Louis Armstrong, way down the river in New Orleans, was working out a similar technique for jazz" (*S&A* 221). From Ellison's perspective, Louis Armstrong—trumpeter supreme, trickster, clown, scapegoat, and wearer of masks—is a kinsman of his boyhood's imaginary roguish Renaissance Man, a live vernacular hero who helped make jazz a paradigm for liberating cultural processes in America by masterminding the fusion of popular and classical traditions. The music of Armstrong and Charlie Christian and Charlie Parker, Ellison contends, grew out of the tension the black musician feels "between his desire to master the classical style of playing and his compulsion to express those sounds which form a musical definition of Negro American experience" (*S&A* 233). The aesthetic counterpart of this tension is the relatively unrecognized conflict between "two separate bodies of instrumental techniques: the one classic and widely recognized and 'correct'; and the other eclectic, partly unconscious, and 'jazzy.'" Crucial for Ellison's literary aesthetic and his theory of social democracy, this conflict of techniques and ways of experiencing the world had given rise to "a fully developed and endlessly flexible technique of jazz expression, which has become quite independent of the social environment in which it developed, if not of its spirit" (*S&A* 234).

For in codifying the subterranean conflicts, unconscious drives, random associations, and unrecorded history of American culture, jazz and the vernacular constituted the alternate reality required by Ellison's growing awareness as a novelist "that the forms of so many of the works

which impressed me were too restricted to contain the experience which
I knew" (S&A 111). He rejected the "rather rigid concepts of reality" at the
heart of the tight, well-made Jamesian novel and the understated forms of
Hemingway's "hard-boiled" fiction for a fluid vernacular reality "far more
mysterious and uncertain, and more exciting, and still despite its raw violence and capriciousness, more promising" (S&A 112). Stirred by the aesthetic
possibilities of American culture's radical forms of alienation, contradiction, and disorder—which Richard Chase hypothesized as characteristic of
the American novel and its Manichaean traditions—Ralph Ellison rejected
the forms of realism and the novel of manners for the "bright magic" of a
marvelous and terrible existential fabling. The American tendency, when
embracing the looser reality of fable and romance, has indeed been to rest
in contradiction, to leave moral problems unreconciled or equivocally so.
But the vernacular gave Ellison a mode of consciousness that indeed rec-
onciled the moral with the cultural order; and he used it to absorb all the
contradictions and extremes into a normative view of American life as a
"delicately poised unity of divergencies"—tragicomic, transcendent, and
protean.

As synthesized in jazz, the vernacular process presents reality through
an elastic sense of time, a deperspectivized space, and a language Langston
Hughes had described as one of conflicting changes, sudden nuances, sharp
and impudent interjections, broken rhythms, riffs, runs, breaks, and hyperbolic distortions. In the terms of Erich Auerbach's magisterial summation
of the Western world's mimetic tradition for representing reality, jazz is a
paratactical mode, part of that recessive but periodically resurgent strain in
Western thought and art which rejects the linguistically organized mind's
syntactical coding of reality into dominative relationships of subordination and stress (Auerbach 70–76). In rejecting the orderly but provisional
reality Western science and mimetic art have built upon, the paratactical
consciousness that jazz expresses maps the chaotic and diverse elements
of experience not through syntactical strategies of hierarchical combination but, as Walt Whitman's free verse "ensembles" attempted, by arranging
them together, side by side, in a sequential democracy of lateral coexistence.
The paratactical mode, though, has historically been linked with archaic,
myth-dominated, authoritarian societies or with movements of reaction
during periods of crisis: that T. S. Eliot's royalist resurrection of myth and

religious certitude adopted a paratactical style akin to jazz modulation was part of Ellison's original attraction to *The Waste Land* (*S&A* 161–62). But what differentiates Whitman's parataxis and Ellison's from that of Eliot, and what suggests a new historical function in American culture for the paratactical consciousness, is its turn from the fall back into authoritarian myth toward the quest, instead, for a particularized and unified human- ity. Ellison's rendering of the jazz metaphysic located in it a kaleidoscopic, communalistic, vernacular rebellion against the art, history, and ethics of a dominative, dis-integrative tradition—an aural counterconsciousness whose subversive and liberating powers Americans had readily intuited if only imperfectly understood.

Although Ellison's metaphysical jazz mythos is counterreactionary and embodies a submerged political record of the black American struggle for freedom, it does postulate a "golden age" when gods mingled with men and set the course of history. In the 1959 essay "The Golden Age, Time Past," Ellison turned a retrospective look at jazz history's famed Minton's Playhouse into a celebration of communal myth, ritual, and revolt—all bound up in the birth of "bop" and the accompanying "revolution in culture" sounded by such resident deities at Minton's as Dizzy Gillespie, Kenny Clarke, Charlie Christian, Charlie "Bird" Parker, Thelonius Monk, Lester Young, Ben Webster, and Coleman Hawkins. As hallowed ground in a time now dead, gone, and misremembered, Minton's in the early 1940s was, as Ellison paints it, a festive wartime sanctuary for jazz musicians, its significance obscured in the sweep of the war effort, the urban riots, the industrial tensions, and the continuing disregard of cultural critics. But it became host nonetheless to an exceptional musical moment when "the world was swinging with change" (*S&A* 199).

The music made at Minton's then Ellison describes as a study in con- trolled fury—"a texture of fragments, repetitive, nervous, not fully formed; its melodic lines underground, secret and taunting; its riffs jeerings . . .; its timbres flat or shrill. Its rhythms were out of stride and seemingly arbitrary, its drummers frozen-faced introverts dedicated to chaos" (*S&A* 201). To the young Europeans who pilgrimaged years later to Minton's in a steady stream, it was, he remarks, a shrine of legendary heroes and events asso- ciated emotionally "with those continental cafes in which great changes, political and artistic have been plotted" (*S&A* 204). But Ellison insists that the proper context for understanding Minton's is as "part of a total cultural expression" representing the national pattern of black cabarets, dance halls, and nightclubs, on the one hand, and, on the other, a ritual ground for the apprenticeships, ordeals, initiation ceremonies and rebirths effected in jazz musicians' jam sessions. A people's complex history came to a focus in jazz, he maintains; and beyond offering the now famous portrait of the jam session as "the jazzman's true academy" (S&A 206), he treats the Minton phenomenon as the locus of a subterranean dialogue about the politics of culture carried on between an older generation of jazz lyricists and a younger generation seeking new identities in the undanceable discord of bebop.

For Ellison the achievement of personal identity and cultural self-expression free of defensiveness and alienation has always been the ultimate objective of the political struggle whose point, he states in DuBoisian terms, is "to be both Negro and American and to bring about that condition in American society in which this would be possible" (S&A 262). In "Harlem is Nowhere," ten years before the essay on Minton's and directly astride the bebop movement, Ellison sees the lyrical, ritual elements of Southern folk jazz as the embodiment of that dreamed of "superior democracy in which each individual cultivated his uniqueness and yet did not clash with his neighbors," while he perceives in "the near-themeless technical virtuosity of bebop" the musical equivalent of "slum-shocked" anomie (S&A 287). "In the perspective of time," he writes, however, in "The Golden Age, Time Past," we now see "that what was happening at Minton's was a continuing symposium of jazz, a summation of all the styles, personal and traditional" (S&A 208). Bop was not birthed out of aimlessness at all but out of a brooding recapitulation of the past which, in the terms Ellison here provides, almost bespoke a "blueprint" in music akin to Richard Wright's manifesto in literature that a commanding theme for black artists would emerge when they had "begun to feel the meaning of the history of their race as though they in one lifetime had lived it themselves throughout all the long centuries" (R. Wright, "Blueprint" 16).

So in the developments at Minton's, Ellison identifies a pattern of generational tensions and external commercial exploitation that might stand for the problems of historical continuity and tactical constraint confronting every phase of the Freedom Movement and the arts at midcentury: introspectively subdued younger jazzmen, often formally trained, their formative years shaped by post-Depression developments, warred for mastery and recognition with exuberant older men whom they mistakenly labeled—as they did Louis Armstrong—Uncle Toms and minstrel men, not artists. As a consequence, in misunderstanding their forebears this way, they misinterpreted themselves and their own emerging art through new myths and misconceptions: "That theirs was the only generation of Negro musicians who listened to or enjoyed the classics; that to be truly free they must act exactly the opposite of what white people might believe, rightly or wrongly, a Negro to be; that the performing artist can be completely and absolutely free of the obligations of the entertainer, and that they could play jazz with dignity only by frowning and treating the audience with aggressive contempt; and that to be in control, artistically and personally, one must be so cool as to quench one's liquid fire" (S&A 209). Ellison imagines the birth of bop energized in part by the despair that "after all, is ever an important force in revolutions"; and he pictures the bopsters, "like disgruntled conspirators meeting fatefully to assemble the random parts of a bomb," confronting the musical piracy of the white instrumentalists and big bands with an aggressive style fashioned from intricate chord progressions and melodic inversions that for a while, at least, were to be a shield against the white music industry's predatory imitators (S&A 203, 209). But the lessons Ellison wanted readers to understand from his celebration of this moment of "momentous modulation" involved not just the names, the place, the mood, or the musical mode, but the significance of jazz as a form of historical consciousness and the ways the meaning of such a phenomenon becomes victim to the selectivity of memory, the arbitrariness of the historical record, and the fragile idealism of tradition and innovation.

Implicit in this exposure of how Minton's golden age succumbed to the processes which make history "ever a tall tale told by inattentive idealists" is that relentless questioning of formulaic thinking that has been the central characteristic of Ellison's dialectical style. Though rejecting Marxian dogma, he has remained Hegelian enough in spirit to believe that error resides in incompleteness and abstraction and that it can be exposed through the contradictions they create. Accordingly, he has devoted much of his literary and cultural criticism to singling out the absurdities and non

sequiturs latent in the fragmentary and one-dimensional theories generated by "that feverish industry dedicated to telling Negroes who and what
they are, and which can usually be counted upon to deprive both humanity and culture of their complexity" (*S&A* xvii). "Since we are more complex than we think we are," he insists, "we are constantly making blunders"
(Ellison, "Alain Locke Symposium" 27). This, together with his uncompromising assertion that human experience is of a whole, that in the mind
as in nature "the heel bone is connected to the head bone," has fueled his
war on those partial and abstract views which reduce the dynamic Gestalts
of personality, culture, history, and art to stereotype. When imposed on
any of these, the concept of race, especially, from Ellison's perspective, has
bred a logic of illusion rooted in social expediencies and psychic repression; and he has confronted it everywhere he has found it. Dialectic has
been his "coping-stone"; and like Plato's and Aristotle's dialecticians, he is
a man who knows how to ask and to answer questions. In the published
exchanges with friends, foes, and interviewers, Ellison has most commonly
engaged them with the proximally psychotherapeutic tactic of forcing a
confrontation between their racial half-truths or facile abstractions and
the general human truths which racist assumption has suppressed or kept
out of consciousness. Or, like Aristotle's *epagoge*, he has pressed and accen-
tuated the contradictions in oversimplified formulations by showing their
helplessness before the concrete and particular.

Ellison's unearthings of the vernacular process are often couched
explicitly in the rhetoric of desublimation, as are his maneuvers in the long
war against racial stereotypy. But in *Shadow and Act*, it is in the skirmishes
with individual opponents—the exchanges with Irving Howe and Stanley
Edgar Hyman and the reviews of work by Gunnar Myrdal and LeRoi
Jones—that Ellison has mobilized the full force of his particularizing anti-
theories and shown his formidable dialectical skills to best advantage. In
"The World and the Jug," for instance, he opens his unsparing rejoinder to
Howe's critical rehearsal of the shop-worn argument over the roles of art
and protest in African American writing by posing three epagogic ques-
tions: "Why is it so often true that when critics confront the American as
Negro they suddenly drop their advanced critical armament and revert
with an air of confident superiority to quite primitive modes of analysis?
Why is it that sociology-oriented critics seem to rate literature so far below

politics and ideology that they would rather kill a novel than modify their presumptions concerning a given reality which it seeks in its own terms to project? Finally, why is it that so many of those who would tell us the meaning of Negro life never bother to learn how varied it really is?" (S&A 115)

Ellison proceeds to drop a rhetorical curtain on the puppet figures of radical agitprop by deftly severing the cords between the critic's prescriptive stereotype of clenched-fist black militancy and those palpably human features of experience and temperament that understandably distinguished Richard Wright's literary sensibility and James Baldwin's from his own. He reveals that what radical formula posited to be a sterile and irremediably agonizing state of "Negroness" was, for him, an emotionally complex, rewarding, and profoundly civilized way of life. To the image of himself and other black writers Jim Crowed into intellectual endogamy, he opposes the image of his own far-flung international and interracial family of literary "ancestors" and "relatives." With none of the ritual rancor and scatology of the dirty dozens, but with all the rhetorical force of its ad hominem stripping away of pretense, Ellison's bravura stand for principles he knew to be more than personal issues raises an army of disproving particulars against abstract racial categories he finds ultimately more oppressive "than the state of Mississippi." Such presumptive categorization left no room for the individual writer's unique existence—"for that intensity of personal anguish which compels the artist to seek relief by projecting it into the world in conjunction with other things; that anguish which might take the form of an acute sense of inferiority for one, homosexuality for another, an overwhelming sense of the absurdity of human life for still another. Nor does it leave room for the experience that might be caused by a harelip, by a stutter, by epilepsy—indeed, by any and everything in this life which plunges the talented individual into solitude while leaving him the will to transcend his condition through art" (S&A 136).

In the more amicable but no less exacting exchange with Stanley Edgar Hyman, Ellison, archetype-oriented writer that he is, nonetheless takes his old friend and intellectual sparring partner to task for consistently oversimplifying the relationship between African American literature and folklore archetypes and, more pointedly, for failing to guide his archetype-hunting with the caution that between literature and the folk tradition "there must needs be the living human being in a specific texture of time, place and circumstance, who must respond, make choices, achieve eloquence, and create specific works of art" (*S&A* 61–62). Ellison rejects Hyman's approach to black literary folklore through the minstrel tradition's "darky entertainer" because, as an ostensible Negro version of the archetypal trickster figure, the minstrel darky was actually an abstract imposition that glossed over the contradicting specificities of American historical and literary experience. For despite the "blackness" in its use of black American idiom, songs, dance, and wordplay, the darky entertainer was, Ellison insists, a negative sign in a comedy of the grotesque and unacceptable, which expressed not the African American sense of the comic but "the white American's Manichean fascination with the symbolism of blackness and whiteness" (*S&A* 62). Pulling away from the detached panorama of universal archetype, Ellison shows that under close inspection, the specific rhetorical situation of minstrelsy serves white needs, not black, that it "involves the self-humiliation of the 'sacrificial' figure, and that a psychological dissociation from this symbolic self-maiming is one of the most powerful motives at work in the audience" (64). Where Hyman insisted that the figure in blackface is related to an archetypal trickster originating in Africa, Ellison counters by specifying its "homegrown, Western, and Calvinist" features which, together with the figure's adjustment to white American symbolic needs, pointed to indigenous developments "far more intriguing" than any abstract, intercontinental tracings (66–67).

If repudiating Hyman's theoretically inspired distortion of cultural fact and literary fiction showed one continuing pattern of Ellison's dialectic, the turn therein away from "the African connection" spotlighted another. For despite his long-lived interest in African art, Ellison persistently rejected as artificial all attempts by literary romanticists, racial mystics, Pan-African ideologues, and cultural anthropologists to establish a systematic cultural kinship between African Americans and Africans. In an exchange in France in 1958, published in *Shadow and Act* as "Some Questions and Some Answers," he defines black Americans as having the world's only "Negro" culture, a culture native to the United States, basically Protestant in religion, Western in its kinship system, American in its sense of time, history, and secular values. What bound American Negroes to the world's other scattered peoples of "partially African origin" was not culture, he argues, but the hatred of European domination shared by most nonwhite peoples, a common denominator which had potent political value but whose cultural value, he claims, was "almost nil" (*S&A* 253–5). Three years earlier, in an interview for *The Paris Review*, he declared that, because America's race problem had now lined up with the anticolonialist struggle of the non-Western world, its possibilities for art had actually increased; but this too had implied no specifically cultural linkages (*S&A* 182).

It is important to remember that Ellison, like Richard Wright, was part of the intellectual cutting edge of a Depression era generation of black literary radicals, infused with Marx's and Freud's demystifying theories, who rejected the primitivist African vogue of the Negro Renaissance and the Garvey Movement as fanciful posturing and a flight from the existential realities of the African American folk and proletarian experience. Like Wright and sociologist E. Franklin Frazier, Ellison rejected Melville Herskovits's later thesis of widespread African cultural survivals in America because he believed, as Wright did, that "it was only by and large in the concrete social frame of reference in which men lived that one could account for men being what they were." Though intrigued by Lorenzo Turner's study of Africanisms in the Sea Islands Gullah dialect, and though he later would find "some validity" in Herskovits's cross-cultural theories, Ellison initially dismissed *The Myth of the Negro Past* because "the context and the way [Herskovits] put it seemed to imply that we needed to apologize—that we needed a past" (Ellison, "Twenty Years After" 6). To a man who felt "no lack" in his cultural heritage as a Negro American, and for whom *all* Americans were "people without a history—but with a new synthesis," the insistence of sociological theorists that he had special African ties which he could never discover in any concrete way made an identification with Africa and Africans that much more problematic (Isaacs 264–65). Years later, remarking that he had never had any question but that he is *part* African, Ellison nevertheless reasserted his belief that the past does not have the relevance in America that it had in Europe and that there is a needless apology implicit in "Negro Americans walking around top-heavy from trying to Africanize themselves when that which is authentically African in them has come down to us through more subtle ways—and *we* are not the only inheritors of it" (Ellison, "Twenty Years After" 6).

It is this sense of a black cultural tradition independent of political ideology—subtle, subterranean, and diffused throughout the social structure—which gave the dialectical animus to Ellison's 1964 review of LeRoi Jones/Amiri Baraka's *Blues People*. Ellison, like Baraka, has always seen the blues tradition as a special repository and focus of a collective history and as embodying a "total way of life." Accordingly, Ellison lauds Baraka's effort to treat the music according to what the Black Arts imam described as a "strictly theoretical" exegesis of the journey in sound from slavery to citizenship. Ellison's final evaluation, however, is that Baraka's theory "flounders before that complex of human motives which makes human history, and which is so characteristic of the American Negro" (*S&A* 246).

In that regard, as is so characteristic of Ralph Ellison, he arms his critique of Baraka's militant abstractions with pointed particularities the former could not contain. Where Baraka's theory attempted to simplify the historical bifurcation of the blues into "country" and "city/classic" forms by imposing Franklin Frazier's pejorative class anatomy of the rise of a self-eviscerating, blues-rejecting black bourgeoisie, Ellison confronts the resulting "rigid correlation between color, education, income and the Negro's preference in music" with the unruly instance of "a white-skinned Negro with brown freckles who owns sixteen oil wells sunk in a piece of Texas land once farmed by his ex-slave parents who were a blue-eyed, white-skinned, red-headed (kinky) Negro woman from Virginia and a blue-gummed, black skinned, curly haired Negro male from Mississippi, and who not only sang bass in a Holy Roller church, played the market and voted Republican but collected blues recordings and was a walking depository of blues tradition" (*S&A* 245).

Where Baraka asserted categorically that "a slave cannot be a man," Ellison counters, "but what, one might ask, of those moments when he feels his metabolism aroused by the rising of the sap in spring? What of his identity among other slaves? With his wife? And isn't it closer to the truth that far from considering themselves only in terms of that abstraction, 'a slave', the enslaved really thought of themselves as men who had been unjustly enslaved?" (*S&A* 247). The implication that the test of theory is its ability to cope with concrete and idiosyncratic experience is the heart of Ellison's dialectic. And the idea of a culture of survival and transcendence built from the possibilities for maneuvering in the face of the inevitable, from affirmative roles and identities irrepressible even in bondage, and from excellences forged under limitation, is the heart of his uncompromising embrace of traditional African American strategies for psychic survival and self-sustenance.

Nor is this an evasion of the political problems of power and freedom or the necessity for social reconstruction. Ellison believes, with Hegel, that "consciousness is all," that "human life is a move toward the rational" (O'Brien 70, 75), and that freedom finally is a creation not of political institutions but of mind: "Simply to take down a barrier doesn't make a man free," he insists; "he can only free himself" (Graham and Singh 86). He or she does so, Ellison believes, in the course of discovering and pushing against the extreme limits of his or her own possibilities, which happens in the context of societies that are not God-constructed worlds but man-made and improvisational "arrangements," inevitably hierarchical through the inheritance of power or talent and always, tragically, productive of victims, guilt, and scapegoats—"whether it's in a democracy, a socialistic society, or a communistic one" (O'Brien 69–70). In contemporary America, where, Ellison believes, the lines of color caste are blurring, class lines grow more rigid, offering the prospect not of an end to the need for victims and scapegoats but perhaps to the practice of designating them by race. Realistically, the human challenge, he contends, is to moderate injustices and inequalities that sometimes may be ineradicable; and this can only be done by "keeping the ideal alive" as a *conscious* discipline (O'Brien 72). For those individuals and groups who, like black Americans, bear disproportionately the human costs of human systems, that keeping of ideals seems, in his view, to be simultaneously a pragmatic strategy of social reform and a mode of transcendence.

The role of art, here, for Ellison, is crucial. Richard Wright, in the often alluded to passage in *Black Boy* where he broods upon the "cultural barrenness of black life," wondered whether such human values as tenderness, love, honor, and loyalty were native to humanity or whether they were in fact "fostered, won, struggled and suffered for, preserved in ritual from one generation to another." Ellison, interpreting Wright's comment as an oblique affirmation of black people's struggle against alienation, visualizes the conflict between black Americans and white society as a ritual confrontation of willed values in which "Western culture must be won, confronted like the animal in a Spanish bullfight, dominated by the red shawl of codified experience and brought heaving to its knees" (*S&A* 103). The arena for this imposition of a black vision on the world is, most properly, in the rituals of art; for, as Malraux had helped make clear to Ellison, "the organized significance of art is stronger than all the multiplicity of the world; . . . [and] that significance alone enables man to conquer chaos and master destiny" (*S&A* 94). When the three volumes of Malraux's *The Psychology of Art* were published in the late 1940s, Ellison paid twenty-five dollars apiece and walked around with holes in his shoes in order to possess what then "was more important than having dry feet"—a revelation, fused in Malraux's art history, philosophy, and politics, of a secret and almost satanic path to power, freedom, and salvation (Ellison, "Essential Ellison" 149).

Malraux's opulent and exacting multivolume tribute to artistic genius vouchsafed the liberating possibility that, now through the power of twentieth-century reproductive technologies, artists for the first time drew on the whole continuum of the world's art. Art works had consequently acquired "a kind of ubiquity," thereby making all men and women both potential "heirs" of the entire world and, more important, creators and conquerors of what had profound social implications—"the first universal artistic culture." This looming, inalienable world of art, in its detachment from the social order, does not imitate life, Malraux maintained, but rather imitates art and reveals life—is in its origins an aggressive negation of the material world and all values opposing its own, so that it is actually allied with whatever denies, destroys, transcends, ordinary human reality. Yet art is, Malraux agreed with Hegel, a vehicle for the perpetuation of spirit and hence a guardian of human values. So the artist, as creator, engages in both negation and human salvation, in the mastery of art and the deliverance of humanity (Jean Leymarie, qtd. in De Courcel 184–203). Art historians critical of Malraux's rapt pronouncements imagined an embarrassing contradiction here, not comprehending Malraux's vatic artist as in fact a rebel Demiurge, a re-creator god who is neither the originator of the world nor an object of worship but the Craftsman who turns chaos into cosmos, rectifying and reorganizing the elements of the universe. As such, in his alliance with the forces of negation, he becomes a gnostic lord of the lower powers, envisioning the rise to sovereignty of forces the surface world would subordinate. Hence the true artist wants no escape from the world into aestheticism but instead a planned conquest of that world, which will compel us to see that the "sustaining, enriching, transforming" image of itself humanity has inherited through art is itself the primary justification of the mystery of human life (Blanchot).

In these terms, Malraux's vision helped canalize Ellison's own demiurgic impulses, helped guide his efforts to interpret and use the cultural inheritance of the slave past and the repressive present as keys for transforming servant into sovereign. History would be an ally, for the African American was and had always been, as DuBois asserted in *The Souls of Black Folk* and again in *The Gift of Black Folk*, "primarily an artist," regardless of his or her other considerable gifts. Benjamin Brawley, the first comprehensive chronicler of African American cultural life, had documented that claim in *The Social History of the American Negro* (1921) and in *The Negro Genius* (1937). Brawley insisted that the pronounced distinction of black men and women in the arts, and their almost exclusively aesthetic influence on American civilization—the exception of enforced labor duly noted—implied, as current accomplishments confirmed, no incapacity for achievement in other spheres but only a peculiar racial genius that destined the Negro "to reach his greatest heights in the field of the artistic" (Brawley 9). Alain Locke, tendering less confidently the old racial mysticism, had reasserted the idea even as the Negro Renaissance went into eclipse, writing in 1929 that

> [I]t is obvious, in spite of the great necessity for practical and economic
> contributions in the future on the part of the Negro, that the main line of Negro
> development must necessarily be artistic, cultural, moral, and spiritual. . . .
> Although he must qualify in all branches of American life and activity, the
> Negro can be of more general good in supplementing Nordic civilization than
> through merely competitively imitating or extending it along lines in which it
> is at present successful and preeminent. Indeed, as what seems to be the special
> race genius matures and gains momentum, it becomes increasingly apparent that
> the Negro's unique experience and heredity combined may have fitted him for a
> special creative role in American life as an artist class, as a social re-agent, and as
> a spiritual leaven. ("Negro Contributions to America" 257).

The racialism and historical romanticism of Brawley's and Locke's position, and what might be interpreted as its subtle acceptance of being relegated to the social role of "darky entertainer," were, of course, anathema to Ellison's generation of radicals—as Richard Wright's credo and the bop revolt emphasized. His political perspectives led Ellison to focus as much on the potential role of African American artistry in the struggle for liberation from American racial oppression as on the undeniable, though historically ironic, black artistic "contribution" to American civilization. Locke himself, by 1938, in the course of retracing the career of black art and literature from Emancipation through Depression, had changed his emphasis on art as showpiece to that of art as a liberating force, acknowledging that "every oppressed group is under the necessity, both after and before its physical emancipation from the shackles of slavery—be that slavery chattel or wage—of establishing a spiritual freedom of the mind. . . . This cultural emancipation must be self-emancipation and is the proper and peculiar function of a minority literature and art" (Locke, "Freedom through Art" 227). From the antebellum black abolitionists to the post-Reconstruction pastoralists to the New Negroes to the New Deal leftists, each generation, with tactics shifting almost each decade in accord with changing social forces, Locke now realized, had been seeking freedom through art.

DuBois, too, his own philosophy transformed by his absorption of Marx and Freud, by the 1940s had exchanged his earlier progressivist faith in a cultural messianism through which the meek black masses would inherit the earth for a theory of humanist, pacific, socialist transformation rooted ultimately in cultivating the explosive freedoms in the inner regions of the spirit—"the dreams and fantasies of mind, of imagination and contrivance, playing with the infinite possibilities of ever-revealing truth" ("The Nature of Intellectual Freedom" 233). In the same year that Locke shifted ground, DuBois proclaimed, in "The Revelation of Saint Orgne the Damned," that "freedom is the path of art, and living in the fuller and broader sense of the term is the expression of art" (112–13). But while DuBois believed that art provided the ends and means for the most complete enjoyment of the possibilities of human existence, his special brand of Marxian humanism made art either defensive propaganda or a grand refuge from the world of material compulsions; and like Locke's cultural reformism, it lacked what Ellison came to see as the active mode of true art—the passionate will to dominate the world and all reality.

Beyond fueling that will, what Malraux's conception yielded when Ellison trained it on the African American cultural predicament and on his own sense of the American national experience was the opportunity to convert the traditionally constrained and compensatory art Locke and DuBois described into an art of redemptive conquest. The rise of a universal artistic culture accessible to any literate person with the energy and will to appropriate it had special implications for communities socially submerged in an American society whose pluralism, fluidity, and relative absence of stable traditions gave literature and the arts and the novel, particularly, an unprecedented role in the development of the nation. In his 1955 *Paris Review* interview session, Ellison concluded by insisting that his devotion to the novel afforded him the possibility of contributing not only to the growth of the literature but to the shaping of the culture as he should like it to be: the novel was literally a conquest of the frontier, *creating* the American experience in the process of describing it (*S&A* 183).

But perhaps the clearest expression of the demiurgic mode in Ellison's aesthetic appeared through a foray into the visual arts in his 1968 exhibition-catalogue introduction to the work of painter-collagist and long-time friend, Romare Bearden. That year of political assassinations, Ellison noted later, had a chilling effect on the comic development of his novel in progress; and in "The Art of Romare Bearden" the tragic and agonistic quality of the times made an obvious imprint. Against this numbing societal backdrop, Ellison pictures Bearden as a demiurgic paradigm—a Craftsman and true creator whose "nature and mode of action [is] to dominate all the world and time through technique and vision. His mission is to bring a new visual order into the world, and through his art he seeks to reset society's clock by imposing upon it his own method of defining the times" (Ellison, *GTT* 229). As a lower-world master of illusion and revelation whose amorphous physical appearance masked his world-absorbing blackness, Bearden labored lovingly to release us "from the prison of our media dulled perception" by reintegrating the forms of experience, so that his ultimate aim was to "destroy the accepted world by way of revealing the unseen" (*GTT* 234). In making manifest that which goes conventionally unseen, Bearden's tradition-steeped but eclectic play with plastic possibility effected a return of the repressed: he masked Harlemites with the abstract faces of African sculpture and totem. His Harlem became therefore "a place inhabited by people who have in fact been resurrected, recreated by art. . . . And resurrected with them in the guise of fragmented ancestral figures and forgotten gods (really masks of the instincts, hopes, emotions, aspirations and dreams) are those powers that now surge in our land with a potentially destructive force which springs from the fact of their having for so long gone unrecognized, unseen" (*GTT* 235).

Bearden's technique, as Ellison imagines it, was an eclectic and ceremonial parataxis "eloquent of the sharp breaks, leaps in consciousness, distortions, paradoxes, reversals, telescoping of time and surreal blending of the styles, values, hopes and dreams which characterize much of Negro American history" (680). It successfully marshaled all the resources of modern art—with Pablo Picasso's cubist and collagist revelations as aids to extrapolation—for exploring the tragic predicament of Bearden's people and did so "without violating his passionate dedication to art as a fundamental and transcendent agency for confronting and revealing the world." As such, Bearden's own collagist masterworks mocked wordlessly the self-willed powerlessness of those would-be black artists whose fascination with, and accommodation to, their "anachronistic" social predicament made them believe the true artist's attitude toward the world is "quite quixotic" (675). Those who will be dominated by reality, Ellison warns, are those who, "in the field of culture, where their freedom of self-definition is at a maximum, and where the techniques of artistic self-expression are most abundantly available," allow the social imbalance to shrivel their sense of possibility and to dominate their thinking about themselves, their people, their country, and their art (674). By contrast, those who will dominate reality are those who, working from the heights of the time and with the most challenging possibilities of form, convert the unassimilated and anachronistic into conscious elements of style captive to their own controlling vision.

The power to dominate reality, social and aesthetic, which is so much the subject of the essay on Bearden's art, was never for Ralph Ellison a mere matter of a field of force acting on inert human objects, nor a matter merely of "positive thinking." It had always been predicated on a relationship, a confrontation of active wills, somewhere on the continuum from antagonism to cooperation, between a wielder of power and those who value the things he or she controls. Power, influence, domination, in life and in art, are always, in Ellison's conscious thought, directed by will and effected by the mastery of organizing techniques. On one level of the political struggle for power in America, the answer to the riddle of black disempowerment rests for Ellison in the failure of black leaders to recognize their true source of power, "which lies, as Martin Luther King perceived, in the Negro's ability to suffer even death for the attainment of our beliefs" (*S&A* 37). On another level, the political potency of a Booker T. Washington and the comparative inability of a W. E. B DuBois to effect his political will are measures, to Ellison, not so much of the values the two men espoused, however close or conflicting, but of their individual technical mastery over structured possibilities (Ellison, "Indivisible Man" 53). Conversely, Ellison eschews organized violence as a means to black freedom and power in the United States because, first, "we are outnumbered and . . . the major instruments of destruction are in the hands of the whites"; and second, most importantly, because black people have not yet collectively willed either political goal—separation or seizure of the government—which would make orchestrated violence "something to think about" (Ellison, "Interview with Ralph Ellison" 163–64).

But then, political violence and the ideologies that seek to wield it as an instrument of power are in Ellison's vision largely aspects of the chaos and illusion that life-affirming acts of self-definition must somehow reduce to redemptive form. On the level of aesthetics, the violence the demiurge does to provisional reality is, at the same time, an act of regeneration and deliverance. Such violence seeks no throne or ideology but only to reenergize the forces of life. Its power is an initiating vision that creates human desire, overcomes human resistances, redirects human actions by reshaping what men and women perceive their interests and possibilities to be. For Ellison as artist and wielder of the word, this power to dominate minds lies in the capacity of technique—the ingenious, guileful, symbolic structuring of emotions and perceptions—to do violence to our "trained incapacity" to perceive the truth. And the revelation of truth—never mere reportage or raw "telling it like it is"—is always a function of style, whose test is not so much beauty as power.

Ellison's awareness, however, of the ambivalence of human experience and our ambiguous perception of that experience extends to power and the word as well. Power, his Invisible Man learns, can be an anodyne or an illusion as well as an instrument of the rational will—and the will itself is never completely free or inviolable but always limited by recalcitrant necessity and always vulnerable to injury and deflection. Moreover, the word, magical and Janus-faced, has the potency not only to revive and make us free but to "blind, imprison, and destroy" (*S&A* 42). As Ellison observed in his interview with Black Arts iconoclast Ishmael Reed,

> During the sixties, the myth of the redeemed criminal had a tremendous influence on our young people, when criminals guilty of every crime from con games, to rape, to murder, exploited it by declaring themselves political activists and black leaders. As a result many sincere, dedicated leaders of an older generation were swept aside. . . . I found it outrageous. Because not only did it distort the concrete historical differences between one period of struggle and another, it made heroes out of thugs and self-servers out of dedicated leaders. Worse, it gave many kids the notion that there was no point in developing their minds. . . . Years ago Du Bois stressed a leadership based upon an elite of the intellect. During the Sixties it appeared that for many Afro-Americans all that was required for such a role was a history of criminality, a capacity for irresponsible rhetoric, and the passionate assertion of the mystique of 'Blackness.' (Ellison, "Essential Ellison" 150).

Here, clearly, and in the published and still unpublished fragments of the projected multivolume novel he labored meticulously over for so many years, Ralph Ellison remained unwaveringly and outspokenly absorbed in the problems of power and leadership in "a land most strange." As ever, the forms of mysticism and militancy that mask political naiveté, personal opportunism, and an ignorance of the past seemed to him merely mirages of power and leadership in the social arena, whose counterparts in the rituals of the word he was distressed to see in the self-pitying sentiment and vapid propaganda of the defensively illiterate writer. If African American writers are to sustain a place in American literature and to become more influential in the broader community, he told James Alan McPherson in a lengthy exchange in 1969 when the war of anti-Ellison invective was still intense, "they will do it in terms of style: by imposing a style upon a sufficient area of American life to give other readers a sense that this is true, that here is a revelation of reality" (Ellison, "Indivisible Man" 49). His hesitancy then to predict future popularity and impact for black wordsmiths rested in his troubled observation that "so many of them seem to be still caught up at the point of emphasizing inwardness," when in his view mastery of the rhetoric of fiction requires also an intricate awareness of the world outside the self and one's immediate community. There is no quarter given here in Ellison's continuing guerilla action against the forms of illusion. And there is no easy target offered by this one-time horn blower and quail hunter turned literary grenadier, this street-corner activist and pamphleteer turned minister of culture, this prideful dance master and raconteur for whom "eclecticism is the word" and "playing it by ear" the mode, this artificer of masks and names and comic chaos, whose shifting guises as synthesizer, celebrant, dialectician, and demiurge seem designed to make any manhunt fixed on this mind in motion as quixotic as wing shooting at shadows.

War is an act of violence intended to compel our opponent to fulfill our will. . . . Rather than compare war to art, we should more precisely compare it to commerce, which is also a conflict of interests and activities; and it is closer still to politics, which, in its turn, is a kind of commerce, but on a larger scale. . . . To introduce into the philosophy of war a principle of moderation would be absurd.

—CARL MARIE VON CLAUSEWITZ, *On War*

Armament is an important factor in war, but not the decisive factor. . . . Man, not material, forms the decisive factor.

—MAO TSE-TUNG, *Lecture*

In guerrilla warfare the struggle no longer concerns the place where you are, but the place where you are going. Each fighter carries his warring country between his toes.

—FRANTZ FANON, *The Wretched of the Earth*

We do not fight for the real but for the shadows we make.
A flag is a piece of cloth and a word is a sound,
But we make them something neither cloth nor a sound,
Totems of love and hate, black sorcerystones.

—STEPHEN VINCENT BENÉT, *John Brown's Body*

Groucho: Do you realize our army's facing disastrous defeat? What do you intend to do about it?
Chico: I've changed to the other side.

—MARX BROTHERS, *Duck Soup*

Chapter Two

THE CONSCIOUS HERO AND THE RITES OF MAN:
ELLISON'S WAR

In the fall of 1947, five years before the appearance of *Invisible Man*, Ralph Ellison published in England's *Horizon* magazine a fictional fragment that prefigured the panoramic novel to come. Nightmarishly surreal, grotesquely comic, hyperbolically absurd, the scenes of this "Battle Royal," for all their Marx Brothers outrageousness, nevertheless had roots in a living social history of routinized color-caste codes and "race ritual" traceable at least as far back as the fugitive slave narratives of the 1840s. Ellison's tale, however, directed attention no more explicitly to its place in a submerged vernacular history than it overtly promised the novel a 1965 *Book Week* critics' poll would ultimately acknowledge to be the most distinguished single work of fiction published in post–World War II America.

The most immediate literary accomplishment of "Battle Royal" was the rhetorical innovation of addressing its midcentury audience from the vantage point of a black memoirist whose intensely personal account of the preceding two decades of depression and world war compressed its deepest meanings into this now famous anecdotal frame: A young black Southern high school graduate, a would-be leader of his people, has been invited to repeat, before the leading white citizens of their segregated small Southern town, his recent graduation speech urging blacks—in the manner of Booker T. Washington—to "social responsibility" and cooperation with

79

the ruling whites. Before being allowed to give his speech, however, he and nine other "little shines" are herded to the ballroom via a servants' elevator and outfitted with trunks and boxing gloves. To get their blood up for what lies ahead, they are then titillated erotically by a garish blonde stripteaser, after which they are blindfolded and led into a boxing ring. There they battle to the last survivor and finally scramble for counterfeit coins on a surreptitiously electrified rug—all for the orgiastic entertainment of the onlooking whites. Delivering his speech at last as a finale to the evening's program, choking on his own blood and saliva, the self-described "invisible man" turns the sideshow atmosphere deadly serious for a moment by accidentally uttering the forbidden phrase "social equality." He humbly retracts it, completes his speech, wins a briefcase containing a scholarship to a black college, and goes home to a night of haunting dreams that prophesy his fate as the butt of a white folk's joke that is to "Keep This Nigger-Boy Running"—under the taunting tutelage of his own outwardly meek but inwardly Machiavellian grandfather.

In contrast to the soberly strident protest fiction Richard Wright had shepherded during the preceding decade, Ellison's experimental yarn revealed much in common with the new metaphysically "black" humor and "tragic farce" toward which postwar literary sensibilities seemed drawn.[1] Its phantasmagoria of perversely sacred and profane public rituals and caste compulsions aligned "Battle Royal" with the developing body of mythopoetic motifs and New Critical concepts then rising to prominence among artists, academics, and reviewers (Wellek, "Philosophy"). Ellison's deflection of explicitly "racial" themes from the realm of moral melodrama to that of comic absurdity, and from the grotesqueries of the reigning American literary race ritual—lynching—to the slapstick antics of the ballroom smoker, made "Battle Royal" seem disarmingly distant from the spectre of black-white confrontation signaled in the then expanding national pattern of organized black protests, boycotts, and Freedom Rides, as well as from the urban race riots that had convulsed Mobile, Los Angeles, Detroit, and Harlem during the war years.[2]

"Battle Royal," however, would attract little critical attention until its reappearance in 1952 as the point of entry into the unheralded experimental novel that, for all its reviewers' emphasis on generic identity crisis, existentialism, political disengagement, and all-American questing for self, nonetheless pursued its larger meanings through the medium of intensely "racial" experience and a corollary nexus of political engagement, failure, and rededication. In the course of moving its anonymous hero from childhood to manhood, from feudal Southern province to Northern machine-age city, from the margins of power toward the center, *Invisible Man* traversed a disconcerting multiplicity of institutional, technological, and psychological environs while leaping experientially across a hundred years of American history, official and unofficial.[3] Like Wright's *Native Son*, Ellison's completed novel would find its explicit politics to be its greatest burden and its most often cited failure of eloquence. But it was precisely in *Invisible Man's* attempt to "politicize" the nonpolitical—to reveal the protopolitical jumble of human motive embedded in the ritual and psychic substructure of American racial codes—that Ellison offered the most startling new insights about American culture. Most crucially, in creating a "conscious hero" able ultimately to comprehend this bewildering modern context and still "believe in nothing if not action" despite all his "sad, lost period" of naive political enthusiasms, Ellison's narrative distilled prophetically the metamorphosing black dissident sensibility whose phoenixlike resurgence in the postwar Freedom Movement would ultimately transform American social and political life.

That such a sensibility would conceive its own circular life history as beginning and ending in riot was a matter of more than the rhetoric of fiction—a matter indeed of a newly consolidated radical black historicism. In recognition of it, the structure of Ellison's narrative was undergirded phenomenologically by a nonmechanistic, nonlinear concept of time that constituted no mere storytelling device but rather what Ellison knew to be an increasingly pervasive element of African American consciousness. In a trenchant mixture of fatalism and hope, Spenglerian echoes of white Western nations spiraling downward on paths yoked contrapuntally to a chiliastic "Rising Tide of Color" had been in popular currency in black sermons and street-corner oratory since the Jazz Age (Moses 251–71). In that tradition, for Ellison's "thinker-tinker" and chronicler of personal catastrophe, what he would call the "boomerang of history" represented his historically minded generation's awareness that, with World War II, what had happened to the Jazz Age "New Negroes" who had preceded them a generation and a world war earlier was repeating itself, only now on a broader and more inexorable scale. The Great Migration from South to North and country to city that had been spurred by World War I and that had been buoyed on hope and had buoyed in turn the Negro Renaissance and Garveyism was now, with the stimulus of World War II, greater and nationwide. The military experience itself, which in World War I opened to black soldiers the internationalizing vistas of European battlefields and cosmopolitan cities, in World War II spread more than a million young black men across the entire face of the globe, altering their worldviews concomitantly. World War I's covert colonialist underpinnings and accompanying "scramble for Africa" had impressed on its black participants the international import of racial ideology and the rising anticolonialist fervor. Correlatively, World War II's undisguised fascist talk of master races, its genocidal Hitlerian assault on the Jews, and the heady symbolism of Mussolini's preparatory war on ancient, unbowed Ethiopia combined to help forge the new consensus among the black war generation that henceforth would inseparably link foreign and domestic racisms and would be dedicated to breaking the cycle of institutionalized white supremacy in America just as the cycle of colonial empire in Africa and Asia would be broken in the aftermath of the war for Roosevelt's "four freedoms" (Weisbord 89–114).

Against this panorama of historic imperatives, the most acclaimed experimental novel of the postwar era took shape. Ellison's imaginary memoir would recapitulate the strivings and debates of a whole generation of black intellectuals who looked out on an expanded postwar world as pregnant with dangers as with new possibilities. For them, unlike Anglo-American intellectuals, it was not a time when the old progressivist faith no longer provided meaning or when consensus politics and an "end to ideology" dominated thought. Rather, it was a time when the twin spectres of world war and race war drove them on a quest for a new kind of leadership that would draw on the rich resources of African American life and liberate them from the myths and psychic shackles of the past. A "useable" past had to be won, the still magnetic career of W. E. B. DuBois taught them, from "the propaganda of the past"; and by fleshing out that proposition in the sweeping Depression-era prose poem of *Black Reconstruction in America* (1935), DuBois had, with partisan rigor, vivified an old millennial vision:

The most magnificent drama in the last thousand years of human history is the transportation of ten million human beings out of the dark beauty of their mother continent into the new-found Eldorado of the West. They descended into Hell; and in the third century they arose from the dead, in the finest effort to achieve democracy for the working millions which this world had ever seen. It was a tragedy that beggared the Greek; it was an upheaval of humanity like the Reformation and the French Revolution. Yet we are blind and led by the blind. We discern in it no part of our labor movement; no part of our industrial triumph; no part of our religious experience. . . . And why? Because in a day when the human mind aspired to a science of human action, a history and psychology of the mighty effort of the mightiest century, we fell under the leadership of those who would compromise with truth in the past in order to make peace in the present and guide policy in the future (727).

Having immersed himself in these issues during the early 1940s as researcher, as polemicist, and as apprentice fiction writer, Ellison enthusiastically witnessed the new black historical consciousness consolidate itself intellectually in the immediate postwar years through allied scholarly assaults on "The White Masters of the World" in the adamantine Pan-Africanist rhetoric of DuBois's *The World and Africa* in 1946 and in the quieter but no less revisionary cadences of John Hope Franklin's *From Slavery to Freedom* in 1947. The new black historicism proposed a global context and a requisite need to "re-tell the story of the evolution of the people of the United States in order to place the Negro in his proper relationship and perspective" (Franklin xi–xiii). The earlier publication of Gunnar Myrdal's *An American Dilemma* in 1943 (the year of the cycle of urban race riots Ellison first helped report and then later recreated fictionally) had documented exhaustively both the ethical "schizophrenia" of the white American mind and the debilitating black adjustments to it that the dislocations of war now made unnecessary and untenable. Acutely attuned to sociological as well as literary assessments of American race relations, Ellison had largely accepted Myrdal's sociopsychological anatomy of the white man's racial dilemma. But his evaluation of the Swedish sociologist's work took issue sharply with Myrdal's account of a rigid psychology of victimization and a corresponding culture of deviant imitativeness ostensibly dominant in black communities (*S&A* 290–302). More in accord with Ellison's interpretations, *Black Metropolis*, St. Clair Drake's and Horace Cayton's mid-decade sociological classic of participant observation, instead described the world of America's black "Bronzevilles" as a complexly differentiated amalgam of defensible norms, values, and prophylactic styles of living. Among them the conscious, uncompromising struggle for "racial advancement"—through the labor union movement, through left-wing politics, through the panoply of New Negro and black nationalist enclaves, and more and more through a radicalized social gospel in the church—was increasingly ascendant. In these contexts "race men" and "race women" reconfigured by modern ideologies of social reform or revolution were increasingly the leadership prototypes for the kind of disciplined public protests and politico-economic organization that ultimately would surface in the energetic civil rights movement of the early 1950s.[4]

The New Negroes of the post–World War I Roaring Twenties, unlike their white counterparts, had considered themselves a "found," not a "lost," generation, as Alain Locke's movement-mounting anthology made clear. Similarly, the New Negroes of the postwar 1940s were energized by a consuming sense of mission and fateful urgency. They repudiated old notions of gradualist racial reform in part because they anticipated, short of a saving revolution in race relations and in the nation's political economy, a predictable fate for black Americans as prime victims of a predicted new depression and consequently as the prime incendiaries in another even more apocalyptic cycle of widely anticipated postwar race riots. Radical disillusion reverberated from such leading voices as Richard Wright, who wrote a bitterly bleak preface for Drake and Cayton's 1945 study not long after renouncing his Communist Party membership—and not long before expatriating himself away from American postwar racism. Indeed the larger truth was that African Americans generally had entered this war, as John Hope Franklin noted, with "no illusions about the benefits they would derive from it" (573–91). But unlike for Ellison, for Wright the changes in the consciousness of postwar Bronzeville and its environing culture were insignificant or invisible. To Wright all of the still segregated black communities were pathology-ridden and intellectually sterile "ghettoes" into which black Americans had been herded by social forces beyond their control, places which, as Myrdal had suggested, incorporated in exaggerated form what Wright considered to be many of the worst facets of American life—conspicuous consumption, a tasteless appetite for the devitalized products of a mass culture, devotion to frivolous trivialities, and a potpourri of escapist religiosity.

Wright's repudiation of postwar American life in Bronzeville and beyond anticipated the terms of E. Franklin Frazier's mid-1950s indictment of the postwar black middle class's nominal "success." Providing the harshest black counterpart of the era's broad sociological assault on American postwar materialism, Frazier mounted a decade of research that ultimately, in *Black Bourgeoisie* (1957), profiled a pathetic subsociety of culturally deracinated, economically marginal, guilt-ridden, and politically apathetic black entrants into the make-believe world of the American middle classes.[5] Amidst the storm of controversy Frazier's study generated, however, he later acknowledged one important aspect of the developing new black bourgeoisie that he had omitted, an omission that his American but not his foreign critics had strangely overlooked: to wit, those "recent accessions to the Negro middle classes who are prominent in the sit-ins and in the other protest movements against racial segregation" (12) and who had evolved, Frazier believed, not so much from the old black bourgeoisie's fusion of mulatto aristocrat and Southern peasant but from the migrating black folk and working classes, newly educated, newly urbanized, and conditioned triply by depression and war and the spectre of race riots (7–14).[6]

It was the emotional history of precisely that pivotal segment of black America that Ellison's panoramic narrative, perhaps more than any other cultural document of the early postwar era, finally made dramatically visible. And in the emotional distance between the fictional portrait of martyr-murderer Bigger Thomas with which Richard Wright had opened the decade of the 1940s and the portrait of the anonymous would-be political leader with which Ralph Ellison synoptically recounted and closed it lay a whole generation's disillusioning experience of migration and work and war and education. But in the imaginative confrontation with this disillusionment also lay the psychological and social roots of an optimistic postwar rededication to political struggle and mass civil disobedience. For that, the long underground "hibernation" of Ellison's prototypical Invisible Man would be, by his own carefully prophetic definition, the "covert preparation for more overt action" that the decade ahead would disclose. As underground guerilla at odds with Monopolated Light and Power, as Brotherhood political operative turned saboteur and traitor like his grandfather, Ellison's unsighted underground guerilla would turn to military metaphors—retreat, reconnaissance, redeployment—to rationalize his "hibernation" and to war and its symbolic equivalents for the emotional terms upon which life in America perforce had to be lived and art's saving graces conceived.

As Ellison would remark many years later in a prefatory essay on the "war-haunted" imagination of Stephen Crane—the one high-caliber American writer between Twain and Faulkner whom Ellison could credit with having looked "steadily at the wholeness of American life"—war and its symbolic equivalents had perennially formed the background for the high periods of the modern novel (*S&A* 74–88). Civil wars especially, Ellison thought—agreeing with Hemingway—because they are never really won, their most devastating engagements "fought within the individual human heart" and continuing long after military hostilities have ceased (*S&A* 79). In accord with the World War II truism that every writer who had seen combat carried in his barracks bag a war novel or a plan for one, Ellison charted his own preliminary foray into the world of fiction with the military experience as his metaphor for and microcosm of that inner civil war he early saw as a conscious obsession in African American life and as a suppressed but no less obsessive force in the literary and political imagination of the nation at large. As oblique preliminaries to "Battle Royal," his early short stories "In a Strange Country" and "Flying Home," both published in 1944, and the framework of his unpublished first novel each dramatized the dilemma of young black men, soldiers, who like Ellison himself had "wanted to contribute to the war, but didn't want to be in a Jim Crow army" (Kostelanetz, "Ralph Ellison" 56–77).

But in none of these were military combat or the atrocities and horrific carnage of modern warfare the experiential or metaphorical focus. Nor was war conceived as some inverted or freakishly alien world apart. Ellison's military tales treated war most crucially as an intensification and continuation of peacetime social existence: war was not a dislocation but a defense and even an entrenchment of the social order's class and caste hierarchies and racial mystique. Ernest Hemingway and André Malraux as war novelists, for all the ways in which their importance as literary "ancestors" would later be acknowledged by Ellison, did not provide that vantage point in space, time, and circumstance from which the prospective black heroes of Ellison's war fiction might come to see how "democratic ideals and military valor alike were rendered absurd by the prevailing mystique of race and color" (*IM* x). Ellison originally conceived his war novel's hero as a captured American pilot in a Nazi prisoner-of-war camp where he, by virtue of rank, is the spokesman for white fellow prisoners who despise him and where, by virtue of a German camp commander's Machiavellian sense of amusement, he is pitted against his erstwhile comrades:

> For him that war-born vision of virile fraternity of which Malraux wrote so eloquently is not forthcoming, and much to his surprise he found his only justification for attempting to deal with his countrymen as comrades-in-arms lay precisely in those old betrayed promises proclaimed in such national slogans and turns-of-phrase as those the hero of Hemingway's *A Farewell to Arms* had found so obscene during the chaotic retreat from Caporetto. But while Hemingway's hero managed to put the war behind him and opt for love, for my pilot there was neither escape nor a loved one waiting. Therefore he had either to affirm the transcendent ideals of democracy and his own dignity by aiding those who despised him, or accept his situation as hopelessly devoid of meaning; a choice tantamount to rejecting his own humanity. (*IM* ix)

Ellison, however, abandoned his gestating war novel in the mid-1940s after his preliminary efforts "to manipulate the structural unities of beginning, middle and end" had led him to a chaotic psychological strata of images, symbols, and emotional configurations before which, as artist-apprentice, he at that point felt helpless. What also drew Ellison's conception away from the privatist preoccupations of most 1940s war novelists, and toward the unifying political focus of *Invisible Man*, were exactly those democratic moral visions of social reconstruction with which so many of the 1940s Anglo-American novelists had become disillusioned. In that conceptual void, race provided the heuristic and the metaphor that pulled Ellison's postwar fictional musings on the problem of collective and individual freedom toward the perplexing social figure of the hero and the democratic quandaries of public leadership.

It was his dubious role as the utterly isolated black ranking officer of contemptuous white fellow prisoners, and his being cast into that position by the force of circumstances which oppose the codes of military hierarchy to the codes of racial supremacy, that made Ellison's unrealized protagonist a potentially pristine study in the ambiguities of authority. Conventional sociopolitical war novels of the era routinely dramatized problems of freedom and authority by bifurcating military society into opposing castes of officers and enlisted men who then acted out the implicit class conflicts of bourgeois society back home. But as Depression-era racialism back home had barred black aspirants simultaneously from even token entry into the ranks of the white privileged and from class unity with white populists, so in Ellison's abandoned war novel the omnipresent race war provided the dramatic "act of complication" that barred the hero's aligning himself with either military caste and consequently ceded him neither an officer's ascribed power of rank nor an enlistee's assumed power of mass solidarity. That this dramatic dilemma foreshadows the later focus of *Invisible Man* on power and leadership is clear. But the evidence for how Ellison's absorption with wartime issues affected the evolution of the novel that supplanted his abandoned earlier effort has remained submerged in the broader currents of his own published recollections and in the decade's still fragmentary literary history.

Sent home to recuperate during the winter of 1944 from the stress of his service in the Merchant Marine, acutely aware that his original idea for a novel would not work, Ellison floundered, he often recounted, "into a state of hyper-receptivity" which yielded two creative seeds: first, an inner voice that declared "I am an invisible man"—in ironic rebuttal to the sociological truism that "most Afro-American troubles sprang from our 'high visibility'"; and second, a realization that "war could, with art, be transformed into something deeper and more meaningful than its surface violence," an insight afforded by a conjunction of brooding recollections about the experience of black soldiers first in the Civil War and then in the war of his own time (*IM* xiii–xiv). Out of a complex train of associations recorded only in shards by Ellison over the years, two other oft-noted "explanations" stand out. He was absorbed with reading Lord Raglan's *The Hero: A Study in Tradition, Myth, and Drama* (1936). And he was, as an outgrowth of the current black struggle with the Roosevelt administration over discrimination against blacks in the war industry and among combat personnel, intensely "concerned with the nature of leadership, and thus with the nature of the hero ... [and] with the question of just why our Negro leadership was never able to enforce its will. Just what was there about American society which kept Negroes from throwing up effective leaders?" (Ellison, "On Initiation Rites and Power" 185).

Ellison's accounts of the genesis of *Invisible Man* have understandably emphasized the knotted artistic process of creation and imaginative integration that ultimately gave him "a vague but intriguing new perspective."

But the sources of *Invisible Man*, its achievement not simply as enduring individual artistry but as the culminating imaginative chronicle of a particular era, lay as well in its author's conscious participation in the decades-old orbit of black political and literary debates that in the 1940s, in Harlem, expressed themselves in the continuing, problematic influence of the Negro Renaissance, in the Federal Writers' Project milieu, and in the Stalinist-Trotskyite radical left. To the extent that *Invisible Man* reflects the creative tension between Ellison's discovery of "invisibility" as an analytic metaphor and his pragmatic awareness of the crisis in black leadership, the novel synthesizes perspectives that were traditional in African American thought, both formal and vernacular, and brought into sharp relief by World War II.

In this last regard Ellison's expressed concern with the problem of the hero and black leadership reflected political anxieties common to Americans at large in the years between the Great Depression and the Second Great War. The flood of studies of the hero-leader by political scientists, mythographers, philosophers, and historians, and the rise of a formalized sociology of leadership during the 1940s are not to be understood apart from the spectacular rise of Adolf Hitler and Benito Mussolini and fascist authoritarianism, of Roosevelt, Stalin, and Churchill, or from the interest rekindled thereby both in the perplexing role of great men in history and in the fatalistic popular attitudes and scientific determinism that denied such heroic interpretations of history.[7] Ellison's encounter with Lord Raglan's effort to separate the myth from the history of heroes took place against the intellectual gyrations of wartime 1943, during which philosopher Sidney Hook's *The Hero in History: A Study in Limitation and Possibility* and historian Gerald Johnson's *American Heroes and Hero Worship*, for example, affirmed the current claim that "never has the world been more in the grip of hero mythology than today, and never has the voice of sense and science been more needed to bring the beast to bay" (Koch 16).

Debated more abstractly as an expression of the ancient philosophical conflict between free will and determinism, heard most often as echoes of Thomas Carlyle's "Heroes and the Heroic in History" and of William James's "Great Men and Their Environment," the 1940s' debates on whether the hero-leader (Hook termed him "the event-making man" as opposed to the merely "eventful" man) was the product of a particular age or of his or her own prodigious will and creativity became polarized between the

touting of the leader's role by contemporary authoritarians and the correspondingly extravagant deification of impersonal "social forces" by Marxist
thinkers. Much of the debate on the hero in history, though, evaded, or
equivocated on, the issues of particular interest to Ellison. The conventional emphases on military and political leadership largely ignored folk
and popular-culture heroes, on the one hand, and, on the other, the role of
ideas and the heroes of the arts, sciences, and religion. A frequent failure
to distinguish the hero from the leader led typically to a confusion of the
former's honor or charisma with the latter's power and to the particularly
American practice of associating honor with democratic heroes and power
with authoritarian ones. Moreover, the overlooked relationships between
the leader and the led, the shifting reasons for their obedience and the personal traits of his or her power, were, as C. Wright Mills shrewdly insisted,
crucial to understanding the pivotal situations in which the hero acts, or
can act, and the symbolic character of the process of "heroizing" by which
the hero's power is socially bestowed (834).

All of these matters, in one formulation or another, beleaguered the
ongoing tactical disputes in African American political life, where leadership
and heroic action, as problem and possibility, had loomed over the processes
of deliberating collective political strategies from the era of nineteenth-
century abolitionist oratory and national conventions to the brief, betrayed
experiment of Reconstruction to the turn-of-the-century Washington-
DuBois controversy and the New Negro-Garveyites clashes of the 1920s.
Alongside the official heroes and leadership of the rising black middle class's
civil rights and racial uplift organizations, a popular tradition of millenar-
ian cult heroes, religious revivalists, charismatic revolutionaries, and skilled
confidence men had evolved. Parallel to and interpenetrating both of these
from below, black folk traditions, shifting and diversifying with migration,
urbanization, and industrialization, articulated the pantheon of alternative
heroic images in tales, toasts, blues, and ballads, which Lawrence Levine's
scholarship on black folk consciousness has helped illuminate.

For Ellison's generation of literary radicals, the confluence of the tangled
traditions of the hero with the perceived crisis in letters and public leadership galvanized both a rebellion against the intraracial old guard and a series
of manifestoes within their own radical ranks that spurred new alignments
of the black political and literary imaginations. Two influential critiques of

black leadership bracketed the decade of Ellison's literary apprenticeship: political scientist Ralph Bunche's anatomy of black organizational leadership and programmatic policies in 1939 and sociologist Oliver Cox's historical overview of black leadership styles and psychological types, which appeared at the end of the decade in 1950 as part of Alvin Gouldner's pathbreaking *Studies in Leadership*. Bunche's bleak assessment described an unbroken chain of black leaders deluded, disorganized, and chauvinistic:

> They flounder about, desperately and often blindly, in their ghettoes of thought, seeking a break in the dams of oppression through which they may lead their flock to a more dignified and secure existence. The tiniest crevice in the barriers is magnified into a brilliant ray of hope. So great is the desperation that daily disillusionments are angrily shaken off; they pound away at impregnable walls, dash triumphantly down blind alleys, yet dare not stop to calculate lest it is learned that ultimate escape is generations, even centuries removed. . . . Color is their phobia, race their creed. . . . They, like Hitler, even though for different reasons, think that "all that is not race in this world is trash." . . . Unless the Negro can develop, and quickly, organization and leadership endowed with broad social perspective and farsighted, analytical intelligence, the black citizen of America may soon face the dismal prospect of reflecting upon the tactical errors of the past from the gutters of the black ghettoes and concentration camps of the future (550).

Cox's less lurid but no less urgent reading emphasized the forces in America antagonistic to "genuine" black leadership, forces which misdirected would-be leaders into a variety of "spurious" attitudes. In Cox's view, after the decay of the heroic abolitionist leadership in the crucial post-Reconstruction years, collaboration, placation, compromise, and opportunism had become the preeminent dynamics of self- and white-appointed black leaders, while the disaffected black masses had been driven increasingly toward the ambiguously emotional politics of revolutionary nationalism and the dysphoric symbolism of martyrdom.

The impact of the war experience and its internationalizing outlook in part made these dilemmas of black leadership seem less a peculiar racial inheritance and more a common condition of modern humanity. Richard Wright's creation of Bigger Thomas in 1940 made the point metaphorically concrete. In his postscript to *Native Son*, "How Bigger Was Born," Wright made Bigger's leaderlessness, his projected hunger for a "highly ritualized and symbolized life" and for the true leader who would organize it, one measure of the global condition in which all Bigger Thomases, black and white, American, Russian, German, were primed to follow the "gaudy, hysterical" magnifico who would promise to fill the void left by vanished moral and metaphysical meanings and by the cataclysms of material change, conflict, and dispossession (xx).

Wright proposed that writers themselves become the leaders of their generation and undertake "the task of creating with words a scheme of images and symbols whose direction could enlist the sympathies, loyalties, and yearnings of the millions of Bigger Thomases in every land and race" (xix). Less imbued than Wright with the image of the artist-hero as the creator of values and a leader of people, Langston Hughes, emphatically reversing the emphasis on the common citizen and the independent artist that he had taken in his 1926 Jazz Age manifesto "The Negro Artist and the Racial Mountain," issued in 1941 a new, more strident manifesto in tune with the temper of the times. Hughes proclaimed "The Need for Heroes" and the social duty of black writers to turn away from the endless depictions of victimization and defeat and "caged animals who moan, who cry, who go mad, who are social problems, who have no guts"—and to document instead "the deep reservoirs of heroism within the race" (194). Citing himself along with his literary peers for insufficient attention to the pantheon of black heroes, historic and contemporary, ordinary and extraordinary, Hughes called for a cycle of literary odysseys about black men and women who, in contrast to Hollywood and popular-culture stereotype, faced life unafraid and unhumbled: "For we are not endlessly funny, nor always lazy, nor forever quaint, nor eternally defeated. . . . For ourselves there is a need, more than anything else, of great patterns to guide us, great lives to inspire us, strong men and women to lift us up and give us confidence in the powers we, too, possess" (185).

The psychology of heroic inspiration both Wright and Hughes advocated, however differently, with its dark, Hitlerian tendencies at one pole and its liberating possibilities at the other, served as an implicit point of reference in the dialogue Ellison and Angelo Herndon shepherded in 1942 and 1943—as editors of the short-lived journal the *Negro Quarterly*— among black and white radical writers concerned about the progress of the war and the developing forms and functions of black fiction (Johnson and

Johnson 125–60). Conceived by Ellison and Herndon as "a review of Negro thought and opinion" and as a medium for the "training and orientation" of young writers, the *Negro Quarterly* recorded crucial aspects of the 1940s attempt to divine the techniques for revitalizing black leadership in letters and life. And it charted, in the essays Ellison contributed, his own conscious progress toward a new war-born concept of heroic fiction.

During the four years prior to joining the *Negro Quarterly*, Ellison's work as a researcher and interviewer for the New York Federal Writers' Project had immersed him in African American history, in the "living lore" of Harlem, and in the legal backgrounds of famous New York trials—all of which enlarged his sense of the varied, interlinking dimensions of historical consciousness upon which narrative might be erected. The publication of the Federal Writers' Project's *The Negro in Virginia* in 1940 and of Richard Wright's *Twelve Million Black Voices* the following year had provided superb models of history and folklore vibrantly fused and compressed, voiced in distinctive accents, and, as in Wright's lyrical saga, eloquently framed by an oracular collective consciousness.

The "New Negro" Renaissance, for all its pride in race, in the folk tradition, and in the African heritage, had cultivated no programmatic literary historicism and, perhaps not surprisingly given the underdeveloped state of black historical scholarship, had produced no genuine historical fiction. As suggested in Ellison's 1941 *New Masses* review, "Richard Wright and Recent Negro Fiction," Arna Bontemps's two historical novels, *Black Thunder* (1936) and *Drums at Dusk* (1936), and Edward Turpin's family chronicles, *These Low Grounds* (1937) and *O Canaan!* (1939), were the 1930s' only significant black fictional vehicles of "conscious history." But Bontemps's tales of slave insurrection dramatized discrete periods long past rather than modern ongoing historical processes; and Turpin's attempts to trace the generations of a single black family through several periods of the country's development betrayed "the lack of a fully integrated world-view" and clung correspondingly to "obsolete technical devices" (Ellison, "Richard Wright and Recent Negro Fiction" 12).

The effect of all the recent black fiction, Ellison felt, was "one of incompleteness, something . . . not fully formed," a disjunction "between the themes of which Negro writers are becoming aware and the technique necessary for their expression" (Ellison, "Richard Wright and Recent Negro

Fiction" 12). Reviewing William Attaway's *Blood on the Forge* (1941) in the *Negro's Quarterly*'s first issue, Ellison made clear his own standards for the integration of technique with conscious historicism. More importantly, in critiquing Attaway's work he apparently moved closer to having discovered his own potential subject matter and conceptual innovations. Ellison acknowledged that, by choosing the Great Migration spurred by World War I as its subject, Attaway's work had effectively made the processes of broad social transformation his historical theme: he showed himself naturalistically adept in depicting both rural and industrial milieus and psychologically scrupulous in identifying symbolically the principal attitudes with which the three farm-family brothers of *Blood on the Forge*—who flee a Kentucky lynch mob to become Allegheny Valley steelworkers—face the changing social factors in their lives. Ellison concluded, however, that Attaway's narrative nonetheless ultimately disintegrated "into a catalogue of meaningless casualties and despairs" and into a simple "lament for the dying away of the Negro's folk values" ("Transition"). The novel left one brother dead at the end, one blind, and the last a mere survivor; and it left Ellison objecting not so much to the author's depicting them defeated by circumstance as to denying any of them a conscious understanding of their experience and, with it, genuine grounds for hope and endurance.

Counterposed here against Attaway's apparent fatalism was Ellison's own contrary belief in fiction's role as a means of "heightening" consciousness and of preserving pivotal historical traditions of black heroism. If not always expressed in the terms Hughes prescribed—of remaining undefeated, unhumbled, unafraid—those traditions always ought to achieve at least the victory of conscious perception, Ellison inferred, even under circumstances of defeat or humiliation. "Attaway grasped the destruction of the folk," he noted, "but missed its rebirth at a higher level." Consciousness was the narrative's potential, albeit unactualized, hero. But in *Blood on the Forge* "there was no center of consciousness, lodged in a character or characters, capable of comprehending the sequence of events" ("Transition"). Foreshadowing the "conscious hero" he himself would create to traverse some of the same symbolic history, Ellison acknowledged that "this, possibly, would have called for an entirely new character." Nor, he intimated, would such a character's higher consciousness be "a mere artistic device; it would have been in keeping with historical truth" ("Transition"). Neither

wish fulfillment nor artifice, then, but historically evolved if not yet incarnated fictively, the consciousness Ellison hypothesized would be one
capable, first, of understanding the chaotic patterns of a complex mechanical world and, second, of distinguishing potential allies from natural
enemies amidst the two types of Western man then waging war—the democrat and the fascist—and between whom the unending social warfare
which had so powerfully conditioned African American lives would persist
("Transition" 91–92).

The potential meaning of such consciousness for black leadership
Ellison probed in directly political terms in a subsequent editorial in the
Negro Quarterly. Under the pressure of wartime experience, he noted, three
principal political attitudes were being expressed by African Americans
toward the forms of violent and discriminatory domestic fascism they
faced. The first was a self-abasing acceptance of racial subordination which
revealed "almost psychopathic" fear or uncertainty along with a "disintegration of the sense of group personality" that, rather than leaders, produced
"the spy, the stool pigeon, and the agent provocateur." The second attitude,
only seemingly opposed to the first, was one of unqualified rejection of
the entire war against fascism as a "white man's war" because of its fascist
racial practices. This, he argued, was "a political form of self-pity," impotent and fatalistic and inclined toward passivity, martyrdom, and "magical"
solutions that promised to make the problem—"Negroness"—simply disappear. The third attitude, implied in group sentiment but barely articulated by figures of official authority, was an unapologetic "manifestation
of Negro nationalism," which proposed to transform both of the others
into strategies of struggle through its triple commitment to the life of the
group's conscious personality, to its nationally redemptive quest for freedom, and to that sense of independent African American interests in the
war for the "four freedoms" which made rational give-and-take possible
on the interracial homefront "in the interest of national unity" (Ellison,
"Editorial Comment" 296–99).

Such an attitude's leadership potential, Ellison contended, then, lay
in carefully equilibrating modern social and technological innovations to
reinforce black actions and objectives, in consolidating the group's historical consciousness as a guide to strategic possibilities and limitations, and
in deciphering psychologically just how those energies necessary for social

transformation might be repressed, channelized, and released through cultural symbols. The ability to centralize and direct group power, Ellison surmised, would come only from those who realized that "much in Negro life remains a mystery; perhaps the zoot suit conceals profound political meaning; perhaps the symmetrical frenzy of the Lindy-hop conceals clues to great potential power—if only Negro leaders would solve this riddle" ("Editorial Comment" 301). The need to see leadership, democratic and fascist, as among other things a matter of symbolic transactions with the led, and thereby linked like hero-worship to shifting social mythologies, dominated Ellison's probings. No mere planner, policy maker, ideologist, or exemplar, the leader he hypothesized here, like the uncreated hero he had proposed for Attaway's unhopeful novel, was first of all a center of consciousness and, by extension, perceptive, self-critical, adaptive, technically skilled. A leader such as this would be disciplined but experimental, would be energized by personal will while directed by a vision of freedom and fraternity, and would be rigorously unsentimental about human virtues and vices.

Ellison's broodings over the idea of leadership, leadership as an explicitly symbological problem rooted in the workings of a society in unprecedented flux, ultimately exploded the uncompleted draft of his unities-bound and more narrowly conceived military novel into a vision of politicized philosophical picaresque that surfaced as he pondered the persona of his prototypic leader and the corresponding dramaturgical need to "work out some imaginative integration of the total American experience and discover through the work of the imagination some way of moving a young black boy from a particular area and level of the society as close as he could be 'realistically' moved to sources of political power" (Ellison, "On Initiation Rites and Power" 171). He needed a model, a "structure of symbolic actions which could depict the various relationships between groups and classes of people." To create it he plunged into the American political and literary past; his Federal Writers' Project immersion in American legal history guided the view he consolidated, in the 1945 and 1946 essays "Beating That Boy" and "Twentieth Century Fiction and the Black Mask of Humanity," that the mystique of race, wedded to that of power, lay at the root of conflict in America between the Anglo-Saxon elite and the newer white and nonwhite immigrant groups, a conflict which the ambivalent, improvisational framework of Jeffersonian democracy had repressed from the outset and which persisted unexamined in American literature, as in the body politic, through "the anesthesia of legend, myth, hypnotic ritual and narcotic-modes of thinking" ("On Initiation Rites and Power" 171).

Aesthetic solutions to the corollary conceptual problems that had bedeviled Ellison's war novel emerged from his enthusiastic absorption of Kenneth Burke's evolving philosophy of literary form and its extrapolated fictional possibilities. Ellison's war novel had been conceived in naturalistic terms that revolved, as Wright's *Native Son* had, primarily around neo-Aristotelian conceptions of the dramatic unities of time, place, and action. Wright, in wanting Bigger Thomas's auditors to feel the story happening "now, like a play upon the stage or a movie unfolding upon the screen," had given his prizefightlike "action upon action" the sheen of unyielding causality by seaming it with the documentary realism of sociological case history and newspaper reportage (R. Wright, "How Bigger Was Born" 864). Unlike Wright's "scientific" focus on the problem of racial oppression, Ellison's "mythographic" focus on the problem of racial leadership became configured as rhetorically speculative, exploratory more than documentary, deductive more than inductive. Lord Raglan's *The Hero* had proposed a universal pattern against which to conceive the particular contingencies of black leadership; and that pattern's unity lay in the time and space of ritual actions otherwise obscured and rendered "invisible" by the competing detail of naturalistically documentable reality. The pivotal political battle in modern America, Wright had suggested, was the struggle between black men and white over the very nature of reality. But Ellison, in agreeing, would choose subjective more than scientific reality, the symbolic more than the literal, as that imaginary field of battle.

Ellison had gleaned how heroic myth might mask pathological leadership through Burke's 1937 critique of Adolf Hitler's autobiography, *Mein Kampf*. The book had become "the well of Nazi magic"; and the rhetoric of Hitler's battle for Aryan ascendancy modeled a masterful insinuation of heroic biography's ritual logic into the quest for power by a man of self-described "domineering apostolic nature" (Burke, *Philosophy of Literary Form* 191–220). Richard Wright, analyzing the Nazi phenomenon in relation to Bigger Thomas's inner void, had admitted being fascinated by Hitler's rhetoric and being "reminded of the Negro preacher in the South telling of a life beyond this world, a life in which the color of men's skins would not matter, a life in which each man would know what was deep down in the hearts of his fellow man" ("How Bigger Was Born" 864). The will to solidarity and certainty central to the oratorical traditions of black leadership were mirrored darkly in the führer's autobiographical rhetoric, and the sense of redemptive mission, along with other psychic forces possibly delusive or dangerous: the evocation of a kingdom to be fought for and won from a tyrant who appears in many guises and is an enemy to all; the total unspoken identification of the leader with the people, of his suffering, his struggles, his rebirth with theirs—and at the same time a denial of his personal ambition; the assumption of specious group unity and the obsession with enemy spies and disunifiers; the sexualization of political conflict fostered in the verbal imagery of the hypermasculine leader-lover of the people who would keep his group "pure" and woo "her" from the seducer-rival; the advocacy of armed violence in the name of reason, humility, peace, and love; the enticing design of religious conversion and self-sacrifice grafted onto the processes of secular empowerment; the satisfactions of ritual itself, detached from moral ends; the studied presentation of the leader's political activities as the creative extension of his artistic ambitions (Burke, *Philosophy of Literary Form* 191–220).

Because the ingredients of leadership might, through such word magic, concoct a "snake oil" as well as a curative for the body politic, Ellison conceived his novel as a Burkean "comic corrective" to the various pathologies of actual and idealized leadership impinging on the prototypic central character. As an attitude toward experience, Burke's comic frame modeled a method of study that, in its constant two-way measurement of human aspiration against human limitation, counteracted one-dimensional polemicism and made it possible for human beings to become conscious "observers of themselves"—able to transcend being cheated or brutalized by turning such losses into the asset of "experience" and, by observing themselves while acting, able to convert passiveness into maximum consciousness (Burke, *Attitudes toward History* 170–71).

It was just such an attitude, ritualized in the blues, that Ellison saw intimated in Wright's *Black Boy*, published in 1945, the same year Ellison began *Invisible Man*. It would become the attitude with which he would endow the disembodied narrative voice of the novel whose ritual progress, like the blues, would become "an autobiographical chronicle of personal catastrophe expressed lyrically." That voice's comically corrective self-disclosures would give form in *Invisible Man* to what, in *Black Boy* again as in the blues, was an "impulse to keep the painful details and episodes of a brutal experience alive in one's aching consciousness, to finger its jagged grain, and to transcend it, not by the consolation of philosophy, but by squeezing from it a near-tragic, near-comic lyricism" (*S&A* 90).

Ellison's 1944 short story "King of the Bingo Game" left him confident of having mastered technically the narrative means for projecting, in his own distinctive voice, a stylishly tragicomic and surreal rendering of modern life's absurdity. Three years later Ellison was finally able to unveil the Burkean "representative anecdote" that compressed into a single dramatic scene the whole system of symbolic actions his meditations on war, leadership, heroic action, and the nation's hidden history had precipitated.[8] The idea of war as a grim microcosm of society and the soldier-hero as the prism through which to view it had given way finally to the image of a social "Battle Royal," of human beings still warring but having disarmed themselves militarily and ideologically and facing each other instead in painfully comic confrontation. As the first clearly crystallized prototype of his newly conceived picaresque world, the Battle Royal was manufactured race riot and Dionysian orgy and coon show and circus entertainment and scapegoat sacrifice. It was an object lesson in humiliation, a sexual torture and castration rite, an acting out of crab-barrel sociology, and, as Ellison would later name it in its structural context, a "ritual in preservation of caste lines, a keeping of taboo to appease the gods and ward off bad luck . . . and the initiation ritual to which all greenhorns are subjected" (*S&A* 175).

Perhaps most importantly, it dramatized a preliminary answer to Ellison's controlling query, "[W]hat was there about American society which kept Negroes from throwing up effective leaders?" The political lesson, inculcated earlier in Ellison's essays, that his fictive would-be Booker T. Washington fails to learn in the course of this grotesque graduation into adult life and leadership, the failed lesson that will dog him as cursedly as his grandfather's deathbed admonition, is that, in a ruling Anglo-American culture dominated by ethical schizophrenics fearful of deep thought and feeling, political issues assume nonpolitical forms; ideologies are masked in sexual, cultural, and pseudo-religious guises. And in that white world of officially sanctioned repression and among its leaders, it is practically impossible to think of entertainment, of sex, of economics, of women or children, of crime, or of social equality or social responsibility or sweeping sociopolitical changes "without summoning into consciousness fear-flecked images of black men."

The Battle Royal Ellison's novel proceeded to chronicle—confined quite precisely by the narrator's chapter 1 exposition to the years between 1930 and 1950—pushed the events of World War II outside its conscious margins. But the book's denouement was no less a picture of apocalypse. Ellison's nameless narrator closed his metahistory of the Depression and World War II decades with not the slightest allusion to the cessation of international military hostilities or the onset of the Atomic Age and the Cold War, or to the rise of suburbia, corporate culture, and an expanding consumer society. The closing scenes of the novel instead are of the initiatory battle royal exploded finally into full scale urban race war—the wartime race riots that actually convulsed Harlem in 1943 transmuted here into nightmarish scenes of black-white conflagration with all the military-minded incendiary strikes, deployments of racial combatants, guerrilla maneuvers, and, perhaps most crucially, the loss of faith in political alternatives that such warfare presumes.

That *Invisible Man*, however, does not rest in apocalyptic disillusion, that the historical consciousness framed in the book's circular prologue and epilogue finally posits the rebirth of the hero-leader and not his sickness unto death, discloses no unreasoning authorial leap of faith, no unearned catharsis, no indecipherable sociological mystery.[9] Rather, it simply but insistently inscribes a full imaginative sensitivity to the peregrinations of consciousness that so unexpectedly and "mysteriously" spawned the generation of hero-leaders Martin Luther King, Jr., would soon come to symbolize, those "accidents of history" who emerged from their invisibility in the official accounts of postwar consensus historians to "boomerang" the nation's psyche.[10] In the confidence games, shape changing, and "spiritual technologies" of Ellison's urban trickster, B. Proteus Rinehart, *Invisible Man* intimated also the rise to power of King's leaderly alter ego, Malcolm X—alias Malcolm Little, alias Satan, alias Detroit Red, alias El Hajj Malik el Shabazz—though Ellison's fictional emphasis on the misleaderly dark side of Rinehart's multifarious omnicompetencies seemed thereafter to shade the novelist's recorded commentary on the Muslim minister's public odyssey from insurgent princeliness to martyrdom.[11] In Ellison's view, the belief that leadership, any more than progress, could ever again be stable, predictable, programmatic, defied the logic of modern change. The illusions on which such faith was based had been shattered by the Depression and World War II; and Ellison in the mid-1950s reiterated the sobering view he had consolidated more than a decade earlier during the war years:

> In fact there is no stability anywhere and there will not be for many years to come, and progress now insistently asserts its tragic side; the evil now stares out of the bright sunlight. New groups will ceaselessly emerge, class lines will continue to waver and break and re-form. . . . The fundamental problems of the American situation will repeat themselves again and again and will be faced more or less by peoples throughout the world: Where shall we draw the line upon our own freedom in a world in which culture, tradition, and even history have been shaken up? At how fast a pace should we move toward social ideals? What is worth having and what worth holding? Where and in what pattern of conduct does true value, at a given moment, lie? (*GTT* 272–73)

It was out of this sense of an age of anxiety's crisis in letters and leadership that Ellison's career as a fictionist had evolved in the late 1930s and early 1940s. As the genesis of *Invisible Man* reveals, World War II brought to a focus tensions in African American literary thought that had developed over the course of three decades. If critical historians are correct in describing the 1940s as a productive period for black novelists, characterized by heightened technical merit and less chauvinistic perspectives, then in Ellison's maturation we see how much that achievement was forged out of black writers' sense of their collective engagement in a war within a war. That war for leadership in letters and in life was fought double-consciously both at the level of the international politico-military conflagration over fascism and at the level of black artist-activists grappling simultaneously with the obdurate rhetoric of fiction as well as with the unshouldered, reciprocal responsibility on both sides of the DuBoisian veil of color for leaders and the led to confront political realities that Americans, white and black and otherwise, had conditioned themselves not to see.

A few years at least before embarking on his novelistic experiment, Ellison had come to believe, with Kenneth Burke, that race relations were captive to the "trained incapacity" (a concept Burke appropriated openly from Thorstein Veblen) of most Americans to "see" alternative ways of sharing social space and material resources. In *Permanence and Change* (1935), Burke's evolving "dramatistic" explorations of order, property, guilt, redemption, and victimage led him, and subsequently Ellison in concert, to construe the "scapegoat mechanism" visited by poor whites especially upon Negroes as a function of such trained incapacity: it was thereby subject to remediation or reversal only through some "perspective by incongruity" capable of "shattering" and reorienting the limiting "visions" and "methodical mis-namings" of social possibility (Burke, *Permanence and Change* 7–9, 14–16, 69–70). Burke described "perspective by incongruity" as a "magical" but nonetheless utilitarian process that he associated with certain "kinds of hermeticism," with "logonomical purgatory," with the "realm of gargoyles," and with the rituals of exorcism. Cultivating these perspectives by incongruity required, accordingly, a heightened receptiveness to startlingly new orientations and apprehensions; and he balanced the "purely rational or intellectualistic elements" of this process against the "deep emotionality of the search for new meanings" (69–70).

It was perfectly congruent, therefore, that the "psychogenesis" of *Invisible Man*, Ellison reiterated periodically through the years, lay in a World War II furlough's tonic state of "hyper-receptivity": sent home from the Merchant Marines in the winter of 1944 to recuperate from wartime stress, Ellison had "floundered" into a powerful intuition. Then at work on his recalcitrant war novel, he linked his aesthetic conviction that "war could, with art, be transformed into something more meaningful than its surface violence" (*IM* xiv) to a punning inner voice that brooded over the whirling conundrum of black soldiers fighting for the right to fight for freedom in a war effort designed to return them home unfree—and discovered, "I am an invisible man." This "logonomical" rebuttal of the sociological truism that most African Americans' troubles sprang from their "high visibility" would become the creative heuristic—the perspective by incongruity—that helped Ellison abandon his planned war novel for a highly experimental, panoramic, and picaresque fictional memoir concerned more broadly, as its author had become, "with the nature of leadership, and thus with the nature of the hero" and with those unplumbed "mysteries" of American society that forestalled the development of powerful, effective black leaders

(Ellison, "On Initiation Rites and Power" 185). Absorbed in parallel with Lord Raglan's *The Hero: A Study in Tradition, Myth, and Drama* (1936), Ellison turned his explorations into the mythic and ritual substructure of American caste codes and political culture toward the specific locus of normative "race ritual" that subsequently yielded, as a narrative embryo, the grotesque high school graduation rites undergone by a young, would-be leader-of-his-people in the "Battle Royal" tale Ellison sent to *Horizon* magazine in 1947, five years before the appearance of the novel it would eventually introduce.

With contrapuntal riffs on Lord Raglan's schematic myth of heroic biography guiding the ritual understructure, and with the Battle Royal as a reverberating point of entry, Ellison devised a carefully articulated skeleton for the body of the narrative he then encircled with prologue and epilogue:

> I began with a chart of the three-part division. It was a conceptual frame with most of the ideas and some incidents indicated. The three parts represent the narrator's movement from, using Kenneth Burke's terms, purpose to passion to perception. These three major sections are built up of smaller units of three which mark the course of the action. . . . The maximum insight on the hero's part isn't reached until the final section. After all, it's a novel about innocence and human error, a struggle through illusion to reality. Each section begins with a sheet of paper; each piece of paper is exchanged for another and contains a definition of his identity, or the social role he is to play as defined for him by others. But all say essentially the same thing, "Keep this nigger boy running." Before he could have some voice in his own destiny he had to discard these old identities and illusions; his enlightenment couldn't come until then. (*S&A* 177)

The "blues-toned laughter-at-wounds" Ellison created to narrate the tale becomes the controlling consciousness, the organizing principle of the underground memoir. But his "identity" is only nominally its subject: the operative subject is the proper conduct of his battle royal for freedom and full consciousness in a modern picaresque world of flux and contradiction where identity itself is strategy more than entity, and selfhood a synonym for improvisation. As if to illustrate Carl von Clausewitz's psychology of guerrilla war (the first American translations of Clausewitz's *On War* appeared during World War II and selectively infiltrated the war-born novels of the era), the narrator's wounding movement toward enlightenment reveals progressively the psychic need for the materially weak to be morally strong in the face of an adversary and to subordinate potentially suicidal military conflict to social, political, and economic engagements in what ultimately is a war of wills. The Invisible Man's attempt to master his world's meanings and patterns, to acquire a conscious philosophy and a pragmatic code of living in it—and to lead—becomes an inadvertent Clausewitzian study in the conduct of war by other means. His is a struggle to keep the will to struggle from being destroyed by an ambiguous enemy's insidious psychological warfare.

In this connection the legacy of the Civil War is one of the great under-stated themes of *Invisible Man*. The politico-military *agon* traceable in the dramatic historical reversals from Civil War battlefields to Reconstruction politics to Reconstruction's subversion, in turn, by armed terrorism and political compromise is reconstituted in the riddling "orders" the hero's dying grandfather bequeathes him and is prefigured in the grandfather's fierce divulgence to all his heirs that "our life is a war and I have been a traitor all my born days, a spy in the enemy's country ever since I give up my gun back in the Reconstruction" (*IM* 16).

The premise that, with giving up the gun, politics necessarily becomes the substitute for war—and potentially its antidote—controls in part the particular ways in which Ellison's novel alters the conventions of pica-resque and of heroic myth. The world of *Invisible Man* recreates the famil-iar picaresque miasma of a warring society, only nominally civilized, in which life, death, incest, fornication, treachery, insanity, prostitution, labor strife, scatology, mutilation, political violence, and riot are all inescapably intermingled. And in a society so construed, the true picaro—the con man, Rinehart—is the ultimate warrior and predator, as well as a subversive antitype to Lord Raglan's hero of tradition, who is, archetypally, a royal warrior on an epic quest and an unquestioned embodiment of his future kingdom's deepest religious and political values. Historically, the modu-lated picaresque alternative to the destructive rogue from the social under-ground had been a rational, upwardly mobile potential bourgeois, whose roguery was less criminality than pragmatism, and more a maneuvering around the obstacles to his full assimilation in society than an attempt to destroy society itself.

In neither incarnation was the modern picaro necessarily a conscious rebel; and even when most subversive, he or she was never "politically" oriented. Moreover, the hero of picaresque had little sense of community or family and was too engrossed with the arduous struggle to survive and with winning the social war to seek any satisfactions in heterosexual love beyond the merely biological or honorific. Utterly caught up in the pressures of the present, he or she lacked any abstract sense of the macrocosmic workings of society and any historical consciousness. In American fiction, Twain's moralized use of picaresque conventions in *Huckleberry Finn* incorporated the picaro as an obstreperous, contrabourgeois, "white trash" scamp who remains "pre-ideological," as well as ultimately unamenable to life within society. In *Invisible Man* Ellison's contrasting commitment to a formally educated black protagonist, politically impassioned and struggling toward philosophical awareness, yielded instead a rising bourgeois hero, closer to Quixote or Candide or Gulliver or Melville's Ishmael than to a congenital rogue—though he is ultimately impelled to roguery by circumstance. He is a hero for whom even temporary life outside society is what finally becomes untenable and for whom the animating goal in life is that preeminently bourgeois aspiration—public leadership—which appears most typically in conventional picaresque as an object of ridicule.

What indeed is programmatically ridiculous about the situation of Ellison's Invisible Man derives from his being, functionally, the bourgeois hero of *bildungsroman* displaced, incongruously, into the realm of picaresque. His apprenticeship to life and leadership, in the lenient logic of *bildungsroman*, would have allowed him numerous mistakes of judgment and repeated chances to right himself without undue suffering. Instead, his novitiate is hyperbolized into a chronicle of comic catastrophe by the brutal logic of picaresque—where all errors unerringly bring pain and where only the true picaro, who is *born* knowing and needs no education, does not err. The heroic expectation of overcoming and the comic hope of not being overcome collide at nearly every point of crisis in Ellison's black and blue tragicomedy, crisis determined here neither by episodic happenstance nor naturalistic law but by the alternate and no less rigid determinism of the ritual process. The narrative patterns of heroic myth and the picaresque converge in this context. For the picaresque, even without the schematic mythology Ellison employs, characteristically retains elements of ritual, especially rites of passage, which test, often mock-heroically, its protagonist's "mother wit" and wisdom.

Ellison's protagonist, more pointedly than other laughers-at-wounds with whom he is juxtaposed all along his road of trials, is, from his rude Southern beginnings to his rising fame and fall up North, a thoroughgoing mock-heroic counterpart to Lord Raglan's hero of tradition. With a slave's genealogy of shame to mark and mock him dynastically and with no family traditions save his ex-slave grandfather's secret role as traitor and spy and agent provocateur, he enters the world "no freak of nature or of history," but born of parents who are, if not unknown, then unnamed and otherwise unnecessary to his ritual progress. His preinvisible childhood days are a blank spent miming his grandfather's steely meekness until vague promptings to leadership propel him, as initiate, into the nightmarish battle royal of life. With his grandfather's riddling counsel still to be deciphered along the way and the word-magic of his native oratorical powers to sustain him, he moves away from the seemingly stable and naturalistic world of the rural South and Negro miseducation (really a semifeudal "flower studded wasteland" seething with disorder). Fortuitously deceived, he embarks on a journey *up* north geographically but *down* existentially into a nether world of human and mechanical monsters and mis-leaders who preside over surreal forms of establishment and antiestablishment chaos. In his search for a place in the world, he finds himself unceasingly embattled, alone, and displaced. Outside the maze of misnamings that his treacherous allies lay before him, he remains nameless. His own self-chosen moniker—a mock title, not simply a name—links him to a mock kingdom by way of a salient greeting-response ritual common in 1930s and 1940s black communities: "How are you today, my brother?"—"Like Jack-the-Bear: just ain't nowhere" (*S&A* 285).

He is, however, succored at crucial junctures by symbolic foster parents and by the survival wisdom of the maternal folk community he at first foolishly repudiates but ultimately reaffirms. He wins all his victories through such self-affirming eloquence as he commands; and all his reverses spring from self-abnegating acquiescence. He rises to a brief reign as a presumptive orator-king over an uptown realm of restive Harlem subjects; is deposed suddenly by his unbrotherly "Brothers"; is then exiled downtown to what that misnamed Brotherhood considers to be the ideological backwaters of the "Woman Question." He finally vanishes, first, metaphysically, into the urban wonderland behind a pair of magical sunglasses, and then literally, when driven underground by his rebellious subjects and into sepulchral hibernation. Ultimately, he resurrects himself from the ashes of his political failures and personal dissimulations by inscribing a "code of laws" in the form of his codified life story—the memoir that becomes his ranter-turned-writer's memorial.

If Ellison has given his narrator all these ritual trappings of the mock-mythical hero, the context enforces certain riffing variations on Raglan's twenty-two-part biographical pattern. The hero's potentially Oedipal antagonism toward the father-king and his desire for the surrogate mother-queen are inverted sexually, because the king to be deposed and his potential deposer are crossed in Jack-the-Bear's world by racial as well as incest taboo. The same antagonism is deflected politically, because Ellison's rising hero misleads himself repeatedly not to rule but to be ruled. A rabble-rouser, not a warrior, he makes speeches instead of making war; and he fails his many trials comically more than tragically because all his reverses are self-generated "boomerangs"—bruising but inconsequential pratfalls. A creature of the age of mass ideology and modern technology, he models a comedy at the brink of tragedy which is less akin to Odysseus's heroic saga of comic wiliness and adaptability or to Aristotle's comic "species of the ugly which is not painful" than to the image Ellison found in Henri Bergson's *Laughter* of human behavior become mechanized, rigid, life-denying, robotic, and, hence, comically maladjusted.

If Jack-the-Bear is not the martial hero fated to found kingdoms, destroy his enemies, kill his father, or dispel plagues, neither is he the rutting picaresque hero of play and waggish sensuality, prone to the pleasures of the senses and the lure of bawd and belle alike. Politics is his passion, ritualized and romanticized. And he disciplines himself against dissipation, averting in youth his college roommate's more natural passion, when "the grass is green," to seek out "broad-butt gals with ball-bearing hips" (*IM* 104). He weakens in later years only before the pandering allurements of enemy sibyls or the "political" necessity for fornicational reconnaissance. The ritual hero's latent paranoia, its Freudian implications largely skirted by Raglan, becomes somnambulistically real and not wholly irrational in Ellison's tragicomic rites. The narrator's dim suspicions of conspiracy, betrayal, and persecution are nearly always innocently disregarded then painfully confirmed, congealing finally in the consummatory castration dream that punctuates his ritual progress.

Ellison's awareness of the suppressed psychic and symbolic "power of blackness" attuned him, far more than Raglan had been, to the dark side of heroic myth, to its demonic and demiurgic possibilities. Accordingly, he found a major role in his conception for what in Raglan's ritual drama had been a minor character: the Spielman, a figure half trickster, half devil, who, like the Norse god Loki, is the sacred plotter and wily father of artifice who sets the conflict in motion and drags the giants and demoniacal powers into the play and onto the assault that entails their ultimate defeat. And in Mephisthophelean fashion, though he plays no part in the drama, the Spielman is the motive power behind key characters that inspires them to tabooed acts and leads them to ruin. As ritual prompter and stage manager appearing in different guises throughout, Ellison's Spielman—speaking in the voices of the prologue's "singer of spirituals," the Golden Day's mad veteran, the cartman "Peter Wheatstraw-the-devil's-son-in-law," Tod Clifton after his plunge outside history, or the omnipresent mocker-mentor figure of the narrator's grandfather—persistently utters the magic words that goad the hero to act.

The Invisible Man's acts of attempted leadership mark the stages of his ritual progress "from purpose to passion to perception"; and they chronicle collaterally his developing relationships with the procession of leaders variously representing the shifting material conditions and states of consciousness that mark post-Reconstruction black history in America. The narrator's continuing meditations on the methods and mysteries of leadership, the complex patterns of animal and mechanical and aesthetic imagery that give emotional texture and covert structure to his experience of power and authority, and the periodic eruptions of unofficial leadership which counterpoint the parade of official power brokers and the narrator's obsession with them jointly expand the narrative's range of political commentary. *Invisible Man* probes the "character" of leadership strategies as well as the relationships between the leaders and the led, identifies the spectrum of tactical constraints within which political maneuvers must be devised, and makes utopian as well as pragmatic leadership the object of satiric dissection. A trio of heroic images from the black past—Frederick Douglass, Booker T. Washington, and Marcus Garvey—provide a genealogy of authentic political leaders. And a pantheon of heroic performers—Louis Armstrong, Paul Robeson, Joe Louis, John Henry—suggest, if only as names or cameo images, certain attitudes, techniques, and attributes proper to the movers and shakers of humanity.

Quite naturally, the nameless narrator's problem of identity, which is bound up at one level with his progress in reintegrating into his life the traditions of his repressed folk past, on another level must be resolved concretely in the personal drama of his leadership ambitions. One lesson implicit in his boomeranging movement across the social landscape is that the *identity* he seeks, like the leadership to which he aspires, is not a fixed and palpable *entity* but a shifting pattern of transactions with other people. At its most life giving, leadership entails a creatively improvised assertion of the leader's whole self within and against the group will; and at its most eviscerating, it retreats into the insecure camouflage of prescribed social roles.

As he turns his talent for oratory into his tool for leading, the narrator's attempts to harness the power of words record his slow progress in consciously unifying the elements of his developing will, wisdom, and technique. The bizarre world he inhabits and the role he blunderingly seeks keep these facets of the *whole* man and the *true* leader fragmented and at odds. The high school graduation speech he repeats at the town smoker after the humiliating rites of the battle royal, while gulping down his own blood and saliva and mouthing Booker T. Washington's Atlanta Compromise Address "automatically" to the unhearing throng of his abusers, is a parody of leadership and of the self-avowed "powers of endurance" and naive "belief in the rightness of things" that together confirm his first attempt at leading as hopeless mimicry and his wordsmanship as the parrot's art. He is, as the Golden Day's mad vet later incisively proclaims, a "walking zombie" who has learned "to repress not only his emotions but his humanity" (*IM* 92). As willing heir to that "great false wisdom taught slaves and pragmatists alike—that white is right," he is ready to do the bidding of such false gods as the white millionaire philanthropist Mr. Norton and his self-anointed appeaser, the black college president A. Hebert Bledsoe. Fittingly, it is Bledsoe who fleshes out the concept of leadership as wellheeled sycophancy that claims the neophyte leader's attention in his college years: "He was the example of everything I hoped to be: Influential with wealthy men all over the country; consulted in matters concerning the race; a leader of his people; the possessor of not one but two Cadillacs, a good salary and a soft, good-looking and creamy-complexioned wife" (*IM* 99).

The mastery of oratorical magic that the narrator associates with such leadership is demonstrated most tangibly for him on Founder's Day in the orotund homiletics of the Reverend Homer Barbee. Barbee's heroization of the exslave-cum-demigod who rose from oppression and obscurity to found a citadel of learning in a hostile wilderness reveals Barbee's panoramic mastery of the myth of heroic biography (Ellison vivified Raglan's ritual pattern here in unerring detail) and its officious power in the college's annual "black rites of Horatio Alger" (*IM* 109). Ellison allows Barbee's oratorical prowess to wax unmocked until the speaker stumbles from the rostrum to reveal his blindness. The author thereby allows the reader to feel *with* the narrator the full powers of Barbee's eloquence, powers which, though yoked here to a finally delusive vision of the race's history as "a saga of mounting triumphs" (*IM* 131), nonetheless hold the promise of leadership for whomever might possess them.

Cast out by Bledsoe from that saga's sacred ground, which the Invisible Man identifies (echoing Candide) as "the best of all possible worlds," he treks north with his confidence and optimism reviving. Not yet aware of how thoroughly he has been betrayed and "kept running," he preserves his enthusiasm for oratory and the art of leadership undimmed. Being a leader is still, he thinks, a matter of "playing a leading role" (*IM* 175), of learning "the platform tricks of the leading speakers" (*IM* 155), of affecting an image of sophistication and hygienic respectability, of stage-managing conversations and contacts with "big men," and of mastering such Bledsoe-like "secrets of leadership" (*IM* 176) as cultivating an aura of mysterious profundity to keep oneself omnipresent in the minds of one's inferiors. Nor, he thinks, could a prospective leader give much thought to love; for, "in order to travel far, you had to be detached" (*IM* 174).

But he is driven to a higher level of consciousness by a cumulation of experiences. The first is his workingman's fiasco at Liberty Paints with Lucius Brockaway and afterward at the factory hospital. The next is his deep alienation from the black fantasy world of upwardly mobile posturing and narcotic self-aggrandizement he encounters among the roomers at the Men's House. Last is the brooding resentment toward Bledsoe that erupts after the narrator sloughs off repressive bourgeois prohibitions against yam eating and in so doing recovers a submerged well of feeling that spurs his virtuoso street-corner exhortation against the eviction of an elderly black couple. The speech marks his transition from a phase of egocentric leadership "for" society to a phase of self-effacing leadership "against" the social order. And his extemporaneous rhetorical pyrotechnics signal his regenerated political will to freedom and his new mastery of oratorical "technique." At last he unites his own unconstrained psychic experience with the complex symbols of his people's emotional history—which he has now perceptively deciphered in the tangled heap of mementos piled before the dispossessed couple. Consequently he is able to articulate a transforming vision which moves a mass of men and women to action that, for a moment at least, breaks the chain of injustice.

On the basis of this effective fusion of controlled anger, abstract principle, and vernacular style, he is ushered immediately into the politics of Brotherhood (whose glorification of archcapitalist Booker T. Washington and whose leader's symbolic Fourth of July birth date warn against any such easy identification with the Communist Party as readers in search of easy political scapegoats might wish). Renamed, relocated, reclothed, and initiated into the doctrinal mysteries of "scientific" political theory the narrator now adopts a new professional leadership role. Ellison dramatizes its successes and tensions in the subsequent rabble-rousing Brotherhood speeches; in the promotional innovations the narrator fosters, such as the People's Hot Foot Squad and the symbolic posters of a future "Rainbow" coalition of America's races; and ultimately in the funeral oration for his martyred Brotherhood comrade, Tod Clifton. Jack-the-Bear's changing conceptions of leadership mirror his shift of allegiance from the example of the Founder (which he secretly adopts in opposition to the Brotherhood's desire to make him another Washington) to that of Frederick Douglass, whose portrait becomes his personal totem. As he becomes ambitious to rise in the Brotherhood hierarchy—he thinks it the one organization in the country in which he faces "no limits"—such changes in role model signal his growing clashes with the group's depersonalizing rigidity and thinly veiled racism.

The Brotherhood veteran Tod Clifton, symbolically "black-marble"-skinned in contrast to the narrator's "ginger" color and a man of action more than words—handsome, sensual, and with the air of "a hipster, a zoot-suiter, a sharpie"—is the "possible rival" who becomes the narrator's true brother and leaderly alter ego. Clifton's tragic plunge outside what the Brotherhood calls "history" sets in motion a chain of events that leads the narrator into self-proclaimed guerrilla war against the Brotherhood and leads the Harlem community into the apocalyptic riots that will be "triggered," like Clifton's death, by a murderous political logic that betrays the weak and then singles them out to be sacrificed in the name of leadership's "higher law." Swept along in these ominous, explosive events that terminate his tale, cornered and about to be killed by Ras the Destroyer's followers, the narrator finds his apprenticeship in leading finally at an end. And now finally wordless, he faces an angry group of the Harlemites he once had hoped to lead as instead "no hero, but short and dark with only a certain eloquence and a bottomless capacity for being a fool to mark [him] from the rest; [he] saw them, recognized them at last as those whom [he] had failed and of whom [he] was now, just now, a leader, though leading them, running ahead of them, only in the stripping away of [his] illusionment" (*IM* 546).

The narrative logic behind his final political failure, however, is not, as so many of Ellison's commentators have somehow concluded, necessarily a cumulative determinism which despairingly assumes all political possibilities doomed to defeat in a world so constructed: to be defeated is not necessarily to be defeatist. The logic is rather that of a rigorous Ellisonian phenomenology of consciousness and strategic style which asserts the irrepressibly human will to refuse the surrender of what is wholly possible to the force of what is merely real. Once understood to be merely momentary or material, defeat alone cannot destroy the sense of autonomy with which individuals and groups conceive their experience and choose (or fail to choose) ideas, techniques, and attitudes that defy whatever limits their possibilities.

The limits imposed on black leaders and political action are hyperbolic realities in the world of *Invisible Man*, experienced directly as the powers of persons and contexts to dominate consciousness first of all. In the narrative's Southern context, power polarizes between the local black baiters who orchestrate the Battle Royal and the Northern millionaire impresarios who bankroll black miseducation in the name of manifest destiny. The logic of such limitation drives the conventional black leadership class— the exsoldiers, lawyers, politicians, preachers, doctors, teachers, and artists the narrator encounters at the Golden Day—either in lockstep into straitjackets and the insane asylum or into the self-humiliating, Janus-faced machinations of a Bledsoe. In the North, the same class, nominally freer and with access to wider strategic alternatives, falls prey to urban alienation and anonymity. They become dissociated from the communities they might otherwise lead and are forced by organizational default, the narrator observes, to fall in line "like prisoners" to the dictates of outside political directorates such as the Brotherhood.

Nor are the prospects for combating these nightmare conditions any less dreary in a broader national context that seems to offer the narrator

> no possibility of organizing a splinter movement, for what would be the next step? Where would we go? There were no allies with whom we could join as equals; nor were there time or theorists available to work out an over-all program of our own. . . . We had no money, no intelligence apparatus, either in government, business or labor unions; and no communications with our own people except through unsympathetic newspapers, a few Pullman porters who brought provincial news from distant cities, and a group of domestics who reported the fairly uninteresting private lives of their employers. (499–500)

Moreover, the "masses," for obscure reasons but with consequences not obscure at all, seemed to tolerate the versions of Bledsoe, Ras, Jack, and Rinehart that cynically or romantically exploited them. Ellison's narrative, in dramatizing this perverse mental landscape, yields the psychic and material forces of political disintegration a commanding sway—and yields the narrator full consciousness and the ability to articulate it only in retrospect.

Implicit in Jack-the-Bear's growth of perception, however, is a restabilizing "calculus" which measures each of the leaders or mis-leaders in the narrative in terms of a complex phenomenological equation that, like a Gestalt, treats leadership as an organized whole whose parts belong together and which cannot function otherwise. As a reaction to the specific realities the novel proposes, in other words, true leadership in *Invisible Man* is finally not a matter of political will or technical mastery or ethical values or inspiration or ideology or analytical accuracy or shared sensibilities—but the whole and creative integration of *all* these elements into an effective, *organic* response. No stranger to psychological theory, Ellison put Freudian and Jungian theories and the role psychology of Harry Stack Sullivan to eclectic rhetorical use in his fiction. And for him, the theory of Gestalt—more than the others a psychology of perception and hence directly relevant to his concept of invisibility and his Burkean view of the ritual process—cogently suggested symbolic techniques for showing his characters in harmonious or unharmonious relationship to their immediate private and political situations. Jack-the-Bear's accounts of his jangling experiences and his political speechmaking accordingly dramatize richly detailed holistic Gestalts of physiological, perceptual, syntactic, emotional, and ideological interaction that measure the unity he is able to achieve, as a leader, in the course of persistently disunified events.

The specific import of such a calculus is that it conceives the problem of leadership and the problem of identity as related aspects of the human organism's struggle for creative unification. The parade of mis-leaders we encounter in *Invisible Man* is not one of fixed types representing unambiguously defective philosophies and completely discardable strategies. They are, rather, types of ambiguity, Empsonian in the ways they personify how warring contraries might either be bound up schizophrenically in a single psyche or be fused in "antagonistic cooperation" to clarify a complexly unitary sensibility. They represent, also, older vernacular or allegorical types of ambiguity that suggest human dispositions strangely distorted, unbalanced, fragmented by some fixed obsession or constitutional disproportion of humours. In Bledsoe, Barbee, Norton, Emerson Jr., Brockaway, Ras, and Jack, vision and impaired vision co-exist, reality and unreality, plausible pragmatism and the perversely irrational. So, Bledsoe's high-handed tricksterism evokes the rich history of folk-fable wisdom to lend it credence. Barbee's grandiloquent eulogy of redemptive progress roots itself in faiths indispensable to group and individual effort. And the strategy with which Lucius Brockaway has made John Henry's martyrdom obsolete and himself indispensable to the Machine is a pragmatic though precarious and inevitably paranoid adjustment to life as a black workingman on the horns of the white man's capitalist-unionist dilemma. Similarly, Ras's fervid Africanity yields accurate assessments of white men's treachery, even though it is blended with a violently quixotic atavism whose results are "not funny, or not only funny, but dangerous as well, wrong but justified, crazy and yet coldly sane" (*IM* 552). Even Brother Jack's mechanistic theory of life as all pattern and discipline and science, though fascistically brutal, conveys truths without which organized political action is inconceivable.

Yet measured against Ellison's paradigmatic leadership Gestalt, all these mis-leaders and their dispositions are absurdly neurotic and politically inadequate representatives of a fractured humanity. Worshippers of control and manipulation, all are rigid, robotized, automatic types, unadaptive and painfully comic in the Bergsonian sense, partisans of some merely provisional tactic or ideology unsuited to endure change or to ensure dignity, incapable of conceiving the world in all its fluid reality, much less of transforming it creatively. Though the narrator's misperceptions keep him from developing such a perspective in the agrarian world of his nonage, there Jim Trueblood provides the locus of value to which the crooked lines of Southern leadership are authorially drawn. Eventually, in the urban technological world that comprises the Northern half of his life's cosmology, Jack-the-Bear himself, his blinders finally falling in the wake of Tod Clifton's senseless death, discovers the corresponding big city locus in the psychic geometries of the three zoot-suited boys he encounters on a subway platform.

In the South, Trueblood's dream-driven act of incest provides a point of dramatic convergence triangulated by the competing imperatives of the three overlords who control the sharecropper's peasant existence: first, the landowning Southern whites who, led by the "boss man" and the sheriff, intercede for Trueblood and make his "unnatural act" of incest a cause for celebration; second, the moneyed Northerners who, in the person of Mr. Norton, atone for betraying Trueblood's ancestral Reconstruction dream of forty acres and a mule by converting the reprobate farmer's sexual misfortune into a hundred dollar scapegoat ritual; and third, the black college community on the hill who, as the narrator confesses, "hated the blackbelt people, the 'peasants,'" for returning the college's efforts to uplift them by doing, "like Trueblood, . . . everything, it seemed, to pull us down" (*IM* 47).

Trueblood's relationships with each side of this triumvirate reveal the political truths behind his metaphorical self-identification with the powerless but still perceiving jaybird he describes, who is paralyzed by yellow jackets' stings "but still alive in his eyes and . . . watchin' 'em sting his body to death" (*IM* 62). The Southern whites regularly confirm their power to rule with such rites as the battle royal and with such bestowals of feudal largesse as sending the scholarship-winning narrator to his miseducation. More crucially, they confirm their delusory "right" to rule with the kind of symbolic magic Trueblood has "accidentally" ceded them by dreaming into being the perversity of his life. And as Trueblood's perverse mishap confirms the power of the Southerners to reenslave him, it confirms the impotence, conversely, of Northern liberalism to free him. For, the first fruit Mr. Norton will see of his investments in the Founder's effort to transform "barren clay to fertile soil" is Trueblood's harvest of sexual sin. That harvest, at the sharecropper's cabin initially and later at the Golden Day, is shown to be, for Norton and his Emersonian ministry no less than for Trueblood and his star-crossed family, a "black 'bomination . . . birthed to bawl [his] wicked sin befo' the eyes of God" (*IM* 66).

Concomitantly, the black college "power house" on the hill, which closes the third side of the triangle around Trueblood's emblematic life, sustains its power with rites of leadership that, again, expropriate and alienate Trueblood's peasant community rather than serve and empower it. Ellison's narrative carefully distinguishes the historical personage of Booker T. Washington from that of the fictional Founder and the Founder's protégé, Bledsoe. But all three are representatives of the same overarching philosophy of racial uplift that historically dominated Southern black education during the age of Booker T. Washington. And Jim Trueblood, in the rhetoric Washington so assiduously cultivated, is the novel's primary embodiment of that "man farthest down" for whom the buckets of racial uplift ostensibly are to be lowered. Yet as Trueblood relates, he once had gone to the Founder's college for book learning and for help with his crops. But instead of leadership he had received contempt and ridicule, subsequently losing the land he once owned, and his independence, in the course of the college's rise to nominal power—and so ironically being lowered into disgrace instead of being lifted to liberty.

The deified Founder in whose name the sharecropper has quite literally been sacrificed—Trueblood's "primitive spirituals" appropriated to sanctify the "black rites of Horatio Alger" and his public shame extirpated from the college's official consciousness—is no mere apostle of wealth or prestige but an energetic cult's supreme oracle and avatar, wielding "the power of a king, or in a sense, a god," but a god who presumably rules benevolently, through faith, not fear (*IM* 116–19). His "living agent," Bledsoe, however, has converted the Founder's utopian vision into a cynical power game engineered with sleight-of-hand, with pandemic fear, and, where black pawns like Trueblood are concerned, with undisguised threats and intimidation. If Bledsoe is "a leader, a 'statesman'" more than just the president of a college, he is also the "coal black daddy" whose "magic" patriarchal leadership becomes a reign of terror capable, he informs the narrator, of having "every Negro in the country hanging on tree limbs" to sustain itself (*IM* 141). Again, it is through Trueblood, who is forced to checkmate Bledsoe's machinations against him with the equally treacherous power of the white bosses, that Bledsoe is first unveiled as Norton's counterpart and accomplice—a shape-shifting, mask-wearing "lyncher of souls."

As Trueblood focuses Ellison's leadership calculus in the Southern context, so the zoot-suited trio in New York's subway underground provides a focal image for dissecting the character of leadership in the urban North. There, in symbolic tableau, Ellison's meditations on Raglan's heroic mythology and the problem of black leadership converge explicitly in a riddle of cultural creativity his 1942 *Negro Quarterly* editorials had proposed as a test in political decipherment for those who would be masters of social movements. Ellison's assertion then that the zoot suit, or the symmetrical frenzy of the Lindy Hop, might conceal "profound political meaning" crucial to black leaders expands here, in the wake of the genuinely tragic death of Tod Clifton (the novel's most idealized figure of political possibility), into a metaphysical consolidation of all those notions of history, culture, consciousness, art, war, and dominion that the ritual progress of the hero-narrator has cumulatively brought to surface.

Looming suddenly before Jack-the-Bear as silent, ambiguous figures with hard conked hair and bodies reshaped by costume into the semblance of "African sculptures, distorted in the interest of a design," the trio moves before the narrator's finally unfettered vision "like dancers in some kind of funeral ceremony" (*IM* 430). They score their movements unselfconsciously with the rhythmic, street-corner staccato of tap dance and share a puzzling and complete absorption in, significantly enough, comic books. The narrator's jolting perception here is one of the book's true epiphanies. He realizes that, though "outside history," like Clifton after his plunge from Brotherhood, the zoot-suiters might actually be "saviors, the true leaders" of an unfathomably irrational counterhistory. This revelation is succeeded by his seeing, too, that they are not anomalies but part of a whole uptown populace of "surreal variations" on downtown styles (*IM* 433). The narrator now no longer sees that populace as a fixed mass to be led but as a mysteriously fluid configuration of personalities and motives in terms of which his own capacities for leading must be recalculated and his ideal of leadership and its genesis reexamined. At this moment, before his belief in Brotherhood has been completely blasted, that ideal is still represented by the talismanic image of Frederick Douglass. But "what was I in relation to the boys," he now must ask himself, and replies, "Perhaps an accident, like Douglass"—glimpsing here that the presumably "scientific" linkage between a leader and the led might, like the boys themselves, instead be outside science and the "groove of history" (*IM* 432–33).

Douglass is the book's only otherwise undiminished historical image of knowledge and power humanely united. (Marcus Garvey, who is fleetingly praised by Clifton for his apparent ability to move a people who "are hell to move" [*IM* 358], is diminished implicitly by association with Ras the Exhorter, just as Washington is diminished by explicit connection with the Founder and the Brotherhood and the Battle Royal.) And Douglass is joined here in the narrator's mind with himself and Clifton, each of them gauged against the cryptic political possibilities of the comic-book reading, zoot-suited boys. Until his experience of Rinehart and then Dupre and Scofield and their cadre of "rational" rioters completes this initial vision, the narrator will have no fuller revelation of leadership's inverse points of reference.

Rinehart, the "confidencing sonofabitch" who is a darker brother of Melville's Confidence Man and who becomes Ellison's "personification of chaos," pushes the calculus of leadership to its logical extreme and the narrator's political consciousness past thinking it his job somehow to get the zoot-suiters and their surreal brethren back inside the groove of history. In his grasp of the "vast seething, hot world of fluidity" beneath official history and in his adjustment to modern life's fullest possibilities, Rinehart is the narrative's ultimate image of social mastery. A connoisseur of techniques and machines and a consummate decoder of the dark recesses of the human soul, he is, as he advertises, a "spiritual technologist" whose ability to manipulate private dreams, public myth, and symbolic structures like the zoot suit, the Lindy Hop, storefront revivals, or sexual fantasy makes him potentially a more powerful leader than so exemplary a man of principle as Tod Clifton. Clifton is acknowledged even by his rival, Ras, as a natural-born leader, a "black prince." And Clifton, like Rinehart, understands the zoot-suiters better than the narrator ever will. But Clifton is fatally misled by his fervent belief in Brotherhood to misread the ulterior motives of his comrades. By contrast, Rinehart's "smooth tongue and heartless heart" and his willingness to do anything bespeak an utter lack of sentimentality about human vices and values and an impregnable cynicism deeper and purer even than that of Ras. Ras "works on the inside" as effectively as Rinehart, and Ras is better able than Clifton or the narrator to penetrate the fog of Brotherhood ideology and to identify his natural enemies and allies. But his atavistic impulses distance him from the hypermodern world of the zoot-suiters and keep him from mastering the pragmatic techniques of empowerment.

In the narrative's agrarian zone, Bledsoe and Norton have proven themselves incapable of accommodating Trueblood's sensibility and its implications for genuine leadership; and in the urban context Brother Jack, Ras, and Clifton all prove inadequate to the task of leadership in zoot-suited Harlem. Only Rinehart is technically and metaphysically equipped to lead, but he is the most demonic mis-leader of all. Correlatively, the narrator's decision to take Rinehart as his model and Rinehartism as his political instrument for undermining the Brotherhood's confidence boomerangs like all his preceding instrumentalities. First of all, he lacks the ruthlessness necessary to carry out the sexual intrigue he plans as a reversal of the Brotherhood's earlier efforts to neutralize him through the agency of a white woman. Then, after discovering a certain horrific sameness between the Brotherhood's real attitudes toward its Harlem constituents and Rinehart's—the Brotherhood's admitted "trick" of leadership is "to take advantage of them in their own best interest"—he finds that his counterapplication of Rinehart's cynical tactics leads not to the destruction of the Brotherhood as he intends but to the apocalyptic riots that the Brotherhood has helped engineer with his and Ras's unwitting complicity, making of Harlem a dark sacrifice to political expediency.

The moment at which Jack-the-Bear commits himself to political Rinehartism, though, is another epiphany of synoptic insight which builds on the perceptions the trio in zoot suits triggered. Here his first full acceptance of his personal past and its humiliations, his sense suddenly of being able "to look around corners," his subsequent look around such a psychic corner to see Jack and Norton and Emerson "merge into one single white figure" of bat-blind absurdity—all these fuse into his first full recognition of his invisibility and into his admission that, though he still did not know what his grandfather's riddling strategy meant, he "was ready to test his advice." That the moment structures an even more comprehensive synthesis, one not yet fully known to the now very knowing narrator, is signaled in the punning metaphor he culls to link the contradictions of invisibility with the political exigencies of the moment: "I was and yet I was invisible. . . . I was and yet I was unseen. . . . Now I saw that I could agree with Jack without agreeing. And I could tell Harlem to have hope when there was no hope. . . . I would have to move them without myself being moved. . . . I'd have to do a Rinehart" (*IM* 496).

Associated here with political rationalization and with the rhetorical process of having to inspire emotion and action in others while remaining detached from the rhetoric of inspiration, this notion of "hav[ing] to move . . . without . . . being moved" that the narrator now links to Rinehart's maneuvers is a provocative echo and revision of the precise terms in which Jim Trueblood had recounted his incestuous, somnambulistic "tight spot" astride his daughter alongside his wife. Trueblood comes to see the phallic dilemma he awakened to as a metaphor for his life in general: having "to move without moving" had been his predicament on the socioeconomic and political ladder, as it had then become his sole salvation from sexual sin. At authorial behest Trueblood expresses here a psychological sense of context akin to the seventh and most ambiguous of William Empson's seven types of ambiguity: that involving absolute opposites which define a center of conflict and which, like dreams in Freudian analysis, place in stereoscopic contradiction what one wants but has not got with what one has but cannot avoid, a conflict unresolvable save in another dimension beyond syntax and logic—in feeling rather than thought, in poetry rather than philosophy.

Short of some such resolving power in another dimension, the only material escape for Trueblood lay in the unmanning possibilities of a gelding knife, a mode of escape from context whose price, for as manly a "daddy quail" as Trueblood feels himself to be, is "too much to pay to keep from sinnin'" (*IM* 59). In his full awareness, then, of the irredeemable cost of freedom from sin and the attendant consequences of freely sinning, Trueblood gives eloquent testimony to his own tragic sense of life and to that need for transcendence that he finally satisfies only in the resolving poetry of the blues. As such, he is marked off in his own mind, as he later will be in the narrator's mind as well, from that world of mastery without limits, beyond ethics and love and art—beyond flesh and blood humanity—that the narrator discovers in the disembodied traces of Bliss Proteus Rinehart. A matter of potent political import for the novel, Rinehart and Trueblood are ultimately the nonpolitical poles of sensibility between which the narrator must mediate his own ambiguous sense of freedom as necessity and as possibility. Despite Rinehart's unmediated freedom and Trueblood's subjection to psychic and social necessity, what Rinehart and Trueblood share is their existential awareness that to be free one must be able to "move without moving," a problem Rinehart *masters* but which Trueblood *transcends.*[12]

In this oblique contrast rests the staunchest fusing power of the narrator's prologue and epilogue to his tale, though Rinehart appears there only fleetingly and Trueblood not at all. The narrator's final declaration that his underground hibernation is at an end along with his prosecution of his grandfather's guerrilla war, that political action and love and responsibility are still possible, is joined with his realization that Rinehart's freedom or Jack's power is not what he really wants. And in so resolving, he recapitulates consciously Trueblood's postincest rededication to his family, to seeing his "black 'bomination" birthed and not aborted, and to accepting his life's agonizing limits as perhaps inescapable but nevertheless endurable. If Trueblood's phallic dream has led him unconsciously to the brink of abysmal sexual sin and he has refused to unman himself to keep from sinning, so the narrator's political tactics—which finally implicate him in Clifton's death and the bloody Harlem riots—lead him unconsciously to the brink of a social abyss; and his phallic dream there of being unmanned girds his final refusal to substitute Rinehart's mode of moving without moving for Trueblood's.

In the epilogue, Jack-the-Bear's will to so refuse is no desperate leap of faith that irrationally denies the cumulative truth of his bruising, boomeranging experiences. Nor is it simply an expression of the bourgeois qualm that Rinehart's nihilism is criminally antisocial. Rather, the narrator's reborn will consolidates the patterned affirmations in his tale, which all along the way have counterpointed the chaotic reversals and explosions of negativity that otherwise dominate his movement through life. These affirmations by no means subdue the forces of negation he has come to know: though recurring throughout, they are momentary at best, isolated from the centers of pragmatic power, and often ambiguous in their own right. Most characteristically, they surface in the stream of resurgent folkloric figures and images from childhood that give his ritual experiences much of their emotional texture and hold him back from cultural deracination.

At their highest pitch they form a rhythm of epiphany and Gestaltic unification that forcefully defies the rule of chaos and destruction and dehumanization. The first and most resounding of these affirmations comes, again, in Jim Trueblood's cathartically sacred and profane riff, his church-song-spawned blues. This creative will to transcendence asserts itself repeatedly in the narrative, often in reaction to, or anticipation of, the most dispiriting circumstances. The narrator, waiting for the hypocritically stage-managed "black rites of Horatio Alger" to begin in his college chapel, drifts, "the bungling bugler of words, imitating the trumpet and the trombone's timbre," into a countervailing reverie of his own that sweeps him away from Bledsoe's officious exercise in cynicism into a loving lyrical paean to the silent, gray-haired campus matron, Miss Susie Gresham, an old "relic of slavery," who is beyond being "fooled with the mere content of words" and who bears "something warm and vital and all-enduring, of which in that island of shame we were not ashamed" (*IM* 111–12). There also at vespers, counterpointing the sterility and meaninglessness of official ritual, he witnesses a sequence of *a cappella* song and spontaneous prayer that simultaneously possesses the unnamed singer—her "voice seemed to become a disembodied force that sought to enter her, to violate her, shaking her rocking her rhythmically, as though it had become the source of her being." Witnessing her reduces the audience to "profound silence" (*IM* 114–15).

Similarly, up North and alone, caught emotionally between his lingering country ways and his citified aspirations, the narrator encounters a loquacious yam vendor, yields to temptation and nostalgia, and then, on devouring the hot buttered yam, experiences an "intense feeling of freedom" and exhilaration. That feeling blossoms into a triumphantly comic fantasy confrontation with Bledsoe and prepares the narrator, unwittingly, for his succeeding eruption of indignation at a street-corner eviction scene, which propels him into a new life as a professional rabble-rouser. Here as elsewhere in the narrative, the moment of affirmation is a moment also of self-unification—of mind, feelings, and physiology harmonized and expressively eloquent. The subsequent progress of his career as a Brotherhood orator is marked by a tension between his self-consciously controlled techniques or ideology and his spontaneous eruptions of compelling emotion: the ideological taboos that Jack imposes and the subject-object separation Rinehart's smooth-tongued rhetoric requires are overborne in the moments of true union with his hearers and with his deepest understandings. He is most moving when moved himself.

Accordingly, at Tod Clifton's funeral the narrator's driving eulogy for his fallen brother is preceded by a moment of transcendent affirmation in which the funeral procession, ambiguously poised between love and "politicized hate," is transformed by the unprompted rise of a single plaintive, anonymous voice and the euphonium horn that rises to accompany it on "There's Many a Thousand Gone" (*IM* 441). The funeral procession becomes, in spirit, a march. The young marchers join the old; the white marchers blend with the black. Singing "with his whole body, phrasing each verse as naturally as he walked," the first singer, an old man, becomes leader and follower simultaneously, unself-consciously voicing "the old longing, resigned transcendent emotion" beneath the words. And by moving the crowd with "something deeper than protest, or religion" the anonymous elder unifies them into a powerful "singing mass"—and moves the narrator to wet-eyed wonder, and to envy also, as he confronts in the otherwise unleaderly, knife-scarred old man the resplendent powers and art of leadership he has struggled so long to master.

In this dramatic image of art and leadership conjoined, the undergirding logic of the narrator's epilogue optimism reveals itself. For the problems of heroic leadership in *Invisible Man* through which Ellison focused his extrapolations from myth, folk tradition, history, and political philosophy ultimately move toward resolution through an assimilation of the myth of the hero's birth to the myth of the artist's birth. Though rarely read on such terms, the novel is, as Ellison has quietly insisted, a "portrait of the artist as rabble-rouser" (*S&A* 179).

That the novel has few of the aesthetic signposts of conventional *Künstlerroman* creates part of the confusion. Save for a brief punning allusion to the prototypic Joycean portrait of the artist, only in the framing prologue and epilogue is the theme of aesthetic idealism explicitly joined in the narrator's mind to his ritual *agon* with politics and invisibility. And there it is not his oratorical art but the music of Louis Armstrong that functions as an index of cultivated sensibility and creative conflict. Ellison was clearly aware that narratives of artistic evolution frequently have a ritual substructure coordinate to that of the mythic hero-king: the genealogy of talent admits the same dramatic dislocations and confusions as the genealogy of hereditary power. As a zone of adventure and contest, the world of artistic means and motives offers its own endemic monsters, mazes, and underworld terrain. And the patterns of quest and conquest inhere in the struggle for technique, style, and aesthetic vision no less than in the world the heroes of myth inhabit. But in *Invisible Man* the psychological drama of the narrator's undesigned, unself-conscious evolution as an artist is veiled by his conscious, designing passion for political heroism. His explicit struggle to master the techniques of oratory, for example, registers only subliminally as an artist's labor to fashion a personal style. He focuses not on creating and expressing his own sensibility but on affecting and directing others. And the object of his artful pragmatism is not to communicate a vision of beauty or unalloyed truth as a subject for contemplation, but to spur the acquisition of practical power by moving men and women to action.

In such a context, he becomes conscious of himself as an artist only when his failure as a hero seems complete. In the prologue and epilogue, as ranter turned writer, he has supplanted his original quest for Washingtonian leadership with a quest for yet-to-be-discovered forms of overt action intimated musically in the heroic lyricism of Louis Armstrong's blues. If here it seems uncertain that he has anything more than revived illusion to sustain a hinted future return to rabble-rousing or to "playing a role," if Armstrong might be only an ambiguous new mirage to "keep this nigger boy running," Ellison's theory- and concept-toting "thinker-tinker" does repudiate his former illusions; and he does draw a cautionary veil of consciousness between Armstrong and himself: Louis has made "poetry out of invisibility" because he is unaware that he is invisible. The implication is that this nescience may give Armstrong a creative edge, at least provisionally. For awareness, Jack-the-Bear has learned, in its initial stages, insofar as it illuminates the awesome forces of chaos and unfreedom without vouchsafing countervailing strategies, need be no boon at all but may rather be a burden, a burden from which Armstrong apparently is free. Jack-the-Bear's own compulsion to "put invisibility down in black and white," he tells us while querying himself, may be an analogous urge to make music of invisibility—his attempt to annex the musician's powers of synesthetic perception to the more limited ones available to a man who has chosen to be "an orator, a rabble-rouser . . . and perhaps shall be again" (*IM* 14).

Jack-the-Bear has been a man of words; but because words cannot contain all of reality, his dependence on them prescribes failures and confusions from which the maker of music is comparatively freer. The word's entanglement with scientific and historical rationality and denotative constraints bars the penetration into time and space that music's relative elusiveness and freedom from official intelligibility make possible. The problem of freedom which his own personal history has made a riddle— and which the prologue's reefer hallucination reframes in the broader allegorical context of racial history's master-slave symbiosis—he knows is unresolvable apart from a decipherment of the culture's and his own consciousness of time. He enunciates time's strategic possibilities in his recollection of a prizefighter boxing a yokel and his seeing the former's vastly superior science, speed, and footwork knocked "cold as a well digger's posterior" when the yokel simply steps inside his opponent's sense of time to deliver a single, telling blow. What the narrator discovers vaguely in the "nodes" and "breaks" of Armstrong's music is just such a sense of time.

Music—bound more than any of the other arts to time and timing— was for Ellison, even more than for his music-minded novelistic exemplar André Malraux, that expressive penetration into ultimate reality whose forms, patterns of evolution, traditions, and metamorphoses supplied the clues not only to the souls of black folk but to the rhythms and style and soul of modern civilization. For such inquisitors of modern life as Hegel, Nietzsche, Spengler, and Yeats, the cycles and spirals and gyres hypothetically circumscribing the course of human events were mimed and ofttimes mocked by the shifting forms of art, literature, and especially of music. For these thinkers the old Romanticist ethos and its expressive theory of art were raised to cosmic significance. In Malraux's view, it was the drama of art confronting the world and refusing to follow the "natural" order that the visual arts, especially, and music more than literature recorded in their own autonomous history. And that history, a history of "style" and the mysterious logic through which style unfolds and imposes itself on the world, is the history whose structured principles in blues and jazz and vernacular signification and folk fable Ellison's narrator ultimately wields against the structure of lies and illusions that have dominated and diminished the sense of possibility he discovered as an invisible man: "My God, what possibilities existed! And that spiral business, that progress goo.... And that lie that success was a rising upward. What a crummy lie they kept us dominated by. Not only could you travel upward toward success but you could travel downward as well; up and down, in retreat as well as in advance, crabways and crossways and around in a circle, meeting your old selves coming and going and perhaps all at the same time" (*IM* 498–99).

Such multidimensional possibilities are visible to the musician more than the man of words because, as the irresistible "club" of reality has impressed on Jack-the-Bear, there is "an area in which a man's feelings are more rational than his mind" (*IM* 560). And music, freed from the constraints of ordinary linguistic thought, maps it more completely than communicative rhetoric. Such rhetoric, however much it strives to expand its symbolic powers, replicates only a fragment of the vast repertoire of human expressive possibilities manifest from grins, growls, and gestures to the masterpieces of high art and the wizardry of machines. The liberating possibilities of music, however, remain untapped because music, he admits, is perceived one-dimensionally—"is heard and seldom seen except by musicians" (*IM* 13). Conversely, as his hallucinogenic hyperperceptivity teaches him, when music's full synesthetic possibilities are grasped by the perceiver, its depredations into time and space may be so overwhelming as to actually inhibit the human actor and defy the political will expressed in the narrator's own undaunted belief "in nothing if not in action" (*IM* 13).

As the "laws" of history impose a tyranny of time, circumstance, and conceptual limitation on humanity, so Armstrong's art, Trueblood's spontaneity, and the spiritual-singer's expressivity, as well as the psychic geometries of the zoot suit, offer escape from the bondage of history not through any evasion of circumstance but through the evocation and consolidation of styles and attitudes for confronting it. In Malraux's psychology of art, which Ellison converted enthusiastically to his own ends in the late 1940s, this "deflection" of history is rooted in a resurrection of the conventional Romantic elevation of creative genius and of the artist as hero: living in time, but also in the presence of the timeless world where art's collective testimony prevails regardless of the change and mortality outside, the artist "escapes" ordinary history—and historical fatalism—in those isolated moments of unique creativity when the expressive gesture liberates him or her from inherited traditions and reveals a style entirely his or her own (Goldberger 234–43). In making such creative gestures, the artist participates in a "history" of creative events, in moments of creative heroism which constitute their own continuity, deflected from, if sometimes parallel to, conventional history.

For Ellison the danger of trying to escape into this antihistory by way of either the creative or the religious imagination was manifest in the African American past where, as he decried in his 1945 review of Wright's *Black Boy*, the special conditions of black life and its consequently "defensive character" had regularly transformed the "will toward organization" into a "will to camouflage, to dissimulate" (*S&A* 93). Creative heroism, for Malraux and Wright and Ellison, could only be energized by a will to confront both the world of circumstance and the world of creative gesture. Creative power manifested itself in the capacity to transcend circumstance—by experiencing it directly, exploring it exhaustively, then reintegrating it by acts of willed imagination in such a way as to remake potentially the culture of which it is a part. The attraction of the blues, their manifest power, lay in their discovery of a style for expressing simultaneously the agony of life and the possibility of conquering it. Rather than a flight into aestheticism or a passive cultivation of sensibility, they were a codified assertion of will—if not overtly political, then nonetheless allied with the political will to convert, through action, conscious experience into felt power.

To unify the political will and the creative will against the backdrop of sweeping historical change and of human values confronting such change was Ralph Ellison's most ambitious intention as a novelist. That his tragicomic judgment of the characters he places under such pressure veers finally toward aesthetic norms and away from the narrowly political links him, of course, to such acknowledged literary ancestors and relatives as Malraux, again, Hemingway, Unamuno, and, more obliquely, Wright. For the former three, the interpenetration into extreme human situations of such aesthetic norms as grace, balance, contemplative detachment, and élan was central to the drama of the heroic. In *Invisible Man*, Louis Armstrong's projective sense of style—which culminates the novel's long series of creative gestures and affirmations in extremity—is Ellison's clearest corollary: it is Armstrong who personifies the narrator's consummatory maxim that "humanity is won by continuing to play in the face of certain defeat" (*IM* 564); and it is Armstrong who, as he "bends" his military instrument into a beam of lyrical sound, carries Jim Trueblood's country blues standard, by phonograph, into the narrative's urban fray.

But Ellison's Invisible Man knows that for all Trueblood's and Armstrong's flesh and bone wisdom and their lyric aplomb, the bluesmen have styled preliminary attitudes and transcendental resolutions of conflicts whose possible solution through material means he, not they, is better suited by proximity to power, by technique, and by consciousness, to undertake. That Trueblood and Armstrong are unaware of their invisibility—as the narrator's grandfather also was—is both their advantage and their limitation. Unlike Rinehart, whose freedom is a destructive freedom that feeds on illusion and breeds chaos and death and whose victory over the material world is won at the cost of absolute self-effacement, Armstrong does not trade on invisibility and does not diminish himself by it. He has transcended defeat by imposing his own personality on his horn and converting its "Bad Air" to communal poetry. In so doing, he has asserted his own undefeated will and defies death itself with an indestructible artistry. Without the strategically crucial sense of space and time that conscious invisibility provides, however, extending his conquest of the world of art into the world of material circumstances remains a hope limited by the ability of his auditors to truly hear.

In Malraux's world, the problem of art's pragmatic relation to the pattern of material existence remained characteristically unresolved. The hero-revolutionaries of his political novels and the artist-heroes of his aesthetic essays are spiritually related but kept consistently apart. The humorless political heroes, inevitably defeated by the failure or betrayal of social revolution, choose consciously to act out doomed commitments they can no longer see as anything but absurd and to martyr themselves, as in *Man's Fate*, to their transcendent passion for the ideal. The hero-artists, by contrast, escape the world of men, in which freedom is finally impossible, steal creative fire from the gods, and, in their own self-constructed world of art, win the freedom that the hero-revolutionaries can only imagine. Ellison's impulse in *Invisible Man* was to reject forms of transcendence limited either to final political martyrdom or to an hermetic world of aesthetics and, instead, to unify the dissevered possibilities in the figure of a political man-of-words-and-action redeemed and reborn through art. If Richard Wright in *Native Son*, like André Malraux and Ernest Hemingway in their novels, cleaved to a secular vision of heroic, or antiheroic, martyrdom, Ellison in *Invisible Man* found it possible, indeed necessary, both to reject the cult of death and to affirm the hope of spiritual rebirth by recording symbolically his group's true pangenerational transcendence of material defeat through the agencies of art.

As his own immersion in his people's and his nation's history had taught him, and as he would later remark, "the art—the blues, the spiritual, the jazz, the dance—was what we had in place of freedom" (*S&A* 247). Rather than proposing any substitutional or merely compensatory role for art, *Invisible Man* makes artistic transcendence the one unsuppressible means through which human freedom is imagined and achieved and human beings are made whole. Its narrator's torturing himself to put down in black and white the chronicle of his abysmal pain and the progress through illusion to perception which enables him to see the pattern in its chaos carries to a higher level that articulate probing of a grievous wound that Jim Trueblood modeled for him with tale and defeat-defying blues. The telling of his own tale—his "buggy jiving"—is the hibernating narrator's initial reengagement with a world that still conspires to defeat him. It is a cathartic release of anger and angst that, through the power of words, converts what begins as an act of war into what he finally knows has become an act of disarmament. And it is, on the terms its author proposes, an act of conscious leadership in which one man's will to selfhood brings to comic and tragic clarity his and his reader-followers' common property in the buggy, jiving, blue-black rites of man.

Is it a fact—or have I dreamt it—that, by means of electricity, the world of matter has become a great nerve, vibrating thousands of miles in a breathless point of time?

—NATHANIEL HAWTHORNE, *The House of the Seven Gables*

I sing the body electric;
The armies of those I love engirth me, and I engirth them;
They will not let me off till I go with them, respond to them,
And discorrupt them, and charge them full with the charge of the Soul.

—WALT WHITMAN, *Leaves of Grass*

The danger of the past was that men became slaves. The danger of the future is that men may become robots.

—ERICH FROMM, *The Sane Society*

Applied Science is a conjuror, whose bottomless hat yields impartially the softest of Angora rabbits and the most petrifying of Medusas.

—ALDOUS HUXLEY, *Tomorrow and Tomorrow and Tomorrow*

I said to the electrocutor: awful lousy crime;
I said to the electrocutor: awful lousy crime;
And my baby asked the judge: was he going to electrocute that man of mine.

—BLIND LEMON JEFFERSON, "Lectric Chair Blues"

Chapter Three

Chapter Three

ELLISON'S SPIRITUAL TECHNOLOGIES

I n "That Same Pleasure, That Same Pain," the interview that opens *Shadow and Act*, Ralph Ellison reflects on his boyhood back in the newly segregated, fading frontier of post–World War I Oklahoma. He conjectures at the outset that his own genesis as an artist rested contrapuntally on two "accidents" of cultural literacy coincident with the rise of the modern mass media and its unforeseen power to subvert the social constraints of caste and color. I will attend to the second of these accidents first. That second happenstance, by no means void of human agency, consisted in the practice by his mother, Ida Ellison, of conveying home to her curious young son a steady stream of opera recordings and *haute couture* magazines—*Vanity Fair* first and foremost in Ellison's recall—that had been discarded by the Oklahoma City white families for whom she worked as a maid. During the early years of the Roaring Twenties, Ellison reminisced, his environment had consequently been extended imaginatively by such "slender threads" into a white world. Those threads, he wrote, were "not really part of my own life: . . . they were things which somehow spoke of a world which I could someday make my own" (*S&A* 3–5).

The form of cultural literacy that those *Vanity Fair* images and ideas dangled before Ellison's boyish eyes comprised a literal cavalcade of 1920s elegance, sophistication, and postwar generational rebellion. Under the

supervision of managing editors such as Edmund Wilson, *Vanity Fair* and
its ilk opened Ellison's imaginative horizons informally to a milieu that
included premier productions of the New York stage, the music of Igor
Stravinsky, the painting and sculpture of Pablo Picasso, and the "Literary
Hors d'Oeuvres," "Satirical Sketches," and critical missives of writers such
as T. S. Eliot, Marcel Proust, Edna St. Vincent Millay, and Kenneth Burke
(Jackson 39). By the time, a decade later at Tuskegee Institute, that Ellison
underwent the demystifying tutelage at the hands of Eliot's *The Waste Land*
that transformed him from a vacillating music major into a conscious dev-
otee of literature, "accident" had become intention. After Ellison followed
Eliot's trail of annotation back to Jessie Weston's *From Ritual to Romance*
and Sir James George Frazer's *The Golden Bough*, Morteza Sprague, the
Tuskegee professor of English to whom Ellison would dedicate his first
collection of essays, furthered the explicatory quest by directing the young
exegete to the world of contemporary literary criticism divulged by Harriet
Monroe, Babette Deutsch, Ezra Pound, and that *Vanity Fair* familiar
Edmund Wilson (Jackson 39).

In this new context Wilson made a singular impress on Ellison's developing literary sensibilities, since by the onset of the Great Depression, the
modernist proselytizer had transformed his earlier journalistic devotion to
"Literature, History, the Creation of Beauty, and the Discovery of Truth"
into his first book's more programmatic dedication to "what literary criticism ought to be—a history of man's ideas and imaginings in the setting of
the conditions which have shaped them" (Borklund 519, 521). *Axel's Castle:
A Study in the Imaginative Literature of 1870–1930* (1931), one of the classics
of modern criticism, would reverberate throughout Ellison's later critical
thinking, along with *The Wound and the Bow* (1941), Wilson's provocative
quasi-psychoanalytic exploration of the thesis that "genius and disease,
like strength and mutilation, may be inextricably bound up together." In
his biography of Ellison's formative years, Lawrence Jackson argues that
Axel's Castle "provided a reader as schematically innocent as Ellison with
a framework to view post-Renaissance Western literature in terms of schools
and groups" (153). Indeed, Wilson had provided Ellison's whole generation
with a path-breaking study of the international origins and development
of the Symbolist school, in particular, and its fusion and conflict with naturalism in the works of W. B. Yeats, Paul Valéry, T. S. Eliot, Marcel Proust,

James Joyce, Gertrude Stein, Auguste Villiers de l'Isle-Adam, and Arthur Rimbaud. Beyond explaining the central role of Symbolism in modern writing and promoting the "widespread acceptance in America of what had been almost entirely a foreign or expatriate movement," *Axel's Castle* also demonstrated how the Symbolist writers' artistic code "brought a new personal rhythm into language" (Adams 272–86). It lent music an overriding influence on modernist poetic development and, Jackson emphasizes, made composers such as Richard Wagner—an early Ellison icon alongside Duke Ellington—as important in shaping the course of Symbolism as any poet (153). In Wilson's stress on the musical nature of Eliot's *Waste Land* experimentation, by extension, lay the seeds of Ellison's own discovery in it of "something akin to jazz modulation"—a revelation pivotal to Ellison's later hybridizing theories about the classical-vernacular amalgam in American culture.[1]

But the import of *Axel's Castle* for the evolution of Ellison's artistic worldview and its generative "accidents" has yet another largely unexplored dimension that which links Wilson's dialectic to the broader tensions between literature and science that also shaped the movements and schools and experiments of modernist literary art. For while Wilson's book proceeded on the notion that the literary history of the modern era must be understood in terms of Symbolism's developmental fusion and conflict with Naturalism, his underlying theory of causation was premised on cyclical patterns in the history of modern science outlined in Alfred North Whitehead's groundbreaking *Science and the Modern World* (1926). Whitehead's book expressed the mathematician-philosopher's profound disturbance over the "new mentality" that had unleashed World War I and harnessed it to the "new science" and "new technology." He grimly traced the preceding three centuries of polarities in Western civilization across the course of a European philosophy that, since the seventeenth-century dualism of Descartes, had continued to presuppose bifurcating scientific assumptions about mind, matter, and energy that had become hopelessly at odds with the revolutions in scientific thinking of the late nineteenth and early twentieth centuries. Whitehead's own research two decades earlier for his *On Mathematical Concepts of the Material World* and his derivation of a principle of relativity alternative to Einstein's general and special theories had piqued his sense of how completely outmoded and dysfunctional the Copernican/Newtonian scientific synthesis had become. In the opening chapters of his new book, Whitehead now thought it essential that the historical cycles of warring cultural action and reaction between a "scientific-classic pole" and a "poetic-romantic one" be resolved by new metaphysical foundations for science more congenial to holistic ecological and environmental thinking—with his own newly apprehended concepts of flux, organism, and event replacing the classical ideas of space, time, and matter.[2]

Edmund Wilson acknowledged at the outset of *Axel's Castle* that the conceptual scheme of Whitehead's *Science and the Modern World* provided the plan of his own book and that in the artistic oscillations *Axel's Castle* addresses "literature [was] rebounding again from the scientific-classic pole to the poetic-romantic one" (3–6). As Romanticism in Whitehead's interpretation reacted against eighteenth-century Newtonian science, so Wilson's Symbolism reacted against the naturalism, Darwinism, and positivism of the nineteenth century (Wellek, *History of Modern Criticism* 107). In their turn, the heirs of the Symbolists—Wilson's cosmopolite cohort of artist-visionaries—assimilated concepts of space-time and relativity from the new scientific metaphysics of Einstein and Whitehead: "As in the universe of Whitehead, the 'events' which may be taken arbitrarily as infinitely small or infinitely comprehensive, make up an organic structure in which all are interdependent, each involving every other and the whole; so Proust's book is a gigantic dense mesh of complicated relations . . . [and] like Proust's or Whitehead's or Einstein's world, Joyce's world is always changing as it is perceived by different observers and by them at different times" (Wilson 221–22). Aligned with the scientific-classic pole, yet not wholly at odds with Symbolism, were writers such as H. G. Wells and George Bernard Shaw "who tried to promote through the new social sciences, in the teeth of the bourgeois world, the realization of those visions of universal happiness which had been cherished by some of the most individualistic of the Romantics" (Wilson 268).

Crucially so for both Ralph Ellison's cultural criticism and the speculative historiography of *Invisible Man*, Wilson saw a denial of social "reality" in late-nineteenth- and early-twentieth-century Realist literature that had roots in the "fallacies of misplaced concreteness" and "crazy" worldview Whitehead dissected in the tandem of cultural action and reaction. Extending Whitehead's logic, Wilson concluded that Symbolism was demonstrably an "elaboration" of Romanticism, a "second flood of the same tide" (2). In Whitehead's reading the seventeenth and eighteenth centuries had been the great period of emerging mathematical and physical theory in Europe; and the literature of the so-called Classical period showed Descartes and Newton to be influences as powerful as the Greco-Roman classics themselves. Poets, like astronomers and mathematicians, had come to regard the universe as a machine set in motion by a detached clock-maker God. The Romantic movement, Whitehead asserted, was really a reaction against scientific ideas, or rather against the mechanistic ideas to which certain scientific ideas gave rise (5).

Whitehead had dropped the story at this point. But, Wilson acknowledged, he had "provided the key to what follows" (6). Accordingly, *Axel's Castle* proceeded to argue that, despite the tensions between them, both Romanticism and Symbolism were "swings of the pendulum" against a dehumanizing worldview of nature and humanity. The leading Romantics had revolted against the eighteenth-century concept of the universe as a faultless machine, while the generative nineteenth-century French Symbolists rebelled against Naturalism:

> In the middle of the nineteenth century, science made new advances, and mechanistic ideas were brought back into fashion again. But they came this time from a different quarter—not from physics and mathematics, but from biology. It was the effect of the theory of Evolution to reduce man from the heroic stature to which the Romantics had tried to exalt him, to the semblance of an animal, again very small in the universe and at the mercy of forces about him. Humanity was the accidental product of heredity and environment, and capable of being explained in terms of these. This doctrine in literature was called Naturalism, and it was put in place by novelists like Zola, who believed that composing a novel was like performing a laboratory experiment. (Wilson 6)

Imbued thoroughly with the positivistic, biologizing spirit of his age, Émile Zola had embarked in 1868 on the creation of a twenty-volume cycle of novels, *Les Rougon–Macquart*, that he rationalized midway in the quarter-century labor of creation with his famous essay *Le Roman Expérimental* (1880). In articulating therein a "poetics" of Naturalism, Zola argued that just as the experimental method had been successfully adapted from chemistry and physics for use in physiology and medicine, so it could be applied strategically to the novel. Novelists should become not only "scientific observers" but "experimenters" navigating their characters through mimetically accurate representations of human situations, which should be orchestrated to demonstrate the ordering of events by the "determinism of phenomena" in accord with scientific knowledge of animal behavior and social relations (Baguley 749–50).

In Edmund Wilson's interpretive scheme, the Symbolist reaction against Zola's Naturalist tradition had "abandoned the detached study of human motives and the expression of those universal emotions which make all classes of people one" to follow instead three distinct trajectories. First was a mediating, quasi-naturalistic strain of social-idealist literature predicated on reform and satire and manifested before World War I by George Bernard Shaw, H. G. Wells, and Arnold Bennett in England and by Anatole France and Romain Rolland in France; but world war had destroyed its influence and vitality (Wilson 286). After the war two present and future forms of Symbolist alternatives had emerged, one a form of counterexperimentation, the other a kind of experiential devolution. Of these, the first comprised "a series of specialized experiments in the domain of 'symbolic expression' and imaginative values attained through the free combination of the elements of language." In a symbolically impoverished environment this new combinatory mode promised literature's survival as a sort of "game"—"just as the development of mechanical devices has compelled us to resort to sports in order to exercise our muscles" (Wilson 284–85). In accord with his book's deflating title, Wilson called this Symbolist alternative "Axel's way," the way of shutting "oneself up in one's own private world, cultivating one's private fantasies, encouraging one's private manias, ultimately preferring one's absurdist chimeras to the most astonishing contemporary realities, ultimately mistaking one's chimeras for realities." The other way, identified with Arthur Rimbaud and his spiritual retreat to the African wilderness, was the way of primitivist exploration—and the only vehicle for explicitly *racial* conundrums and chimeras to surface in *Axel's Castle*:

D. H. Lawrence's mornings in Mexico and his explorations of Santa Fe and Australia; Blaise Cendrars's negro anthology, the negro masks which bring such high prices in Paris; Andre Gide's lifelong passion for Africa which has finally led him to navigate the Congo; Sherwood Anderson's exhilaration at the "dark laughter" of the American South, and the fascination for white New Yorkers of Harlem; and even that strange infatuation with the infantile . . . which has allowed the term Expressionism to be applied at once to drawings done by the pupils in German schools and to the dramas of German playwrights. (Wilson 288).

As *Axel's Castle* moved toward its close, Wilson moved noticeably from historical analysis to strategic prognostication, seeming first to say that, for writers at the onset of the 1930s—facing the future while conscious of the history he had assayed—Axel's way or Rimbaud's were the "only two alternatives to follow." But Axel stood for hermetic experiments that finally reduce art to an elegant private sport; and Rimbaud stood for a deliberate, anarchic primitivism that "tries to leave the twentieth century behind—to find the good life in some country where modern manufacturing methods and modern democratic institutions do not present any problems to the artist because they haven't yet arrived" (Wilson 287). Neither way really answered the collective needs of the moment, nor did the recent literary achievements of the 1920s. Regarding the latter Wilson wrote, "I believe therefore, that the time is at hand when these writers, who have largely dominated the literary world of the decade 1920–30, though we shall continue to admire them as masters, will no longer serve us as guides" (292). Ultimately Wilson did offer some hope that it might be possible for the modern artist to escape Whitehead's oscillation between the "scientific-classic pole" and the "poetic-romantic one":

> As surely as Ibsen and Flaubert brought to their Naturalistic plays and novels
> the sensibility and language of Romanticism, the writers of a new reaction
> in the direction of the study of man in relation to his neighbor and society will
> profit by the new intelligence and technique of Symbolism. Or—what would
> be preferable and is perhaps more likely—this oscillation may finally cease.
> Our conceptions of objective and subjective have unquestionably been based
> on false dualisms; our materialisms and idealisms alike have been derived from
> mistaken conceptions of what the researches of science implied—Classicism
> and Romanticism, Naturalism and Symbolism are, in reality, therefore false
> alternatives. And so we may see Naturalism and Symbolism combine to provide
> us with a vision of human life and its universe, richer, more subtle, more
> complex and more complete than any that man has yet known—indeed, they
> have already so combined, Symbolism has already rejoined Naturalism, in one
> great work of literature, *Ulysses*. (294)

Here again, Edmund Wilson's challenge to the coming generation of American writers spoke in no specific way to the social or psychological or narratological issues that race posed to young black literary intellectuals. Moreover, his notion of possible artistic alternatives omitted any glimpse of the coming golden age of science fiction that would usher a bevy of writers with technical training in science and engineering into the underground world of pulp fiction where H. G. Wells's turn-of-the-century "scientific-poetic" romances such as *The Invisible Man* had survived and would be revitalized in adapted forms. But Wilson's cues to a possible artistic resolution of Whiteheadian cultural dualism helped point Ralph Ellison's way to James Joyce as combinatory synthesizer and salvific experimentalist and to the conceptual journey from Naturalism to Expressionism to Surrealism as a potential narrative strategy for Ellison's own eventual effort to trace novelistically the fusing experience of emblematic American personality moving from medieval to modern society, from country to city, amidst revolutionary technological change. "Joyce, in his new novel," Wilson wrote,

> has been attempting to create a tongue which shall go deeper than conscious spoken speech and follow the processes of the unconscious. It is probably true, as Pater has suggested, that there is something akin to the scientific instinct in the efforts of modern literature to render the transitory phases of "a world of fine gradations and subtly linked conditions, shifting intricately as we ourselves change." In any case, the experiments of men who in their lifetimes have been either received with complete indifference or denounced as practical jokers or lunatics may perhaps prove of equal importance with those scattered researches in mathematics and physics which seemed at first merely whimsical exercises on the margins of their subjects, but which have been laid under contribution by the great modern physical systems—without which these could scarcely have been constructed. Mallarmé's poetry, in its time, seemed no more gratuitous and abstruse than Gauss's fourth-dimensional coordinates—yet it has been built upon by writers as considerable in their own field as Einstein is in his. (295)

In 1936, within months after leaving Tuskegee Institute and his germinal encounters with *The Waste Land* and *Axel's Castle*, Ralph Ellison had, through the mediation of Langston Hughes, met the towering figure of André Malraux and been befriended by the as yet unknown Richard Wright. As Ellison himself notes, Malraux would henceforth become for him the exemplary ideological novelist; while Wright in his turn would convince Ellison of the supreme necessity for writing "consciously"—of mastering not only "technique" but a philosophy of literary form within which writing know-how acquires broader meaning and becomes something more than mystification (S&A 15). Regarding the philosophical significance of race, Wright would drive home his claim that the pivotal dualism in American culture was the struggle between black and white Americans over the nature of reality. Accordingly, one way to conceptualize the structures of "conscious thought" in Ellison's evolving worldview is as a complex mediation between the new artistic codes that seized his attention during the mid-1930s. Although Malraux's novels—*Man's Fate* and *Man's Hope* in particular—would have an early and lasting impact on Ellison's outlook, the riveting cultural criticism in Malraux's multivolume *Psychology of Art* became available to Ellison only at the end of the 1940s, as *Invisible Man* moved toward completion. Before this new revelation both Edmund Wilson's experimental prospectus for "writers of the new reaction" and Richard Wright's "Blueprint for Negro Writers" (1937) supplied manifestoes of formative power; and both were engaged in struggles over the nature of a reality in which oscillations between the Whiteheadian poles of the scientific-classic and the poetic-romantic were implicated. Edmund Wilson's sharper focus on the metaphysics and instrumentalities of modern science, though, provides the crucial link back to the first of the two "accidents" of cultural literacy in Ellison's development with which this chapter's exploration began.

For the year following the 1952 publication of *Invisible Man*, at the presentation ceremony for the National Book Award he had just won, Ralph Ellison told his audience that if he were asked in all seriousness what he considered to be the chief significance of *Invisible Man* as a fiction, he would reply, first, "its experimental attitude" and, second, "its attempt to return to the mood of personal moral responsibility for democracy which typified the best of our nineteenth century fiction" (S&A 111). That his first novel had won such an award he acknowledged as a clear sign of crisis in the American novel, a sense of crisis that he and the other "younger novelists" of the day shared. For himself, on the aesthetic level, his own novelistic experiment had developed out of his personal reaction to a growing uncertainty about the formal possibilities of the contemporary novel—an uncertainty that led him to reject both the forms of the "tight, well-made Jamesian novel" and the "hard-boiled novel" of Hemingway, which Ellison perceived as a center of literary revolt among apprentice writers of the 1930s (S&A 112). Though this particular discord had been only on the margins of the conflict between Symbolism and Naturalism dissected in *Axel's Castle*, Edmund Wilson had distinguished sharply between the psychological novels of Henry James and the forms of psychological experimentation deployed by Gertrude Stein and, through derivation from her, by Hemingway (*Axel's Castle* 252–54). But where Wilson placed Stein and Hemingway on a line of Symbolist influence that moves through "the systematic comic nonsense of Dada" and on to Surrealism, Ellison emphasized Hemingway's ties—and James's as well—to the world of naturalistic surfaces and "rigid concepts of reality" from which Ellison's own novel would flee. The trajectory from Naturalism to Expressionism to Surrealism that *Invisible Man* admittedly traces transports its protagonist from the world of "facts" to the world of dream and nightmare, from the determined to the disordered. But more than in any of the strains of modernist literature save the extrapolated worlds of science fiction, it does so through a technological environment akin to the eschatological dystopia sketched out at the opening of Whitehead's disquisition on the crises of modern science:

> The progress of civilization is not wholly a uniform drift towards better things. It may perhaps wear this aspect if we map it on a scale which is large enough. But such broad views obscure the details on which rest our whole understanding of the process. New epochs emerge with comparative suddenness. . . . Secluded races suddenly take their places in the main stream of events: technological discoveries transform the mechanism of human life: a primitive art quickly flowers into full satisfaction of some aesthetic craving: great religions in their crusading youth spread through the nations the peace of Heaven and the sword of the Lord. (Whitehead 1)

Over the past half century successive generations of scholars engaged in interpreting *Invisible Man* have devoted no small measure of attention to the musical sources of the book's experimental attitude—to jazz and blues, in particular—in part because of the manifest autobiographical impress of musical experience on Ellison's sensibility. They have searched out, with great industry, the vernacular folk traditions and shape-shifting trickster archetypes that, along with jazz and blues players, seem to embody improvisational and experimental stances toward life and art.

And they have betrayed no sign of shyness in excavating the eclectic mosaic of literary models and movements, "ancestors" and "relatives" that demonstrably helped expand Ellison's sense of aesthetic possibility. In this context, however, Ellison's own frequent, almost incantatory allusions to the primacy of "technique" have perhaps helped reinforce narrowly aestheticist readings of the sources of his experimental attitude. But for those who have cultivated such glosses of Ellison's "technique," there may be a joke in this, precisely that kind of wry disjunction between illusion and reality that Ellison routinely turns to comic effect in his fiction and essays.

For if "technique" is, in Kenneth Burke's phrase, a kind of "God-term" in Ellison's critical vocabulary, this is not, I want to suggest, because of any implied suprahuman powers in the how and the what of literary method, style, or manner. To rephrase one of the resonant scriptural texts of African American eschatological traditions, it is not literary technique alone whose ways are mysterious, their wonders to perform. Rather it may be because, in Ellison's use, the concept of "technique" routinely suggests both the literal, organizational, procedural part of executing a work of fiction *and* that much broader system of applied sciences and practical arts by which any society provides its members with those things needed or desired— technology, in other words. Over the course of his career, in critical essays and reviews, in short stories and interviews, in his novel and his novel in progress, Ellison used "technique" as a *synthesizing* term—as a way of making connections between the world of art and the world of our mechanized material civilization—*more* insistently than as a set of operations peculiar to literary text making. As such, in tracking his allegiances as an artist and a man, we should not be surprised to find his notions of technique often less akin to those purveyed by the autotelic New Criticism promoted in the 1930s and 1940s by John Crowe Ransom, Allen Tate, Robert Penn Warren, and company, than to the notions of *technics* and *technology* proffered during the same years in the wide-ranging, often highly speculative cultural criticism about science, utopia, architecture, religion, and "the myth of the machine" that Lewis Mumford developed in the series of books that included *The Golden Day* (1924), *Technics and Civilization* (1934), and *Art and Technics* (1952).

Like Edmund Wilson, Lewis Mumford belonged to the generation of writers who came of age in the 1920s, sharing the hope that American culture would emerge from the shadow of Europe and drawing on the emerging cultural criticism modeled in Van Wyck Brooks's reconstruction of the American literary tradition, in H. L. Mencken's excavations in the American language, and in Gilbert Seldes's studies of the Seven Lively Arts (Menand, "Edmund Wilson" 734). But even more than Wilson, Mumford navigated his way through the revolutions in modern science and technology with the guidance of Alfred North Whitehead—whether writing pioneering interpretations of the recently rediscovered Herman Melville, tracing the history of utopian thought, or configuring the mechanization of modern culture. Driven by his own organicist imperatives, Mumford extended Whitehead's insights beyond the realm of the metaphysical foundations of scientific change into the more mundane operations of the applied sciences, corporate managerialism, and public policy. Carefully attuned to the ways modernist literary thinkers expressed fear, disgust, or indifference over scientific reductionism and mechanization, Mumford often drew attention to the ways they incorporated scientific ideas into their work, often producing "experimental" texts as forbidding and arcanely "technical" as scientific theorizing. As Whitehead had made clear, in some respects the theoretical sciences were more akin to literary art and theory than any of them were to technology. But Mumford made it clear also that the distinction between science and technology was routinely lost in intellectual circles as well as in the public mind. Rarely did literary texts demonstrate deep understanding of the era's increasingly inscrutable science, though the cult of scientism and popular fascination with the wizardry of scientific inventors and engineers drew literary attention increasingly toward what Mumford called the "neotechnic" environment.

Invisible Criticism, Alan Nadel's study of Ralph Ellison and the American canon, provides one of the rare explorations of Ellison's connection to Mumford's "neotechnic" terrain. In a pivotal chapter, Nadel first recounts Mumford's *The Golden Day* as an archetypal drama of the prototypical American locked in losing combat with the ascendant machine age. Then, very deftly, he reads Jack-the-Bear's descent into dreamlike chaos at a Southern bordello—dubbed likewise "The Golden Day"—as a punning Ellisonian riff on Mumford's dismissive treatment of slavery and race as issues in the conflict that led to civil war (Nadel 85–103). Nadel accuses Mumford of writing fiction, not history, in his *Golden Day* account of the culture of Emerson, Thoreau, Whitman, Hawthorne, and Melville. To but-tress this reading of Mumford's book as "an ode to a period that never existed," Nadel quotes a personal letter he received from Ellison himself, excerpted as follows:

> It wasn't that I didn't admire Mumford. I have owned a copy of the sixth
> Liveright printing of THE GOLDEN DAY since 1937 and own, and have learned
> from, most of his books. I was simply upset by his implying that the war which
> freed my grandparents from slavery was of no real consequence to the broader
> issues of American society and its culture. What else, other than sheer demonic,
> masochistic hell-raising, was that bloody war all about if not slavery and the
> contentions which flowed there-from? As a self-instructed student I was quite
> willing for Mumford to play Aeschylus, Jeremiah, or even God, but not at
> the price of his converting the most tragic incident in American history into
> bombastic farce. For in doing so he denied my people the sacrificial role which
> they had played in the drama. (158)

This is classic Ellisonian infighting, and it leaves no doubt about the grounds of difference on which Ellison's send-up of Mumford's *Golden Day* proceeds. It does not, however, gainsay what Ellison *shares* with Mumford about interpreting the culture of the closing three antebellum decades: their absolute import in shaping American values and literature. Nor does it deny the extent to which Ellison shares Mumford's sense of the *omnipres-ence* of technology and the machine and the artist's moral obligation to envision aesthetic possibilities for the machine that will not reinforce the fragmenting, life-denying, dehumanizing conditions created by capitalist technology.

Mumford's notion of the ideal relation between art and technics is in fact closely allied with that revealed in Ellison's work; and it is precisely in Ellison's conceptualization of the "experimental attitude" which culmi-nated in *Invisible Man* that he articulates such a relation most explicitly. "What has been missing from so much experimental writing," he asserted in "Brave Words for a Startling Occasion," has been "the passionate will to dominate reality as well as the laws of art. This will is the true source of the experimental attitude" (*S&A* 105). The clues Ellison has given us about its development in his own life direct us first not to art, but to technology—to the applied sciences, to the systems, mechanical and electrical, whereby our means of transportation and communication, the configuration of our landscape, our very sense of time and space and consciousness were being transformed during the decades of Ellison's boyhood and maturation as an artist. As already acknowledged, those years were also the years of a golden age in science fiction and of a strain of "New Criticism"—best represented in Ellison's gallery of influences by Kenneth Burke—that was not hermetically sealed off from social and political contexts. Finally they were years as well of a French "nouveau roman" that carried the earlier Symbolist experiments Ellison was familiar with into a new territory "ahead of the rest."

If we return again to "That Same Pain, That Same Pleasure," the very first question of that first interview in *Shadow and Act* asked Ellison to clarify "the way in which you as a Negro writer have vaulted the parochial limitations of most Negro fiction." The question itself held presumptions about "Negro fiction" which may have withered over the past four decades; but Ellison responded at the time by proffering the first of those two "accidents" of cultural literacy broached at the outset of this chapter, to which we now turn our full attention. Ellison had begun by insisting that his way out of imposed limitation was first and foremost "a matter of attitude" and then by calmly contradicting any assumptions that his own life might resemble traditional "portraits of the artist." To the contrary, he recalled that

like so many kids of the twenties, I played around with radio—building crystal sets and circuits consisting of a few tubes, which I found published in the radio magazines. At the time we were living in a white middle-class neighborhood, where my mother was custodian for some apartments, and it was while searching the trash for cylindrical ice-cream cartons which were used by amateurs for winding tuning coils that I met a white boy who was looking for the same thing. I gave him some of those I'd found and we became friends. . . . His nickname was Hoolie and for kids of eight or nine that was enough. Due to a rheumatic heart Hoolie was tutored at home and spent a great deal of time playing by himself and in taking his parents' elaborate radio apart and putting it back together again, and in building circuits of his own. . . . It didn't take much encouragement from his mother, who was glad to have someone around to keep him company, for me to spend much of my free time helping him with his experiments. By the time I left the community, he had become interested in short-wave communication and was applying for a ham license. I moved back into the Negro community and began to concentrate on music, and was never to see him again, but knowing this white boy was a very meaningful experience. It had little to do with the race question as such, but with our mutual loneliness (I had no other playmates in that community) and a great curiosity about the growing science of radio. It was important for me to know a boy who could approach the intricacies of electronics with such daring and whose mind was intellectually aggressive. (*S&A* 23–24)

That the impress of technology on consciousness and communion would remain a fixture of his life and finally effect a fusion with the musical and the literary, Ellison had earlier acknowledged in a 1955 essay for *Hi Fidelity* magazine called "Living with Music." The essay had emerged in the course of recalling the intimate battle-history of his audio-system warfare with a musically committed but painfully untalented would-be classical singer in the apartment next door. Ellison also recounted his simultaneous reengagement in the late 1940s with the electronics world that, via a great technological leap forward, suddenly interposed itself between his records, his typewriter, and his ears roughly midway in the course of the ongoing labor with his experimental novel:

> I had started music early and lived with it daily, and when I broke I tried to break clean. Now in this magical moment all the old love, the old fascination with music superbly rendered, flooded back. . . . If I was to live and write in that apartment, it would be only through the grace of music. I had tuned in a [Kathleen] Ferrier recital, and when it ended I rushed out for several of her records, certain now that deliverance was mine.
>
> But not yet. Between the hi-fi record and the ear, I learned, there was a new electronic world. . . . It was 1949 and I rushed to the Audio Fair. . . . I had hardly entered the fair before I heard David Sarser's and Mel Sprinkle's Musician's Amplifier, took a look at its schematic and, recalling a boyhood acquaintance with such matters, decided that I could build one. I did, several times before it measured within specifications. And still our system was lacking. . . . I built a half a dozen or more preamplifiers and record compensators before finding a commercial one that satisfied my ear, and, finally, we acquired an arm, a magnetic cartridge and—glory of the house—a tape recorder. All this plunge into electronics, mind you, had as its simple end the enjoyment of recorded music as it was intended to be heard. I was obsessed with the idea of reproducing sound with such fidelity that even when using music as a defense behind which I could write, it would reach the unconscious levels of the mind with the least distortion. (*S&A* 193–94)

David Sarser and Mel Sprinkle and their "Musician's Amplifier" represented a new phase of audio science and technology in the modern world, which brought high-order musicianship directly into the design processes of laboratory audio engineering. It also brought into the public domain a new cult of audiophile hi-fidelity, which spread far beyond the radio magazines Ellison had absorbed in his youth and into the world of high-culture literacy embodied in magazines like the venerable *Atlantic Monthly*. Sarser was a Julliard-trained, Stradivarius-owning violinist who played in the NBC Symphony Orchestra under maestro Arturo Toscanini. Sarser, in fact, became Toscanini's personal advisor on audio technology and recording—and went on to become the musical director of NBC's *Opera Hour, Hallmark's Hall of Fame*, and to record Frank Sinatra, Bing Crosby, Perry Como, Dinah Washington, and Maurice Chevalier while inventing literally dozens of patented audio devices (Conly).

The experimental Musician's Amplifier that Sarser and Sprinkle designed for sale in kit form in 1949 and that Ellison built and rebuilt while wrestling with his experimental novel grew out of the obsession Sarser shared with Ellison to create a technology of sound reproduction—at that point, focused on the development of "high efficiency vacuum tube triode amplifiers"—capable of producing a spectrum of frequencies beyond both the high and low ends of human audibility which at the same time would render its mechanical and electronic components "invisible" to the listening ear (Sprinkle). When asked if he considered himself an artist, a technician, or a musician, Sarser routinely responded, "I'm a musician. All my formal training has been in music. I've played in many different orchestras. And when war broke out it was my music that saved me. Everything I've done in my life has been because of my music. Everything else has been a hobby" (Newson). In offering a key to his legendary success, he would say, "I was never afraid of what I didn't know."

As Ellison's commentary in "Living with Music" suggests, at the "level of technique" Sarser served as an adult analogue in Ellison's interwoven technologico-musico evolution to his boyhood's crystal-set coexperimenter, Hoolie. Though now, as a mature artist, Ellison understood, as he could *not* have as a boy, that the technical media through which we hear music (the physical systems and spaces) cannot be separated from our ability to experience the music itself. Because music's meaning is *embodied* in its physical quality, we cannot separate music's rhetoric—its "words"—from its physical reality, its "delivery" (Jarrett xviii). The obsession that Sarser and Ellison both confessed became, in those early years of "high fidelity," itself the object of vernacular joking; and audiophile insiders began quipping about a strange new distortion of sensibility and consciousness dubbed "audiophilia nervosa" (Segal), manifest in all the peculiar social behaviors, violations of etiquette, and listening practices of the new cult's fervent devotees—devotees who numbered most significantly, among their representations in fiction, Ellison's reefer-smoking, audio-obsessed dedicated dreamer, Jack-the-Bear.

Psychologically speaking, "the goals that lie at the end of a chain of condensers, resistors, and vacuum tubes" were only partly aesthetic (Segal); and here, as part of a pattern we as readers have probably understated over the years, we can glimpse Ralph Ellison focused for a moment on the first and least acknowledged corner—revolutionary technological modernity—of what he often posited as the triangulating circuit of African American identity, whose complementary corners are, second, the changing fate of being "American," as mysterious and uncertain as that may be, and, third, the "racial predicament," with its complex legacy of oppression, repression, and possibility.

In "Some Answers and Some Questions," for the magazine *Preuves* in 1958, Ellison addressed directly the problematic role of modern industrial evolution in the spiritual crisis of the Negro people of our times and its potential dangers for the future of a "genuine Negro culture." He saw that role to be as ambiguous in African American life as in the life of any modern people:

[I]t depends on how much human suffering must go into the achievement of industrialization, upon who operates the industries, upon how the products and profits are shared and upon the wisdom used in imposing technology upon the institutions and traditions of each particular society. Ironically, black men with the status of slaves contributed much of the brute labor which helped get the industrial revolution under way; in this process they were exploited, their natural resources were ravaged and their institutions and their cultures were devastated, and in most instances they were denied anything like participation in the European cultures which flowered as a result of the transformation of civilization under the growth of technology. But now it is precisely technology which promises them release from the brutalizing effects of over three hundred years of racism and European domination. Men cannot unmake history, thus it is not a question of reincarnating those cultural traditions which were destroyed, but a matter of using industrialization, modern medicine, modern science generally, to work in the interest of these peoples rather than against them. Nor is the disruption of continuity with the past necessarily a totally negative phenomenon; sometimes it makes possible a modulation of a people's way of life which allows for a more creative use of its energies. . . . One thing seems clear, certain possibilities of culture are achievable only through the presence of industrial techniques.

It is not industrial progress per se which damages peoples or cultures; it is the exploitation of peoples in order to keep the machines fed with raw materials. It seems to me that the whole world is moving toward some new cultural synthesis, and partially through the discipline imposed by technology. (S&A 255–56)

However our own experience of machine society may lead us now to evaluate this technological ethos Ellison embraced at midcentury, his own reflections then seem bound up with those of Lewis Mumford in the same kind of "antagonistic cooperation" that characterized so many of Ellison's engagements with leading thinkers of the era. Mumford's monumental studies of the development of technology and the history and culture of the city; his extra-academic readiness to trespass constantly across disciplinary boundaries in the effort to define "organic" connections between different realms of thought and experience; his troubled awareness of the historic abuse of technology and the apparent human inability to control the aggression and power-lust that threaten ecological disaster and global conflagration; his utopian strain of belief in the redemptive possibilities of a humane technology mediated by a new "vitalistic," "Gestaltic" perception of the "complicated interdependences" of all things—these facets of Mumford's thought all seem to resonate on the *cooperative* side of Ellison's intellectual confrontation with the author of *The Golden Day*.

But lest I overstress that convergence, I want to turn for a moment to the pivotal juncture where Ellison's technological ethos and Mumford's ultimately diverge. The impetus of Mumford's career carried him from an early focus as a critic, primarily of American literature and the arts—with painting, architecture, and technology as simply *part* of the mix—to ever larger questions of human history and destiny *centered* increasingly on the origin, meaning, and potential of technology. The fate of urban culture, the possibility of constructing a global technological utopia that was not technocratic, the hopes and frustrations of large-scale urban planning—all impelled Mumford toward a collectivist, macrocosmic vision that made the specific technology and symbolism of *architecture* his prime nexus for locating and evaluating the social meanings of the machine (Casillo).

The *artisan*, then, not the artist, became the locus of Mumford's utopian hopes for democracy; and he professed a profound ambivalence about the modern artistic imagination as a means of "human salvation" from the depredations of the machine and technologized science. "Though each new invention or discovery may respond to some general human need, or even awaken a fresh human potentiality," he wrote in "Utopia, the City, and the Machine,"

> the only group that has understood those dehumanizing, totalitarian threats are the *avant-garde* artists, who have caricatured the system by going to the opposite extreme. Their calculated destructions and "happenings" symbolize total decontrol: the rejection of order, continuity, design, significance, and a total inversion of human values which turns criminals into saints and scrambled minds into sages. In such anti-art, the dissolution of our entire civilization into randomness and entropy is prophetically symbolized. In their humorless deaf-and-dumb language, the *avant-garde* artists reach the same goal as power-demented technicians, but by a different route—both seek or at least welcome the displacement and eventual elimination of man. (Mumford, "Utopia" 257)

For Ellison, if frequent forays into the world of cultural criticism inclined him at all toward Mumford's salvific grander "organicism," his vocation as a novelist drove him instead to seek the "universal" in the particular, the macrocosm in the microcosm, and drove him less to dreams of artisanal utopia than to psychotherapeutic models of personal healing mediated by the artistic imagination. "More than any other literary form," he argued in 1957 in "Society, Morality, and the Novel," the novel "is obsessed with the impact of change upon *personality*. . . . Man knows that even in this day of marvelous technology and the tenuous subjugation of the atom, that nature can crush him, and that at the boundaries of human order the arts *and* the instruments of technology are hardly more than magic objects which serve to aid us in our ceaseless quest for certainty" (*GTT* 244–46).

It was not, then, technology as a vast alienating system of machines moving through history with implacable force that preoccupied Ellison. It was technology as an extension of human lives, as something *someone* makes, *someone* owns, something *some* people oppose, most people *must* use, and *everyone* tries to make sense of. However dreamlike and surreal, the processes of living, through which technology acquires personal and social meaning, are what prevail in Ellison's "experimental attitude." And more than architecture, it is the impact on personality of the new technology of electrification and the machinery of the electric age that defines the crucial contexts of value in his novelistic experiment with the forms of fiction, consciousness, and democracy.

One of the things differentiating *Invisible Man* most dramatically from the other African American fictions of its time is this absorption with the immediate effects of the technological environment on the human imagination and spirit and on the blurring line between reality and illusion, the natural and the artificial—as the "technoscape" replaces the landscape, and as the very nature of human perception is changed by the pervasive presence of the artificial. During the years of Ellison's literary novitiate, other black writers created fictions rooted in the ethos of blues and jazz—Langston Hughes in *Not without Laughter*, for instance. Other black writers fabricated characters immersed in the tales and trickster traditions of African American oral lore—perhaps none more extensively than Zora Neale Hurston. Other black writers such as Chester Himes in *If He Hollers* and Richard Wright in *The Long Dream* brought the world of dreams to center stage; and other writers—here William Attaway's *Blood on the Forge* served as Ellison's reference point—dramatized the epic migration from the feudal Southern landscape to the urban, industrial modern North. None, however, attuned these crucial facets of African American life as consciously as Ellison would to the new world of social and psychic meanings created by technological change, and none attempted to fuse them all into the odyssey of a single black personality whose distinctive consciousness is mediated pervasively by modern technology.

In *Invisible Man* the conflicts between personal and public values, between psychic power and political power, between the ethic of material progress and the spiritual potential of the solitary soul, are dramatized through technological experience. From the punning structural and thematic frame appropriated from H. G. Wells's science fiction classic *The Invisible Man* to the controlling optical metaphors and hyperilluminated underground "sound stage" of Jack-the-Bear's monologue-in-flashback, technologically altered perceptions reverberate and dominate. The confrontations with human antagonists like the Southern white bigwigs at the Battle Royal, like A. Hebert Bledsoe, Mr. Norton, Lucius Brockaway, the Liberty Paints doctors, and the Brotherhood's Jack, reflect the challenges to "natural," autonomous values and self-consciousness presented by the new "artificial" environment of machines and by what Mumford calls the "megamachines"—the machinelike human organizations that convert the "raw material" of humanity into automatons, robots, and "zombies," as the crazy vet at the novel's "Golden Day" calls Jack-the-Bear. Such "character" as he becomes conscious of emerges from the dramatic series of *agons* with machines and technology, including the electrified rug, the electric gauge-laden paint boiler, and the electrifying hospital machine that gives him the equivalent of a prefrontal lobotomy. Transported from site to site in his new Northern home by electrified streetcars and subway trains, and driven finally underground by the boomerangs of fate, Jack-the-Bear ultimately grapples with the forms and formlessness of his life and identity in the artificial illumination made possible by electrification.

Why electrification and electric machinery more than the other technologies of the time? Let me offer some suggestions, the first of which Ellison understood from deep personal experience. The period from 1880 to 1940, as David Nye's history of that new technology details, was the period when, spurred by startling scientific inventions and an aggressive new social class of entrepreneurial engineers, we embarked upon the vast technological process of "electrifying America." Americans adopted electrical technologies across a vast spectrum of social, political, economic, and aesthetic contexts, reconfiguring the whole texture of national experience. Electricity changed the appearance and multiplied the meaning of the landscapes of ordinary life, its aboveground and underground transport systems. Electricity created new ties between city centers and separated outlying districts such as Harlem, created the vast network of electric cables and transformers that made possible assembly-line factories (like Liberty Paints), electrified homes, and produced the new experience of night-space that fascinated painters and photographers and spawned a new species of phantasmagoric public spectacles along the "Great White Way" (Nye 51). Electrification created the "mass media" as we know it—the radio, the phonograph, the telephone, the movies—along with a newly verbalized entertainment taste for onstage "live wires," "human dynamos," and "electrifying performances"—the taste that Ellison, during his boyhood in a small town on the edge of the Oklahoma frontier, was attempting to gratify in the early 1920s by obsessively mastering the techniques and concepts of crystal-set circuitry, vacuum tubes, and winding coils.

The impact of electrification on Ellison's maturing literary imagination, though, had other sources, contemporary and historical. If during Ellison's coming-of-age electricity was, in the public mind, a sign of Thomas Edison's inventive genius and the hallmark of specifically *American* progress, it was also a "mysterious power Americans had long connected—as far back at least as Mumford's mid-nineteenth century Golden Day—to magnetism, the nervous system, heat, power, . . . sex, health, and light" (Nye 155–56). In his own day Mumford himself was not immune to the supernal allure of urban electrification, as he rhapsodized autobiographically in his *Sketches from Life*: "I saw the skyscrapers in the deepening darkness become slowly honeycombed with lights until, before I reached the Manhattan end, these buildings piled up in a dazzling mass against the indigo sky. . . . Here was my city, immense, overpowering, flooded with energy and light. . . . The world at that moment opened before me, challenging me, beckoning me. . . . In that sudden revelation of power and beauty all the confusions of adolescence dropped from me, and I trod the narrow, resilient boards of the footway with a new confidence" (129–30).

Prospects for electrification notwithstanding, such confidence had been more elusive for the Civil War generation; and the "golden day" was ended, Mumford wrote, by a war "between two forms of servitude, the slave and the machine. . . . The machines won; and the war kept on. . . . The slave question disappeared but the 'Negro' question remained" (Nadel 88). Mumford read the Jacksonian era's abolitionism as unenlightened moral righteousness "oblivious to the *new* varieties of slavery . . . practiced under industrialism" (90–94). But Ellison's own ancestral moorings in the "golden day" inverted Mumford's allegory of dark and light, blindness and sight. Instead, Ellison read the social crises of the "golden day" more in accord with the phalanx of transcendentalist millenarians, social reformers, spiritualists, and antislavery apostles who aligned themselves with Emerson's "Party of Hope," and who heeded Whitman's call to "sing the body electric" as an anthem to the new democratic vistas in which electricity—"the demon, the angel, the mighty physical power, the all-pervading intelligence," one of Hawthorne's characters calls it (qtd. in Nye 1)—would be bound up with the realm of human spirit more profoundly than the machine ever had been.

At the same time that Ellison's moral allegiances to the literary lights of the "golden day" reinforced his allegorical sensitivity to the tropes of electrification, his ties to the Jazz Age artists against whom his own literary experiment had to be defined—Hemingway and Fitzgerald in particular—made the electrified technoscape an almost inevitable site of interpretive confrontation and revision. Ellison's critique of the 1920s writers resounds throughout his critical essays but perhaps nowhere more cogently than in the aforementioned "Society, Morality, and the Novel," where he contends that the "organic" moral-aesthetic struggle during the "golden day" against slavery both in *this* world and in the world of spiritual values had its trajectory broken by the failure of Reconstruction and the signalizing Hayes-Tilden Compromise of 1876. The consequent moral evasions and materialism of the Gilded Age, Ellison posits, "prepared for the mood of glamorized social irresponsibility voiced in the fiction of the twenties, and it created a special problem between the American novelist and his audience. . . . [The] novel, which in the hands of our greatest writers had been a superb moral instrument, became morally diffident and much of its energy was turned upon itself in the form of technical experimentation" (*GTT* 252). In Hemingway's case, Ellison contends, "the personal despair which gave the technique its resonance became a means of helping other Americans to avoid those aspects of reality which they no longer had the will to face" (*GTT* 255). The unfaced and enduring problem of race and its relationship to the health of democracy looms largest here in Ellison's mind. Despite that element of Hemingway's "technique" which recognizes that what is left out of a fiction is as important as what is present, the want of a black presence in Hemingway's pivotal images of America marks the moral evasion Ellison detected as psychologically real and aesthetically indefensible.

To see F. Scott Fitzgerald in Ellison's eyes requires a closer acquaintance with the "little man at Chehaw Station," the hypothetical cross-bred connoisseur, critic, and trickster whom the Tuskegee concert pianist Hazel Harrison foisted pedagogically on Ellison during his college days as the ideal audience and goad for would-be American artists. Internalizing the little man as an alternate authorial persona, Ellison notes that, in Fitzgerald's *The Great Gatsby*, the narrator, Nick Carraway, "tells us, by way of outlining his background's influence upon his moral judgments, that his family fortune was started by an Irish uncle who immigrated during the Civil War, paid a substitute to fight in his stead, and went on to become wealthy from war profiteering." Quick to see the symbolic connections between this ancestral moral legacy and Gatsby's illusory rise and fatal end, Ellison's little man represents a possible "saving grace" for both Fitzgerald and his doomed protagonist:

> The little man, by imposing collaboratively his own vision of America upon that of the author, would extend the novel's truth to levels below the threshold of that frustrating social mobility which forms the core of Gatsby's anguish. Responding out of a knowledge of the manner in which the mystique of wealth is intertwined with the American mysteries of class and color, he would aid the author in achieving the more complex vision of American experience that was implicit in his material. As a citizen, the little man endures with a certain grace the social restrictions that limit his own mobility; but *as a reader*, he demands that the relationship between his own condition and that of those more highly placed be recognized. He senses that the American experience is of a whole, and he wants the interconnection revealed. (*GTT* 14)

Fitzgerald's imaginative failure, however, to incorporate the little man's experience into his own diminishes his fiction for readers of the highest standard, Ellison counsels; and, by the little man's corollary logic, Jay Gatsby, whose murder by mistake might have been averted—had the black man who witnesses the real driver of the death car *not* been left voiceless and disconnected from the novel's action—pays with his life.

Now, in case it seems that I have strayed too far from Ellison's own electrified technoscape, let me try to make the connections clearer. For both Hemingway and Fitzgerald, as for many of their American peers, electrification helped chart, fictively, "the changes in values and self-perception that came with modernity" (Nye 284). But for them, as for writers such as Eugene O'Neill, the very real connections between the modern drama of electrified technological change and the modern drama of race went unperceived. O'Neill, who "electrified" his own early career with three "Negro plays"—*Emperor Jones, The Dreamy Kid,* and *All God's Chillun*—also produced a play called *Dynamo* in 1929, in which the stark contrasts between tradition and modernity, between the certainties of Protestant fundamentalism and the morally indeterminate universe of Darwin, Freud, and Einstein, are dramatized onstage in the opposing images of two family homes, one pious and unelectrified, the other fully electrified and infused with the worship of electric power. The worlds of O'Neill's "Negro plays" and *Dynamo*, however, are kept mutually exclusive in his dramaturgical imagination: the characters of the "Negro plays" are kept confined to the Expressionist jungle of Jungian primitivism, while the electrified world of *Dynamo* is kept imperturbably white.

In Hemingway's work, also, electrification takes on broad spiritual and metaphysical import divorced from racial implication. One of the classic examples of Hemingway's style and technique especially pertinent to Ellison, the much anthologized 1933 story "A Clean, Well-Lighted Place," deploys electric light not just as a pragmatic substitute for older forms of illumination, but as a sign of the existential force that in a modern world darkened by the loss of meaning at once holds back the void and, within the frame of enveloping spiritual darkness, solidifies and confirms the fragile reality of human existence. Two waiters sit in a Spanish cafe, one old, one young; one wise but wearied by the ways of the world, the younger one naively confident about his life and its prospects— "I have confidence. I am all confidence," he declares (Hemingway 480). The older waiter is no longer religious but still seeks human communion, the younger one is void of empathy and absorbed in personal pleasure. The two converse about a customer after he leaves, an old man who has recently attempted suicide and whom the two waiters, at the insistence of the younger, have put out of the bright, cheery bodega so they can close for the night.

Arguing that they should have permitted the customer to stay and to share the cafe's lighted communion rather than sending him home to drink alone, the older waiter acknowledges that he, too, is one of those "who like to stay late at the café . . . with all those who do not want to go to bed. With all those who need a light for the night" (Hemingway 480). After the young waiter leaves, the older one stays on, reluctant to close, and, after asking himself *why* he needs a "clean, well-lighted place," realizes that it offers the aura of order in answer to "a nothing that he knew too well." On his own way home in the darkness, without the light, he holds back the void by reciting a parody of the Lord's Prayer—"Our nada who art in nada, nada be thy name thy kingdom nada thy will be nada in nada as it is in nada" (Hemingway 481)—before retiring sleeplessly to await the light of day.

Like Hemingway and O'Neill, Fitzgerald recognized that the new technology of illumination "was far more than a utilitarian prop for home economics": electricity confronted the modern world with new ways to express and understand the self (Nye 284). David Nye points to *The Great Gatsby* as a modern fable in which electricity becomes literally a tool of self-creation. Nick Carraway's first images of Gatsby come from the extravagant lawn parties where caterers mount "enough colored lights to make a Christmas tree of Gatsby's enormous garden" (Fitzgerald 39). The lights conjure up the mood of grand spectacle for Gatsby's guests, who equate the parties with Coney Island amusement. His lights advertise Gatsby's success to the world. Making them more intensely visible makes that success *seem* more real—and more able to fascinate Daisy and draw her to him from across the bay. They blaze brighter the closer he comes to regaining her and brightest on the night a rendezvous is arranged. Gatsby's spectacular lighting asserts the self he has fabricated, multiplies his sense of worth, and answers Daisy's green light flashing at him across the bay. Gatsby *believed* in that green light, Nick Carraway concludes, as it marked a way to "the orgiastic future that year by year recedes before us" (Fitzgerald 182).

From this juncture, the web of allusive connection to Ellison's worldview and fictional universe, if not absolutely straightforward, can be readily demonstrated; so some shorthand should serve to bring our excursion here to a close. Ellison connected himself to Hemingway and Fitzgerald and their Lost Generation peers partly through a counterpointing sense of novelistic mission: "Ours is a task," he wrote, which "whether recognized or not, was defined for us to a large extent by that which the novels of the twenties failed to confront; and implicit in their triumphs and follies were our complexity and our travail" (*GTT* 257). In *Invisible Man*, Ellison confronted the modernist tropes of electrification in Hemingway's "A Clean, Well-Lighted Place" and Fitzgerald's *The Great Gatsby* with revisionary narrative riffs bright with counterpointing implication and anchored in the particular experience of technology and its social contexts that mark three centuries of African American life in the alloy bowels of the machine and that mark black men and women themselves, Ellison reiterated through the years, as in many ways hypermodern, self-fabricated creations as far from the "primitives" of popular stereotype as Lewis Mumford's utopian "neotechnic" age is from neolithic ooze. Alongside all the other things it would become, *Invisible Man* would also constitute a gloss on the "techniques" and technological consciousness of the American novel from the "golden day" to the Jazz Age and beyond; and Ellison's fictive experiment in "revolutionary technological modernity" would heed most carefully the goad of the "little man at Chehaw Station" to incorporate the experience of multiple "others" into its own—and with the combinatory energy of plural truths—to synthesize new thresholds of consciousness.

The famous framing prologue of Ellison's novel nigrifies, hyperbolizes, and renders comically surreal and ironic the controlling motifs of Hemingway's "clean, well-lighted place," as Robert O'Meally's work on the Hemingway-Ellison connection has suggested ("Rules of Magic"). The social and spiritual assumptions upon which the violence, social cynicism, and understatement in Hemingway's work were based—assumptions rendered questionable to Ellison by his place in the social order—were rejected by Ellison's creation of an entirely new kind of figure in American literature: a theory- and concept-toting, gadget-fabricating black "thinker-tinker," kin to Henry Ford, Edison, and Benjamin Franklin, he quips, and sufficiently deft with the techniques of electrification to shunt off enough purloined electricity from Monopolated Light & Power's local station to charge the 1,369 light bulbs he has wired the ceiling of his underground retreat with, to "shed light on his invisibility." "Light confirms my reality," Jack-the-Bear tells us, "gives birth to my form" (*IM* 6). But the insight that has led him to this consciousness he has won from the master of formlessness, Bliss Proteus Rinehart, that "spiritual technologist" and man of multifarious parts who, with electrified guitar music and glowing neon signs—dark *green* neon signs—fishes Harlem street-corners for "marks" ready to "Behold the Invisible."

Rinehart orchestrates the Ellisonian riff on Gatsby's green light, with the *mise-en-scène* of electric illusion transported from Gatsby's hyperilluminated manicured lawns to Rinehart's Harlem storefront, "where a slender woman in a rusty black robe played passionate boogie-woogie on an upright piano along with a young man wearing a skull cap who struck righteous riffs from an electric guitar which was connected to an amplifier that hung from the ceiling above a gleaming white and gold pulpit. . . . The whole scene quivered vague and mysterious in the green light" (*IM* 486). Both Jack-the-Bear's and Rinehart's "spiritual technologies" suggest one final facet of Ellison's fictive confrontation with the myth of the machine and the forms of the novel that readers should bear in mind. That will to personal power and agency, which their shared facility with electrical power mirrors, manifests itself most directly in Jack-the-Bear's and Rinehart's *inventiveness*, their experimental *ingenuity*. "When you have lived invisible as long as I have, you develop a certain ingenuity. I'll solve the problem," Jack-the-Bear tells us. Unlike Rinehart, "that confidencing sonofabitch" whose own ingenuity knows no moral boundaries and no human loyalties, Jack-the-Bear commits himself to community. If by projecting himself as a "thinker-tinker" akin to Ford, Edison, and Franklin the narrator leads us to presume *that* community to be something other than his own race, Ellison hints at one last underground illumination from his people's underground past. In the prologue, Jack-the-Bear makes a point of having wired his ceiling "not with fluorescent bulbs, but with the older, more-expensive-to-operate kind, the *filament* type. An art of sabotage, you know" (*IM* 7).

Ellison knew from his early 1940s research and writing labors alongside Roi Ottley, Waring Cuney, Claude McKay, and company (for the Works Progress Administration Federal Writers' Project manuscript which culminated in the publication of *The Negro in New York*) that, despite disclaimers to the contrary which rendered black technological innovators historically invisible,

the bewildering array of technical inventions, which altered human life within a brief span, found Negroes in the vanguard. . . . But the machine age, which did so much to bring about divisions in the ranks of labor, put men out of work and caused protest from sections of the laboring population, [and] also brought whites new reasons to bolster their hatred of blacks. . . . When the "third rail" [the electrified rail carrying current to the motor of a railway or subway car] was invented and electricity replaced steam on the elevated railways in this city, the white men, who lost their jobs as steam locomotive engineers because of the innovation, heaped all manner of abuse on the whole Negro race because its inventor was a Negro. After its installation, Negroes were not safe on the streets of New York. They were frequently attacked by persons aware only that a new-fangled electric device invented by some "damn nigger" had taken away their jobs. Violence subsided only when the company finally rehired the old engineers and taught them the new job of motormen. The inventor, Granville T. Woods, a native of Ohio, had arrived in New York in 1880 and soon after invented a system by which telegraphing was made possible between trains in motion, technically known as "induction telegraph." During the next thirty years, until he died in New York City in 1910, he perfected twenty-five inventions, . . . was employed by Thomas Edison[,] . . . and while working at his laboratory . . . the American Bell Telephone Company purchased his electric telephone transmitter. (Ottley and Weatherby 140–43)

One of Wood's black thinker-tinker peers, Louis Latimer, a draftsman who was the son of an escaped slave, not only made the drawings for the first Bell Telephone from a design by Alexander Graham Bell but superintended the installation of the electric lighting systems of Philadelphia, of several Canadian cities, and of London, as well as of New York City itself—as *The Negro in New York* details. Though the "collective authorship" of this Harlem-based Federal Writers' Project enterprise effaces specific contributions by individual writers, Ellison's typescript notes demonstrate clearly his authorship of this segment of the broader chronicle.[3] The pertinent passage in *The Negro in New York*, with notably Ellisonian markers of diction, phrasing, and style, reveals that Latimer had patented his own pioneering electric lightbulb as early as 1881, that he became associated with Thomas Edison in 1896, and that, as a member of the "Edison Pioneers," it was he, the "Black Edison," who perfected the revolutionary carbon "filament," which made the intense, smokeless, fireless, glowing orange "Edison light" throw off an illumination unlike anything seen before (Ottley and Weatherby 141–43).

The spiritual cost of that carbon-filament illumination is what Jack-the-Bear's guerrilla war levies against Monopolated Light & Power. Ultimately for him, acts of sabotage and the art of illumination become inseparable facets of his own "spiritual technology" and, for us as readers, the site of one more "electrifying" Ellisonian joke—evidence that, waking or dreaming, in this thinker-tinker's theory- and concept-toting world of high fidelity and calculated distortion, the ways of invisibility remain willfully and invariably mysterious, their "accidents" and wonders to perform.

Where does the drama get its materials? From the "unending conversation" that is going on at the point in history when we are born. Imagine that you enter a parlor. You come late. When you arrive, others have long preceded you, and they are engaged in a heated discussion, a discussion too heated for them to pause and tell you exactly what it is about. In fact, the discussion had already begun long before any of them got there, so that no one present is qualified to retrace for you all the steps that had gone before. You listen for a while, until you decide that you have caught the tenor of the argument; then you put in your oar.

—KENNETH BURKE, *The Philosophy of Literary Form*

I feel a lot better about our struggle though; mose is still boycotting the hell out of Montgomery and still knocking on the door of Alabama U. . . . Something is happening and it's so very good to know that mose's sense of life is too strong to be held in. . . . Mose is fighting and he's still got his briar patch cunning; he's just been waiting for a law, man, something solid under his feet; a little scent of possibility.

—RALPH ELLISON, Letter to Albert Murray, March 16, 1956

So just as with writing, I learned from Joe and Sugar Ray (though that old dancing master, wit, and bull-balled stud, Jack Johnson is really *my* mentor, because he knew that if you operated with skill and style you could rise above all that being-a-credit-to-your-race-crap . . .). Here I'll also learn from your latest master strategists, the N.A.A.C.P. legal boys, because if those studs can dry-run the Supreme Court of the U. S. and (leave it to some mose to pull that one) I dam sure can run skull practice on the critics.

—RALPH ELLISON, Letter to Albert Murray, May 18, 1956

Chapter Four

THE MAN OF LETTERS AND THE
UNENDING CONVERSATION

I n 1955, two years after winning the National Book Award
for *Invisible Man*, Ralph Ellison won the Prix de Rome
Fellowship from the American Academy of Arts and
Letters. With additional Rockefeller Foundation support, he was able to live
in Rome with his wife until 1957. There he worked on a new novel that
pushed its main characters closer to the centers of political power in
American life than he had thought was "realistically" feasible in the World
War II decade when he was developing the concept of *Invisible Man* (*GTT*
45). During the war, he later recalled, African Americans had been "involved
in a terrific quarrel" with the federal government over not being allowed
to participate as combat personnel or to work in the war industries on an
equal basis (*GTT* 44). That "quarrel" had led directly to Ellison's obsession
with the nature of black leadership in America, on the one hand, and to his
parallel concern about the responsibilities of novelists to the democratic
process, on the other. As he would later tell an audience at West Point,
"for novelists, for poets, for men of literature, something else obtains"—a
more expansive "quarrel." In his mind it fused the "unending conversation" that Kenneth Burke postulated as a dramatic framework for human
interchange in general with the dispute that novelist Henry James singled

161

out as imposed no less consequentially on artists and citizens alike by the more specific force of American social ideals:

> We have upon our shoulders the burden of conscientiousness. I think in your motto you say "duty," a sense of duty, a sense of responsibility, for the health of the society. You might not like the society; invariably we Americans (as Henry James pointed out, and as others have pointed out) have a quarrel, we have an on-going quarrel with our lives, with the condition that we live in. At our best moments we have a quarrel with how we treat or fail to treat and extend the better part, the better aspects, the better values, the good things of the society, to all levels of the society. (*GTT* 47)

Invisible Man had been one way of engaging the unending conversation and advancing the quarrel. While in Rome, "putting his oar in" again as a novelist, he found himself, as a "man of literature," taking up the quarrel no less conscientiously amid the mid-1950s controversies about the supposed "death of the novel" and the possible forms of its salvation. In "Society, Morality, and the Novel," an essay written there in Rome during the nation-wide quarrel back home over the spreading civil rights movement, Ellison quarreled expansively with the neoconservative aesthetic and political assumptions behind Lionel Trilling's critique of the "liberal imagination" and the modern novelist's formal and ideological prerogatives. Unlike the exchange six years later in "The World and the Jug," which he wrote to parry Irving Howe's direct attack on him and James Baldwin in "Black Boys and Native Sons," Ellison was taking on here the less personal but no less provocative debate over the nature of "reality in America" that Trilling's "new liberal" initiative had been advancing since the late 1940s, before the 1950s civil rights movement emerged to disrupt the Cold War consensus about the state of the nation. As the most prominent literary critic of the Cold War era, and the most visible leader of a new corps of culture critics that Howe dubbed "the New York Intellectuals," Lionel Trilling was a formidable adversary indeed. His credentials for Anglophile literary leadership had firm support both among the assimilated Jewish American intellectuals who had finally begun to penetrate the institutionalized anti-Semitism of American higher education and within the publishing networks of academy and community-based periodical forums that were coming to dominate the organs of American cultural critique.

Writing a decade before the explosion of radical Black Arts journals and magazines, African American critics of culture during the 1950s lacked the journalistic forums and institutional bases that Anglo-Jewish New York intellectuals enjoyed. The old warrior W. E. B. DuBois was now past eighty; and the most visible black intellectual, Richard Wright, had chosen exile. But alongside Ellison an unconfederated circle of distinctive African American critical voices was emerging nonetheless: Trinidadian expatriate and Trotskyite disciple C. L. R. James, whom Ellison and Richard Wright had met in New York early in the 1940s; Anatole Broyard, the Louisiana creole "ex-colored man" who passed into the postwar circle of Anglo-Jewish commentators on the strength of his insider revelations about the ethos of "inauthentic Negroes" and cool jazz; Harlem-born exevangelist James Baldwin, whose autobiographically driven reviews, critiques, and open letters became staples in the *New Leader, Commentary,* and *Partisan Review* before and after he followed mentor Richard Wright to Paris; Nathan Scott, Jr., an academy-based disciple of theologians Reinhold Niebuhr and Paul Tillich who was forging a distinctively theological brand of cultural critique rooted in American religious experience but rigorously universalist and fixed on the international avant-garde; and Albert Murray, a close colleague and correspondent who (though not a classmate) shared Ellison's Tuskegee Institute background and musical and literary interests and who, though his cultural criticism would not reach major publishing outlets until the 1970s, became Ellison's staunchest collaborator in constructing a comprehensive theory of American vernacular culture. In free-floating but sometimes tense alliance, Ellison participated with all of them in what—a generational step ahead of the incipient Black Arts rebellion—would become a shifting, triangular war of words first against the increasingly conservative New Liberals led by Trilling, then against the opposing "adversary culture" of apocalyptic white and Jewish New Leftists, and finally against a crusading Southern segregationist contingent of self-proclaimed "agrarian" and "fugitive" New Critics led by Allen Tate, John Crowe Ransom, and Robert Penn Warren.

Within the loose circle of black cultural critics Ellison frequented, C. L. R. James focused on reviving traditions he traced to Alexis de Tocqueville's nineteenth-century *Democracy in America.* James used his special brand of anti-Stalinist Trotskyite dialectics to create programmatic "notes on American Civilization" that addressed, first, the national contradictions between the officially sacred "right to life, liberty, and the pursuit of happiness" and, second, more ominously, the violent, totalitarian impulses manifest in the American popular culture media of radio, comic strips, and pulp fiction.[1] Those totalitarian impulses marked a fascinating dislocation, James theorized, from the nineteenth-century "democratic vistas" of Walt Whitman and Herman Melville. Though James lacked the deep familiarity with African American cultural forms—the body of folklore, vernacular idiom, spirituals, blues, jazz, and others—that was foundational to Ellison, James's absorption with the antebellum Anglo-American authors of what Lewis Mumford called the "Golden Day" provided the two of them with an alternate point of common critical reference, Melville in particular. And James's cosmopolite dismay with the failure of contemporary American art and philosophy to engage an international audience drawn more intensely to "Dostoyevsky and Kafka, Picasso and Matisse, Kierkegaard, Heidegger, Marx and Freud, [and] the philosophy of Existentialism" resonated with Ellison's own cosmopolitan orientations. James's book, *Mariners, Renegades, and Castaways* (1953), published a year after Ellison's novel, had grown out of public lectures and private musings that he had shared with Richard Wright and Ellison during the 1940s. James had written it while incarcerated on Ellis Island awaiting deportation. Wielding it as a weapon of radical demystification, he interpreted Melville's *Moby Dick* and *Benito Cereno* as prophetic antitotalitarian political allegories whose radical psychosocial import Ellison had intimated in the epigraphs to *Invisible Man*.

Ellison's friend Anatole Broyard was a New Orleans–born son of light-skinned creole parents who had migrated, at the height of the Harlem Renaissance, from a black neighborhood in the French Quarter to Brooklyn. Broyard had watched his father "pass" through the color barrier into the all-white New York carpenter's union, and he had adapted his father's stratagem to the worlds of literary Manhattan and bohemian Greenwich Village. An early disciple of postmodern culture, he had absorbed European avant-garde literature and cinema as a teenager and became an avid proselytizer for "the movements toward sexual freedom and toward abstraction in art and literature, even in life itself" (Dobson 134). As revealed in *Kafka Was the Rage* (1993), his memoir about the postwar decades in the Village, Broyard gravitated to the New School for Social Research and to European émigrés such as existentialist psychiatrist Erich Fromm and his classes on the psychology of American culture, as well as to Max Wertheimer, the Gestalt psychologist with whom Broyard underwent psychoanalysis in the late 1940s. Wertheimer's phenomenological approach to splits and polarities within seemingly stable personalities provided Broyard with some key insights for interpreting the bohemian netherworld he inhabited, and he adapted them for his subsequent psychological forays into the underground worlds of hipsters and cool jazz. In "A Portrait of the Hipster" and "A Portrait of the Inauthentic Negro," Broyard blended the figure-ground aesthetic metaphors from Gestalt theories about relationships between psychodynamic "fields" of human experience with the Husserlian phenomenology that Jean-Paul Sartre employed in his "Portrait of the Inauthentic Jew" (1948). These tools enabled Broyard to create intriguingly stylized Gestalt portraits of offbeat personalities inside African American culture that crystallized in his striking images of the "lucifugous" underground men of the "hip" world ("Portrait of the Hipster" 723). But whereas Ellison's portraits of hipsters usually affirmed their versatility and hypermodern elegance, Broyard's hepcats typically embodied, at the level of personality formation, the transference from "sincerity" to "authenticity" that Lionel Trilling was busily defining as modern culture's surrender of the more stable and organic hereditary mode of being for the fragmentary, role-playing, antinomian style embraced by the "adversary culture" and the New Left (Krupnick 155–65).

Despite Broyard's iconic status in the eyes of New Left proselytizers such as Norman Mailer, Broyard actually seemed to align himself with Trilling's neoconservative moral consciousness in the profiles Broyard presented of the hipster's incipient Satanism and the inauthentic Negro's "minstrelized" soul and Sartrean "bad faith." What, in Gestalt terms, was the "unfinished business" of having suppressed his own ancestry and family ties seems to have insinuated itself into Broyard's cultural criticism as well, with consequences of a kind that Ellison dissected from another angle in the counterfactual *Going to the Territory* essay "What America Would Be Like without Blacks." In his series of *New York Times* reviews surveying Trilling's literary and cultural criticism after the Columbia don's death in 1975, Broyard extolled Trilling's body of work as a welcome "gift" that made American life feel "infinitely more dimensional" than Broyard had once supposed and taught him "that the occasional ugliness of American life is part of the chiaroscuro, so to speak, of our eccentricity" ("Four by Trilling"). From Broyard's vantage point, Trilling had become a "master of large views, . . . aerial, spacious, a cartography of culture," and a "great conciliator, a labor mediator of imagination" in a time given to walkouts and wildcat strikes. Sitting on Broyard's shelf, Trilling's collected works gave him "a secure feeling" and "an ever ready source of conciliation" ("Books: Lionel Trilling Encores"). As a coda Broyard cited his favorite passage from the Trilling quartet of *Matthew Arnold, The Opposing Self, A Gathering of Fugitives,* and *Beyond Culture*: "It is a commonplace of modern literary thought that the tragic mode is not available even to the gravest and noblest of our writers. One reason may be that we have learned to think our way back through tragedy to the primal stuff out of which tragedy arose" (qtd. in "Four by Trilling").

The shaded contrasts between Broyard's interpretive framework and Ellison's were even sharper between Ellison and James Baldwin. Despite many of the thematic points of focus they shared, from the outset of his career Baldwin developed a more autobiographical template for his nonfiction critiques of American culture. He expressed his preoccupation with issues of identity less in the language or concepts of psychoanalysis Ellison favored than in that of Calvinist redemption. Baldwin was devoted to Henry James even more fervently than Ellison was, and he reformulated in racial terms James's familiar dialectic of American identity as a conflict between Old and New World compulsions. Where Ellison's espousal of secular existentialism was never posed in contradistinction to his personal grounding in the orthodoxies of the African Methodist Episcopal (AME) Church, Baldwin framed *his* attraction to secular existentialism as a form of energetic opposition to the prior Christian pentecostal fervor he had espoused in Harlem's Temple of the Fire Baptized. Where Baldwin, like both Ellison and Wright, acknowledged an indebtedness to Miguel de Unamuno as a pivotal influence in shaping his understanding of the tragic element in African American blues and jazz traditions, Baldwin's view was ultimately closer to Wright's than to Ellison's: while Ellison was drawn to the comic and tragicomic counterbalances in Unamuno's tragic vision, Baldwin's interpretations of the blues in particular stripped them of Unamuno's leavening comic and Quixotic apprehensions.[2] In broader debates on the state of the nation's culture or character, the rhetorical strategies Baldwin used to position himself in the ambiguous space between racially divided American audiences reflected the contrast with Ellison as well. Baldwin's signatory use of the narratorial "we" in his exchanges with white liberal audiences served both as a marker of black-white psychic symbiosis and as leverage for racial polemics targeted on white guilt. Ellison's rhetorical strategies focused less on the legacy of white liberal guilt than on the ongoing processes of psychological repression, amnesia, and "trained incapacity" he espied in white communities. And Ellison's rhetorical vantage point on the black-white symbiosis positioned him unequivocally as a "race man"—though one who was at war with racialist myopia and "blood thinking"—atop the interethnic battle royal.

In the struggle with Trilling and his disciples over the nature of "reality" in America, Ellison shared many of Trilling's Freudian assumptions about the structures of human consciousness and motivation, but he warred over their cultural implications. By contrast, Baldwin's mid-1950s outlook in *Notes of a Native Son* (1955) allied the expreacher with Trilling's attack on the sentimental naiveté of the conventional liberal imagination, but pulled him away from Trilling's and Ellison's "Freudian Man" as a fundamental ground of analysis toward Jamesian analogues for the theological categories of redemption, damnation, apocalypse. In a letter to Albert Murray in 1952, Ellison shared his perception that the *Partisan Review* and *Commentary* circles of the New York Intellectuals seemed to think "that there's something not quite right about Baldwin and Broyard" (*TT* 31). In the debates over American culture and its artists, he and Murray had something very right and very unique to contribute about the formal and metaphysical dimensions of the blues tradition—especially since the critical confusion instigated by *Invisible Man* showed that these things were beyond comprehension to Philip Rahv and other members of the Trilling circle. The distinctive blend of secular existentialism and vernacular theory that Ellison and Murray were cocreating gave that contribution broadly demystifying appeal.

Moreover, what I suggest might be called their "vernacular existentialism" was not necessarily antithetical to theologically aligned perspectives on modern culture, as the special new strain of criticism by Nathan Scott demonstrated. A precocious midwesterner who had completed two undergraduate degrees by the age of eighteen (a bachelor of arts and a bachelor of divinity), Scott had migrated from Michigan to New York in 1944 to pursue graduate study in theology and modern literature (M. Harris 121). There he had drunk more deeply at the sources of the New Liberal imagination than perhaps any of his black peers. As a student of Reinhold Niebuhr and Paul Tillich at Union Theological Seminary, and of Lionel Trilling at Columbia, he had absorbed Niebuhr's rightward-drifting cautionary gospel on "the nature and destiny of man" and Niebuhr's dialectic of "love and justice" in history, along with Tillich's belief that theology can provide telling insights into the religious character of secular cultural creations. And Scott absorbed at first hand the commitment Trilling had taken up from Matthew Arnold to devote one's critical energies to preserving the highest cultural values in the face of modern anarchy and social crisis. After completing his Ph.D. at Columbia, Scott began a scholarly career first within the still segregated theological confines of Virginia Union University and then at Howard University in the late 1940s, where he began creating, almost single-handedly, a new "genre" out of the older theological tradition of philosophical anthropology and the new existentialism. Over the course of time, Scott merged the demands of Episcopalian priesthood with the Christian existentialist postulates of Tillich and Dietrich Bonhoeffer, and he extended those postulates during the 1960s to rigorous readings of Richard Wright and Ralph Ellison.

Beginning with his book *Rehearsals of Discomposure*, published in 1952, the same year *Invisible Man* appeared, Scott opened a new literary front on the critical controversies of the Cold War years. He made the global *existential* crisis his exegetical focus, and writers from Kierkegaard to Kafka, D. H. Lawrence to T. S. Eliot, from Fyodor Dostoyevsky and Sartre and Camus and Malraux to Melville, Hemingway, Faulkner, and Saul Bellow his preferred terrain for exploring the modern "literature of estrangement." Though his published work showed comparatively little interest in the vernacular and popular culture sources that were pivotal to Ellison's literary enterprises, Scott echoed Ellison's comparatist and anti-chauvinist speculative concerns perhaps more than any of Ellison's other intellectual peers, with the possible exception of Albert Murray. Scott's commitment to the philosophical anthropology of Nietzsche, Bergson, Max Scheler, and Unamuno paralleled Ellison's attraction to the symbological definitions of man and "the dramatic study of comparative humanity" espoused by Kenneth Burke and Ernst Cassirer. In addition, Scott's existentialist Christian interest in the "revolutionary novels" of André Malraux, Arthur Koestler, Ernest Hemingway, and Ignazio Silone formed a provocative counterpart to Ellison's own political and artistic preoccupations. The trajectory of Scott's elegant critical overviews during the 1950s and 1960s offered an oblique but companionate gloss on Ellison's private canon of international authors and philosophical concerns, as they surfaced in the course of his new novelistic enterprise and ongoing critical exchanges. As with Ellison, Scott's personal combination of "aristocrat" and "peasant" values reflected an easy communion between classical and vernacular influences in his private life and a disinclination toward the "highbrow-lowbrow" divide that discomfited New York Intellectuals such as Trilling and Philip Rahv. Ellison considered Scott a "prime example of the modern sensibility in all its complexity," a man who had never become alienated or sidetracked from the universal themes of modern intellectual discourse and who had never once "forgotten where he came from" (Bims 46).

Hailed in a *Phylon* review by Arthur P. Davis as the first black critical thinker to produce a "thoroughly and uncompromisingly modern" study of literature "through the perspective of Freud, Kierkegaard, Tillich, Sartre, and the so-called 'new critics,'" Scott was also, in 1951, the first to challenge Trilling's critique of the liberal imagination (Davis 337). Here and in his subsequent commentaries, Scott assented to Trilling's representation of himself as a *committed* liberal anatomizing the *deficiencies* of liberal ideology: its partisanship on behalf of the rude pragmatism of the American working class; its devaluation of intellect as aristocratic and unreal; the considerable gap between its inspiring ideals and the mediocre achievements, in actual practice, of its democratic institutions and literary representations of a complex and various human "reality" (Scott, "Lionel Trilling's Critique"). But Scott would not assent to Trilling's refusal to embrace "any sort of religious position" or to recognize the extent to which "the best secular wisdom in the modern period has failed"; and he charged his former teacher with what, from his own vantage point, seemed a fundamental evasion: "[O]n no occasion, of course, has he consented to confront any of the great religious geniuses of the tradition: for all of his wide-ranging culture, Augustine and Pascal, Kierkegaard and Barth, Tillich and Niebuhr are quite as if they had never been: so confirmed is he in the prejudices of a man of the Enlightenment that not even, as a Jew, does he pay any attention, say, to a Moses Hess or a Franz Rosenzweig, to a Martin Buber or an Abraham Heschel. . . . His procedure, inevitably, seems in a strange way to be like that of the great theological doctors of the Negative Way" (Scott, *Three American Moralists* 157, 204–05).

When he compared Trilling's views of "reality in America" with those of Ellison peers such as Norman Mailer and Saul Bellow, Scott pictured Trilling's "anxious humanism" as an Old Guard conservative reaction on behalf of Arnoldian stability and order, and a reaction against a younger avant-garde insurgency of antirationalist and existentialist apocalypticism. Scott himself was as skeptical of New Left premises about the human condition and about African American culture, in particular, as he was of Trilling's premises. He read Mailer's hipster manifesto, "The White Negro" (published in Irving Howe's *Dissent* in 1957, the same year Ellison published his retort to Trilling) the same way Ellison, Baldwin, and Lorraine Hansberry did—as a mark of the "adversary culture's" antinomian racial romanticism (Scott, *Three American Moralists* 46–51). But Trilling's evident Edwardian aversion to literary modernism and the new existentialist models of reality and human freedom left Scott ultimately at odds with the former's centrist conservatism, and left him also convinced that what Trilling and ally Arthur Schlesinger imagined to be "the vital center" of American political and literary life, in fact, was irretrievably "broken." In *Rehearsals of Discomposure*, Scott's starting premises about the "disinheritance of man in the modern world" shared Trilling's perception that the American liberal imagination had yet to confront the modern circumstance as what Scott termed a "tragedy in terms of dereliction and estrangement and exile." But disconcertingly for Scott, Trilling himself had failed to see that tragedy must be conceived "not in terms of alienation within a stable world," nor in terms of an unstable world whose stability was even potentially recoverable, but must be seen rather "in a world where 'things fall apart' . . . where man's deepest tension is not social or economic but an *angoisse métaphysique*" (Scott, *Rehearsals* 1–2). As surer guides to the spiritual facts of this new dispensation, Scott directed Trilling to the existentialist visions of such thinkers as Miguel de Unamuno, Jean-Paul Sartre, Max Scheler, Martin Buber, and Karl Jaspers—wherein wiser definitions of human freedom and the capacity for transcendence, definitions beyond those of the liberal imagination, might be apprehended.

Despite this unflinching critique, Scott's acceptance of other grounding assumptions about "the nature and destiny of man" that Trilling borrowed from Reinhold Niebuhr set him nonetheless apart from Ellison's rigorously blues-based existentialist temper. It was the indigenous folk-based, secular existentialism of the African American blues tradition, not some borrowed European ontology or phenomenology or avant-garde literary technique that gave *Invisible Man* its originary power. As Ellison told Albert Murray after realizing the critical confusion his novel had produced, neither the old liberals or the reformed New York Intellectuals grasped the difference: "[T]he prologue has caused some comments, but I don't think Rahv has decided what he thinks about the book as a whole. He does know that it isn't Kafka as others mistakenly believe. I tell them, I told Langston Hughes in fact, that it's the blues, but nobody seems to understand what I mean" (*TT* 31). For Scott and for Trilling's disciples, as well as for most of the adversary-culture adherents (with the possible exception of Saul Bellow), the fault line in American literary culture lay between "the tragic sense of life" it had yet to fully grasp and its merely sentimental or melodramatic attempts at high seriousness. Or, they argued, the divide in the culture's literary life lay between its bourgeois attraction to the classical tragic traditions borrowed from Europe and its more genuine emotional moorings in indigenous American lowbrow or regional "humor." But none of these critical modalities comprehended a homegrown African American consciousness that blended tragic high seriousness with roguish vernacular humor. So for Ellison the crucial collision was between all of these debilitated interpretive modalities and the unifying, enabling, *tragicomic* sense of life and picaresque modes of apprehending the jarring new realities of the age that became for him a foundational alternative.

When he turned his attentions in 1957 to the sixteen Trilling essays in *The Liberal Imagination*, Ellison had other things of high importance on his mind. As his correspondence with Albert Murray makes clear, while working in Rome on his new novel he was paying particular attention to the growing civil rights movement back home and to embattled congressional efforts to advance or frustrate integration (*TT* 95). On a suggestion from Robert Penn Warren, whom he now regarded as having finally "thought his way free of a lot of irrational illusions" about race and nation, Ellison was at work on "a piece about desegregation" that would eventually be published in 1965 as "Tell It Like It Is, Baby" (*TT* 95, 157). Ellison was also reflecting with Murray about the political import of Richard Wright's engagements with the black French intellectuals of *Presence Africaine* and about Wright's participation in the international conference of Third World leaders at Bandung, which the radical expatriate covered in the new book he published that year, *White Man, Listen!* As a consequence of these converging forces, Ellison was keeping the national and international dimensions of the black freedom movement coupled in his mind with his own longstanding allegiances: "[H]ere Africans and West Indians are taking over governments and Montgomery Negroes are showing their quality. . . . Well, man, world events are justifying our position and interests of the thirties, not those of the administration or the campus heroes and politicians; we are operating out of a different sense of time and on a different wave-length" (160).

Ellison made that different wavelength and sense of time manifest in "Society, Morality and the Novel," despite the fact that, as men of letters with credentials both as novelists and critics of culture, Trilling and Ellison, too, had striking points of commonality. They shared a humanist faith in the power of literature as an organ of social insight and healing power, along with firm convictions about the integral relationship between literary technique and moral vision. Both had been committed leftists and Communist Party "fellow travelers" during the heyday of Stalinist-Trotskyite literary radicalism and Popular Front organizations in the 1930s. And both had found their modernist "deviancies" from doctrinaire Socialist Realism a source of tension and eventual disassociation from organized communism, though not from all of its social ideals. They were both powerfully attracted to the revolutionary theories of Sigmund Freud and his psychoanalytic disciples. They had each developed an insistently dialectical view of culture and history and in each case a sense of American literary genealogy focused on the novelists and romancers of F. O. Matthiessen's newly excavated nineteenth-century "American Renaissance." Moreover, both had a clear aesthetic preference for the "scenic" theories and layered architectonics of Henry James over the driving Naturalist machinery of Theodore Dreiser's novels. Nevertheless, their evolving views of the nature of American democracy, of the proper relationship of literary art to changing social realities, and of the nature of "reality" itself had put them on collision course back in the mid-1940s, after Trilling first published the essays that would reappear in *The Liberal Imagination* as "Manners, Morals and the Novel" and "Reality in America" and after Ellison initially drafted his own challenge to the liberal imagination in "Twentieth Century Fiction and the Black Mask of Humanity" in 1946.

By the onset of the 1950s, Trilling had become more closely identified than any other major critic with flaying the literary idols of the 1920s and 1930s and with forecasting the "death of the novel"—the source of Ellison's special animus for "Trilling and his gang" (*TT* 157). *The Liberal Imagination* became a critical and creative manifesto for the Cold War era—and a best seller in the process. Granville Hicks, the Old Left standard-bearer Ellison had known since his days writing for *New Masses*, made it clear in his own review of *The Liberal Imagination* when it first appeared that he was opposed to Trilling's moralizing critical stance and derogation of old-style liberalism in general (Hicks, "Shortcomings"). Hicks had followed suit in a chastening review of Trilling's *Freud and the Crisis of Our Culture* for the *New York Times* in 1956 (Hicks, "Grounds" 7). When Hicks approached Ellison about contributing an essay for a forthcoming anthology that would extol "the living novel" and which would include Ellison comrades Saul Bellow, Herbert Gold, and Wright Morris, among others, Ellison, for his own reasons, accepted the invitation (*TT* 177). A decade earlier in "Twentieth Century Fiction and the Black Mask of Humanity," he had agreed with Richard Wright that there was "in progress between black and white Americans a struggle over the nature of reality," a struggle that Ellison understood then as a dialectical necessity of "that democratic process through which the nation works to achieve itself" (*S&A* 44). Accordingly, the confrontation with "Trilling and his gang" presented an evolutionary opportunity (*TT* 157).

"Reality in America" was Trilling's lead-off essay in *The Liberal Imagination*. In it he pressed his case that the old liberalism had become "Stalinoid" and reductive at a time when worldwide massive societal assaults on the uniqueness and autonomy of the individual required instead a liberal imagination attuned to "variousness and possibility, which implies the awareness of complexity and difficulty" (Trilling, *Liberal Imagination* xii). With a confidence certain to stun readers today looking backwards a half century, he announced that liberalism was "not only the dominant but even the sole intellectual tradition" in the United States and that there were "no conservative or reactionary ideas in general circulation": the "conservative impulse and the reactionary impulse," Trilling opined, "do not, with some isolated and some ecclesiastical exceptions, express themselves in ideas but only in action or in irritable mental gestures which seek to resemble ideas" (*Liberal Imagination* vii). Moored in the Enlightenment's Lockean and Hegelian pieties about the rational nature of man and the course of human history, classical liberalism had become a ruling, uncritical body of optimistic middle-class opinions touting inevitable progress, collectivism, and humanitarianism. Modern "reality," however, insistently presented a more complex, dangerous, and ambiguous set of prospects subject instead to the tangled motives and actions of the human creatures Sigmund Freud had revealed to be fundamentally irrational and biologically driven. A literature rooted in rosy liberal assumptions evaded the darker, deeper, more paradoxical and tragic human truths and took a passive attitude toward reality by striving merely to "reflect" or "mirror" it. The whole syndrome, Trilling argued, was evident in the canonized *Main Currents in American Thought* (1927–30) of literary historian Vernon Parrington and in the conventional liberal elevation of the proletarian novels of Theodore Dreiser over the highbrow novels of Henry James.

Parrington used antiquated political and artistic formulas to reduce complex, chaotic literary creations to simplified representations that were praiseworthy or blameworthy depending on how well they conformed to his liberal's sense of a stable, uniform reality. So he indicted writers such as Emerson, Hawthorne, Poe, and Henry James for "turning away from reality" for one reason or another—ambivalent romanticism, psychological aberration, intellectual or aristocratic pretension, and convoluted style, among others. And Parrington lauded Dreiser for his humanitarian attentiveness to the solid workaday reality of the urban poor and the problems of economic inequality. Such rudely materialist and politically pragmatic judgments might seem to have some social utility, Trilling acknowledged. But they narrowed the public understanding of highly differentiated and turbulent *subjective* experiences. Parrington disparaged writers working in the more genteel or academic traditions, and in the case of Henry James, particularly, he devalued gifts of great subtlety and moral refinement as aristocratic and unreal while praising simpleminded democratic platitudes. Moreover,

Trilling added, besides misunderstanding the true achievements of classic nineteenth-century American writers, such conventional liberal notions of reality and artistic merit were totally inadequate for understanding the monumental literary figures of the twentieth century—Marcel Proust, James Joyce, D. H. Lawrence, T. S. Eliot, William Butler Yeats, Thomas Mann, Franz Kafka, and others—all of whom "have their own love of justice and the good life, but in not one of them does it take the form of a love of the ideas and emotions which liberal democracy, as known by our educated class, has declared respectable" and acceptably real (*Liberal Imagination* 94). Ultimately, what was at stake was the failure of the liberal imagination to embrace human life fully, in all of its intractable and perhaps inexplicable multiplicity and irrationality. And that failure, Trilling warned, had consequences that were dangerous politically as well as artistically in the new Atomic Age and the era of the Cold War.

Since there was much in this part of Trilling's assessment that he agreed with (though certainly *not* Trilling's presumptions about the impotence of conservatism and reaction), Ellison focused his attention on the implications of Trilling's arguments as they extended to the craft and objectives of the working novelist in "Manners, Morals, and the Novel." There, the fault lines between Ellison and Trilling lay deeper, especially where Trilling outlined some of his prescriptions for revitalizing the liberal imagination and forestalling the "death of the novel." Here, Trilling's preference for the nineteenth-century novel of manners and its version of reality over the unruly experimental novels of twentieth-century modernism became clear, despite his Freudian convictions and his remonstrances against delusions of orderliness and stability in the liberal imagination. Trilling's arguments now worked in lockstep: first, what he meant by "manners" was "a culture's hum and buzz of implication," that part which is "made up of half-uttered or unutterable expressions of value" that are "hinted at by small actions, sometimes by the arts of dress or decoration, sometimes by tone, gesture, emphasis or rhythm, sometimes by the words that are used with a special frequency or a special meaning" (*Liberal Imagination* 194–95). These are the "things that for good or bad draw the people of a culture together and that separate them from the people of another culture." Second, since Trilling admitted that there was "not a single system of manners but a conflicting variety" which he could address only selectively, he selected "the manners of the literate, reading, responsible middle class of people who are ourselves" and the novels *they* read to draw his conclusions (*Liberal Imagination* 195).

Third, since the problem of reality—"the old opposition between reality and appearance, between what really is and what merely seems"—is central to all great literature and established itself as such in forefathers of the novel such as Miguel de Cervantes's *Don Quixote*, the novel itself was therefore established as "a perpetual quest for reality, the field of its research being always the social world, the material of its analysis being always manners as the indication of the direction of man's soul" (Trilling, *Liberal Imagination* 196–99). Dissecting illusions of reality created by the snobbery of class was the high calling the novel created for itself, as is evidenced in the varied achievements of the English, French, and Russian novel. Ultimately, while no such tradition of the novel as he described it "has ever really established itself in America," the development of a "moral realism," grounded in the kind of socially attuned "tragic" sensibility made manifest in Henry James's novels of manners, pointed a more "socially aware" way to a successful future for American novelists than the contemporary "modernist" work of Hemingway, Fitzgerald, and Faulkner and promised also the best alternative to obsolescence. The "hard, bedrock, concrete" reality preferred by the liberal imagination worked in dialectical opposition to the reality pursued in the novel of manners and, since "it is inescapably true that, in the novel, manners make men," Trilling posted a final caution: "[I]n proportion as we have committed ourselves to our particular idea of reality we have lost our interest in manners" (*Liberal Imagination* 203–04).

Nearly every turn of this argument troubled Ellison, who began his response by distinguishing "the drive of the critic to create systems of thought" from the novelist's contrasting drive "to re-create reality in the forms vision assumes as it plays and struggles with the vividly illusory 'eidetic-like' imagery left in the mind's eye by the process of social change" (*GTT* 239–40). His tongue deep in cheek, Ellison conceded critics to be "on the whole, more 'adult' types" than novelists, for whom capturing the reality of human life is "a game of hide-and-seek" in which they eternally play "the sometimes delighted but more often frustrated 'it.'" Where "some of our more important critics" (he left Trilling unnamed until nearly halfway into the essay) pronounced the novel to be dead, he detected "a Platonist '*Let* it be dead,'" equivalent to a willful death sentence or, worse yet, an assassination. In counterpoint to Trilling's definition of the novel, Ellison offered his own: rather than being an artifact of perception—a reflection, mirror, or such—the novel instead is "basically a form of communication" (*GTT* 242) and hence a collaboration with readers: inherently dynamic and unstable. Moreover, though the novel is indeed, as Trilling asserted, obsessed with the relationship between illusion and reality, that relationship is revealed "in duration, in process," not in the seemingly stable, surface "facts" of experience that the novel of manners traditionally emphasized, nor in the "hum and buzz of implication" that Trilling was advancing as a genuine penetration to the reality beneath the social surfaces.

The novel's true origin and development as a form of art, Ellison insisted, lay in "seizing from the flux and flow of our daily lives those abiding patterns of experience which, through their repetition and consequences in our affairs, help to form our sense of reality and from which emerge our sense of humanity and our conception of human value" (*GTT* 243–44). "More than any other literary form," he continued, "the novel is obsessed with the impact of change upon personality" (*GTT* 244). Prior to the breakdown of feudal society and the accelerated process of historical change that resulted, there had been "little need for this change-obsessed literary form," he proposed. Though the rising middle class had appropriated it to their own needs, the novel was not their possession but the creation of a total civilization; and during the nineteenth-century moment of greatest middle-class stability—"a stability found actually only at the center and there only relatively, in England and not in the colonies; in Paris rather than in Africa, for there the baser instincts, the violence and greed could destroy and exploit non-European societies in the name of humanism and culture, beauty and liberty, fraternity and equality while protecting the humanity of those at home—the novel reached its first high point of formal self-consciousness." Far from being dead, in our time it had become "the most articulate art form for defining ourselves and for asserting our humanity," as well as for dealing with the irrational (*GTT* 246).

It was the nineteenth-century novel of manners that was dead, Ellison countered, because it had "little value in dealing with our world of chaos and catastrophe." With that he moved from offering theoretical and definitional challenges to energetically dismantling Trilling's interpretations of the specific novelists put forward as objects of emulation or disparagement—James, Hawthorne, Faulkner, Hemingway, Fitzgerald. Of Trilling's paradigmatic novelist of manners, Henry James, Ellison made a special case, if only to turn it back against Trilling's claims about the famous catalogue of American cultural deficiencies which James had glossed from Hawthorne. James had turned the catalogue into American novelists' great "joke" on Old World notions of social reality. What was most surprising to Ellison about Trilling's recourse to James was that Trilling seemed not to have understood the great American joke at all, so it had now become a joke on Trilling himself (*GTT* 266). That American society appeared void of the time-worn European manners, morals, and institutions was a sign not of deficiency but of new novelistic possibilities, first and foremost those relating to that dark and raucous "social field" of racial and cultural variousness that Trilling's hoped-for New Liberal imagination might otherwise entertain but which remained in the repressive underground of Trilling's own surface gleanings of American social reality. Ellison proceeded therefore to dissect the critic's dismissive readings of Mark Twain and William Faulkner, to demonstrate just how Trilling's inattention to the pivotal racial implications in Twain's *Huckleberry Finn* and Faulkner's *The Bear* led him finally to misunderstand the profound "moral realism" achieved in both—precisely that quality of tragic understanding and empathy that Trilling's theory of the novel and American reality ostensibly made paramount.

Ellison refrained from raising here what he would draw sharp attention to a few years later in his exchange with Trilling confederate Irving Howe in "The World and the Jug": Trilling's studiously effaced Jewishness and the ambivalence about it that apparently adulterated his critical sensitivities in symptomatic instances. The son of Orthodox Jewish émigrés from Europe who ultimately experienced the American Dream as a disillusioning reversal of high expectations, Trilling had turned sharply away from the extensive writing and lecturing on Jewish identity and its place in literature that he produced for the *Menorah Journal* at the beginning of his literary career ("Lionel Trilling" 826). Repudiating the economic system that betrayed his immigrant parents' dreams of New World success, he had become, like Howe, a committed Marxist before his growing attraction to the culture of Western humanism effected a fulsome identification with the Anglophile tradition's ultimate icon, Matthew Arnold (Pinsker 208–09). As his autobiographical lectures late in life acknowledged, Trilling's college

years had been a time of "intense and pervasive questioning of the prevailing way of doing things—that is to say, of the majority's way of doing
things" (Pinsker 209). He had ultimately rationalized his dissociation from
what Howe termed "the world of his fathers" by adopting "the belief still
preeminently honored that a primary function of art and thought is to liberate the individual from the tyranny of his culture in the environmental
sense and to permit him to stand beyond it in an autonomy of perception and judgment" (Pinsker 209). Standing beyond it had not protected
him, however, when, after becoming the first Jew appointed to the English
Department of Columbia University, its predominantly "liberal" faculty
had invoked the prevailing rules and quotas of WASP exclusivity to deny
him tenure in 1936 and to dismiss him summarily for being "a Freudian, a
Marxist and a Jew" who would be "more comfortable" elsewhere ("Lionel
Trilling" 826 ; Pinsker 209). Trilling had not overtly protested the bigotry of
his dismissal, and he successfully convinced the faculty to reverse its decision. But, as his own later testimony and that of his wife in *The Beginning
of the Journey: The Marriage of Diana and Lionel Trilling* (1993) make clear,
his outward self-confidence remained riddled underneath with self-doubt,
even as he prosecuted his extended war of retaliation against the "liberal"
imagination.

As Ellison fully understood, Trilling's "new" liberalism had not confronted its divorce from Jewishness and conscious ethnicity, nor its uneasi-
ness in the face of modernist challenges to Matthew Arnold's Anglophile
orthodoxies and monocultural myopia. Nor had he confronted its new
obsession with "reality" and "moral realism" and the "snobbery of class"
in the American novel—to the utter disregard of color-caste and race and
the plurality of other American cultures buzzing and humming with implication. Moreover, the closing paragraphs in "Manners, Morals and the
Novel" voiced covert warnings to its intended WASP audience about the
"dangers" lying in wait for "our most generous wishes" of "greater social
liberality"—as strong a hint as Trilling was able to mount about the
unvoiced social turbulence outside generated by the growing force of the
civil rights insurgencies—but a hint nonetheless of his own reactionary impulses and Arnoldian fears of looming social anarchy. In "Art and
Fortune," later in the *The Liberal Imagination*, where he defended the earlier
essay and took up again the disputes over the novel of manners and the

"death of the novel," Trilling dissociated himself to some extent from the prophecies of novelistic doom and revisited the "great joke" at the heart of the novel's investigation of reality and illusion through manners. But that joke, for him, remained confined to social origins and incongruities visible most pertinently in Shakespeare and Cervantes: "I have suggested how for Shakespeare any derangement of social classes seems always to imply a derangement of the senses in madness or dream, some elaborate joke about the nature of reality. This great joke is the matter of the book which we acknowledge as the ancestor of the modern novel, *Don Quixote*; and indeed no great novel exists which does not have the joke at its very heart" (*Liberal Imagination* 243). And he still asserted that "in this country the real basis of the novel has never existed—that is, the tension between a middle class and an aristocracy which brings manners into observable relief as the living representation of ideals and the living comment on ideas. . . . With the single exception of the Civil War, our political struggles have not had the kind of cultural implications which catch the imagination, and the extent to which this one conflict has engaged the American mind suggests how profoundly interesting conflicts of culture may be" (*Liberal Imagination* 245). Trilling took a step closer here, finally—but no more than that—toward the cultural terrain Ellison saw as fundamental to grappling with the reality of American experience. And Trilling came close again a few paragraphs later when he considered an alternate explanation for the death of the novel and brought the modern world's Jewish question starkly to the surface:

> The façade is down; society's resistance to the discovery of depravity has ceased; now everyone knows that Thackeray was wrong, Swift right. The world and the soul have split open of themselves and are all agape for our revolted inspection. The simple eye of the camera shows us, at Belsen and Buchenwald, horrors that quite surpass Swift's powers, a vision of life turned back to its corrupted elements which is more disgusting than any that Shakespeare could contrive, a cannibalism more literal and fantastic than that which Montaigne ascribed to organized society. A characteristic activity of mind is therefore no longer needed. Indeed, before what we now know the mind stops; the great psychological fact of our time which we all observe with baffled wonder and shame is that there is no possible way of responding to Belsen and Buchenwald. The activity of mind fails before the incommunicability of man's suffering. (*Liberal Imagination* 249)

The eye of Trilling's camera had indeed finally stopped before the horrors of the German concentration camps, but it had yet to discover an angle of vision on the horrors and suffering of Georgia and Alabama and Mississippi. Though the African American literary imagination, liberal or otherwise, remained invisible to Trilling's scrutiny, his brief allusion to the Civil War as a locus of cultural conflict at least broached again some revealing links to the novels of Twain, Faulkner, and James. Trilling would discuss *Huckleberry Finn* at length in *The Liberal Imagination*; and the chapter he devoted to James's *The Princess Casamassima* as a political novel mentioned briefly its companion piece, *The Bostonians*, for which Trilling wrote an important introduction in 1952 developing further his notions about the "cultural implications" of the Civil War in Henry James's imagination. Though Ellison's reflections in "Society, Morality and the Novel" would limit themselves to Trilling's readings of Twain and Faulkner, it was Trilling's subsequent take on the cultural implications of civil war in *The Bostonians* that dramatized even more the divide between them over the nature of reality and the purposes of the novel. When Ellison wrote his essay on "The Novel as a Function of Democracy," published separately a decade later, he reexamined the reverberations of the Civil War in the novel James himself felt had never received "any sort of justice"; and Ellison completed his circle of reasoning begun for *The Living Novel* by framing it in a broader context for *Going to the Territory*.

Trilling had begun his introduction to *The Bostonians* by acknowledging the novel's largely unwelcome reception by American reviewers in 1886, despite James's expressed intent "to write a very *American* tale." While Trilling regarded that intent suspiciously, he recognized that the book was "marked by a comicality which has rather more kinship with American humour than with British humour, or with wit of any transatlantic kind" (Introduction viii). Though Trilling's introduction barely hinted at it, the novel's thematic originality lay in a central love triangle that made it one of the earliest American novels to deal—even obliquely—with lesbianism: Olive Chancellor, a feminist reform leader in 1870s Boston, has discovered a remarkable platform orator and what she believes is a kindred soul in Verena Tarrant, a young alabaster beauty who, while passive and indecisive, can hold audiences spellbound in the cause of women's rights. Olive contends for Verena's commitment and affections against a gracious but

reactionary Mississippi plantation owner and Confederate veteran, Basil
Ransom, whose masculine powers ultimately woo Verena away from Olive
and the feminist sisterhood for a return to postwar Dixie. As a political novel—a surprising departure for James, Trilling suggested—*The
Bostonians* treated the world of post–Civil War reform movements in New
England with a "dialectical" cast of mind Trilling thought was characteristic:
"[H]is fiction is composed out of the setting against each other of two great
elemental principles of life. . . . They may be thought of as energy and iner-
tia; or spirit and matter; or spirit and letter; or force and form; or radicalism and conservatism; or creation and possession; or Libido and Thanatos"
(Introduction ix).

Trilling's specifically Freudian interjection here allowed him to interpret James's closely observed social satire of the novel's "movement of
female emancipation" in postbellum America not just as the bitter total
war of the sexes that August Strindberg and D. H. Lawrence anatomized
later on, but as Freud's concept of sublimated family romance exploded
into large-scale cultural conflict, and linked to the ghosts of the Civil War
by the eroticized presence of the symbolic Southern plantation owner,
Ransom. The Mississippi ex-slave-master was, James had written, "as a representative of his sex, the most important personage in my narrative"; and
around him, Trilling proposed, "the fear of the loss of manhood," the "dis-
trust of theory," and a "tragic awareness of the intractability of the human
circumstance" all revolved. Trilling introduced a psychobiographical twist
by intimating that, during the novel's gestation, the central conflicts of
The Bostonians had been extrapolated from James's traumatic loss of, first,
his ailing mother and then his "sacred old Father," so that, when blended
with the political theme James had selected, the novel ultimately became,
to Trilling, "a story of the parental house divided against itself, of the key-
stone falling from the arch, of the sacred mothers refusing their commission and the sacred fathers endangered" (Introduction xiv–xv).

Trilling's interpretation extended the logic of *The Liberal Imagination*
in such a way as to remake James's "lean, pale, sallow, shabby, striking young
man, with his superior head and sedentary shoulders" into Mississippi's
"proto-martyr" for the "lost cause" of the Old South and the bearer of "a
kind of realism which the North, with its abstract intellectuality, was for-
getting to its cost" (Introduction xii). To Trilling, Ransom had the courage

of the "British line of romantic conservatives" and seemed "akin to Yeats, Lawrence and Eliot in that he experiences his cultural fears in the most personal way possible, translating them into sexual fear, the apprehension of the loss of manhood" (Introduction xii) evident in Ransom's complaint that "the whole generation is womanized.... [T]he masculine tone is passing out of the world; it's a feminine, a nervous, hysterical, chattering, canting age, an age of hollow phrases and false delicacy." Trilling's reading was diametrically opposed to Ellison's in "The Novel as a Function of Democracy," which began instead by emphasizing the extent to which such frames of reference repressed or displaced the immediate impact on James of actual Civil War battlefield deaths, of the volatile abolitionist movement, and of the powerful impact of political crisis and political ideas:

> [I]t was forgotten, however, that James came on the scene at a time when the abolitionists were coming in and out of his father's house, that he was part of a period in which there was great intellectual ferment, religious ferment, civil rights ferment. Few critics recalled that in that war James lost one of his older brothers, who had been a member of Colonel Shaw's Massachusetts regiment of free slaves. It was also forgotten that James's second published story, "The Story of a Year," was based on an incident which occurred in the Civil War.... He recognized—as demonstrated in his novel ... that in his time the United States had reached a moment of crisis and, in fact, that he was writing during a new period in the life of the nation, when the lyrical belief in the possibilities of the Constitution and the broadness of the land was no longer so meaningful. Mindful that hundreds of thousands of men had died in the Civil War, James knew for his own time what Emerson knew for his. Emerson constantly reminded Americans that they had to discover the new possibilities of the new land. What James realized was that the old enduring evil of the human predicament had raised its face.... This evil could no longer be confronted in the name of religion, in the name of kingship or of aristocracy—although James was himself an aristocrat. James recognized that each and every individual who lived within the society had to possess, and to be concerned with, the most subtle type of moral consciousness. (*GTT* 313–14)

At bottom, Trilling construed "reality" in James as neither Ellison nor Richard Wright imagined it—formalistically or morally. Wright used James's prefaces and scenic methods regularly to great effect, fully aware of, but unperturbed by, their creator's aristocratic "snobbery of class"; and in his own Jamesian afterword to *Native Son*, "How Bigger Was Born," Wright

appropriated the Hawthorne-James catalogue of American cultural nega-
tivities as ground for formulating his own punch line to the great American
joke: "the Negro is America's metaphor." For Ellison, alternatively, the punch
line Trilling seemed not to grasp was: *America, therefore, is the undiscovered
country*—an imaginative frontier analogous to what remained repressed
about pluralist democracy in Trilling's critical efforts to define "reality in
America." Where Trilling expressed open suspicion about the authenticity
and sincerity of James's specifically American sensitivities and emphasized
instead the novelist's expatriate outlook, Ellison filtered his own Jamesian
understandings through the panoramic specificities rendered so knowingly by the James of *The American Scene* (1907). And where Trilling's dialectic between culture and psychology relied on Freud's *Civilization and Its
Discontents* (1930) to emphasize the primacy of libidinal forces as cultural
dangers, which required strict policing of the reality principle by the super-
ego, Ellison and Wright adopted instead Wilhelm Reich's countermanding
theory, expounded in *Character Analysis* (1933) and *The Sexual Revolution*
(1935), that relationships between the ego drives and the reality principle
could be emancipatory rather than repressive.

With *Civilization and Its Discontents* as a cautionary hermeneutic,
Trilling treated James's novel as a mannerly drama of sublimated bourgeois
and aristocratic desire circumscribed by the conventions of social reform,
heterosexual courtship, and upward mobility. By contrast, eight years
earlier, when Ellison presented his draft of "Twentieth Century Fiction
and the Black Mask of Humanity" to the 1945 Conference of Psychologists
and Writers (Jackson 344), he had absorbed Freud's insights about the
"resemblances between the psychic lives of savages and neurotics" and had
begun filtering Twain, Faulkner, Hemingway, and James through the alternate hermeneutic of *Totem and Taboo*. The representations of American
experience and the portrayals of black people were revealed thereby not as
images of functional reality, but as neurotic counterfeits: "[T]hey are projected aspects of an internal symbolic process through which, like a primitive tribesman dancing himself into the group frenzy necessary for battle,
the white American prepares himself emotionally to perform a social role"
(*S&A* 45). What Trilling was inclined to read as a renunciation of instinct
in service to a regulatory reality principle, Ellison saw instead as a ritualiza-
tion of instinct in deference to the "omnipotence of thought" that Freud

associated with the power of the id's unconscious force in human culture and personality.

Accordingly, when Ellison refracted *The Bostonians* through the lens of *Totem and Taboo*—with Frazer's *Golden Bough*, Émile Durkheim's *Elements of Religion*, and John Dollard's *Caste and Class in a Southern Town* for theoretical supplementation—the "manners" of civilized society became markers of primitive ritual compulsions and symbolic prohibitions rooted in "magical" notions of purity and pollution—all seen through the "frog perspective" of Nietzsche and Richard Wright or "from the briar patch" and metaphysical "warm hole" of Jack-the-Bear. Indeed, Ellison had highlighted such perspectival shifts in *Invisible Man* through the ritualized phantasmagoria of the Battle Royal and the Golden Day and through Jim Trueblood's orgasmic reversal of fortune. The locus in each instance was Trilling's same superordinate "social field" but viewed instead from beneath the threshold of social propriety—in picaresque hyperbole, so that the "manners" of social superiors are satirically unmasked in "realistic" detail to demonstrate their complicity in oppression and the maintenance of social power, or their primal origins in explosive bodily attractions and repulsions. In that respect, *Invisible Man* became a novel of manners in reverse: the culture's "hum and buzz of implication" seen from the bottom up, stripped of its rationalizing constructs and cosmetic allurements—a social order rendered as dynamic and provisional rather than static and secure, as barbaric and ruthless rather than modulated and compassionate. The underground of racial implication that remains understated in the "psychological realism" of James's *Bostonians* is instead hyperbolized modernistically by Ellison—through Expressionist and Surrealist distortion—to reveal the truths beneath the surface "realities" of bourgeois social manners.

This conflict of visions between Trilling and Ellison over the nature of "reality in America" could be traced earlier in their contrasting readings of Melville, Twain, and Hemingway as well: in Ellison's insistence on the quintessentially moral and humanist *necessity* of Huck's choosing to steal Jim a second time instead of turning him over to Miss Watson versus Trilling's granting the same plot device merely some "formal justification"; in opposition, too, to Hemingway's calling that same scenario excisable and "just cheating." Ellison's critiques of the rhetoric of race relations in "Beating that Boy" (1945) and of the mechanisms of literary stereotype and the institutional suppression of public memory in "Twentieth Century Fiction and the Black Mask of Humanity" show how Ellison's reading of Freud shaped his own theory of reality in America and of the American novel in ways fundamentally at odds with Trilling's Freudian refractions. But Ellison had not only *read* Freud's works, he had been engaged pragmatically in efforts to make Freud's ideas the working tools of real-world human transformation and healing: first through his work experience as an office assistant and file clerk for Harry Stack Sullivan in the late 1930s and then through his collaboration with Richard Wright and forensic psychiatrist Fredric Wertham in founding the LaFargue Psychiatric Clinic in Harlem during the late 1940s and early 1950s.

In *Trading Twelves*, Ellison's comments to Albert Murray about the European obsession with "purity" point to yet another frame of opposition over the nature of "reality" in America and the social and philosophical "problem of the one and the many." Purity as a component of "classical realism"—and of the Manichaeism that Miguel de Unamuno and André Malraux deplored—came to connote for Ellison on the abstract level a dangerous Platonist privileging of essence over existence, of unmixed modes, genres, categories of identity or being over the hybrid and syncretic: of tragedy and comedy, for instance, over *tragicomedy* as modes of expression, despite the latter's closer approximation to the ambiguous actualities of lived human experience. The purist's either/or Manichaeism, when extended to the social sphere, promoted an abhorrence of mixing social classes, castes, and identities and, as Ellison insisted in "On Initiation Rites and Power," ensured that "a great part of the society was controlled by the taboos built around the fear of the white woman and the black man getting together" (*GTT* 61). That almighty taboo had been jokingly subverted in *The Bostonians* by the novel's closing capture of the alabaster Verena by the Mississippi freebooter Basil Ransom, who, as James's narrator slyly divulges, from the very first had been guilty of "prolonging his consonants" and "swallowing his vowels" and of such corollary "elisions and interpolations" as made his discourse seem "pervaded by something sultry and vast, something almost African in its rich basking tone, something that suggested the teeming expanse of the cotton-field" (James 18). Trilling, once more, showed no sign of having grasped this final Jamesian joke. But it was precisely the kind of subterranean riff Ellison turned routinely to raucous effect—and to political meditation as well, since it buzzingly implied a miscegenated outcome of slavery and civil war that the wielders of official power, North and South alike, steadfastly refused to recognize, along with Lionel Trilling.

Richard Chase, Trilling's foremost critical disciple, extended his mentor's theory of American culture as a dialectic of repressed *class* conflict and bourgeois family romance in *The American Novel and Its Tradition* (1957), published the same year Ellison's rebuttal to Trilling appeared. A year thereafter, in honor ostensibly of Trilling's imaginative gifts to the national discourse, Chase converted the monologic voice of *The Liberal Imagination* into a multivoiced fictional "dialogue" on the "the life of the mind, *en famille*," published in book form as *The Democratic Vista* (1958), with a titular nod to Walt Whitman's moody meditation of 1871 on the state of democracy in the wake of the Civil War. In an attempt to simulate a sort of Socratic dialogue between spokesmen for key contending cultural traditions in American democracy, Chase contrived a fictional weekend retreat at the summer place of one middle-aged WASP couple (Professor Ralph Headstrong and his social-worker wife) with a second, younger couple of their "solid citizen" friends from the "new generation" (George and Nancy Middleby), together with a glamorous "amateur and woman of projects, out of the gay past" (Maggie Motive) and a newly naturalized immigrant engineer and social "optimist" (Rinaldo Schultz) (*Democratic Vista* xii). Sporting a tone and *mise-en-scène* straight out of "fabulous fifties" family sitcoms such as *Ozzie and Harriet* and *Leave It to Beaver* but with hardly a chuckle in sight, Chase spun out an almost farcically stilted series of exchanges between the liberal-radical views of the Chase-Trilling surrogate, the conservative middlebrow views of the solid citizen, the countercultural whimsies of the faded bohemian, and the cautious dreams of the hopeful émigré—all intended to dramatize Trilling's concept of American culture as a complex dialectic rather than a stream or confluence.

As a dedicated New Liberal following Trilling's lead, Chase attempted to discuss the crises of American Cold War culture as a network of intergenerational, crossgender, native-born versus immigrant tensions without raising even the spectre, let alone the living force, of racial or ethnic conflict and the unending African American quarrel with constitutional democracy—even as the post–*Brown v. Board of Education* movement for civil rights pushed into high gear in American streets and on television screens worldwide. In the preface to his earlier book on Herman Melville, Chase claimed that no one who had read Melville could have voted for Henry Wallace and the left-wing Progressive Party of 1948—an expression, presumably, of the New Liberal's "tragic awareness" of the "innocent" fallibility of socialist utopianism in the face of the totalitarian Soviet juggernaut. There, Chase seemed more attuned to Ahab's Manichaean vision of the White Whale in *Moby Dick* than to the anarchic ambiguities of *Benito Cereno* and *The Confidence Man*, which so entranced Ellison. Where Chase, following in Trilling's wake, exercised himself subsequently to pursue the dialectic between "novel" and "romance" in American literary narratives, Ellison confronted the leader of the New Liberal gang over the divide between the reality hypothesized in the novel of manners and the contrary vision and imperatives that inclined Ellison toward the "rogue reality" of his own ritualized new form of metaphysical picaresque.

As a man of letters and literary critic in his own right, Ellison found his own perceptions about American literary history ratified more studiously in works such as English scholar John McCormick's *Catastrophe and Imagination: An Interpretation of the Recent English and American Novel* (1957), which Ellison read in Rome while drafting "Society, Morality and the Novel" (*TT* 157–58). McCormick's book addressed the "death of the novel" and the dispute about the novel of manners in a richer comparative framework than Trilling's. It tracked the evolution of the modern novel in terms of McCormick's alternative dialectic between "novels of social comedy" (which celebrate the integration of individuals and society) and "novels of social tragedy" (which mark the dissolution of ties between individuals and society), a dialectic that resolves itself in the development of "novels of ideas," which create self-conscious formal structures for posing the conflicts between individuals and society as well as the ontological conflict between appearance and reality. In McCormick's view, Trilling had falsely pathologized the American novel and overstated its variance from its British analogues. Trilling was "culturally an Edwardian," McCormick concluded, and had prejudicially narrowed the scope of traditional social comedy to the more restricted novel of manners and then ignored the emergence, especially in America, of novels of ideas that performed precisely the analysis of the "social field" and the conflict it posed between appearance and reality that Trilling's own criteria demanded (McCormick 70–74): "[T]he development of American satire since 1945 in the work of Mary McCarthy, Randall Jarrell, Flannery O'Connor, Elizabeth Hardwick, Saul Bellow, and Ralph Ellison, together with the increasing intellectualization of recent American fiction, demonstrates the degree to which American and English writers have come to share similar, if not identical, impulses, just as these events measure the area into which Trilling and his followers are unwilling to penetrate" (McCormick 75). Moreover, as a demonstrably accomplished novel of ideas intriguingly akin to *Invisible Man* on some levels, Trilling's own Cold War tale of "Stalinoid" radical faith and neoconservative disillusion, *The Middle of the Journey* (1947), presented creative countertestimony "which neither his theory nor other theories of the death of the novel take into account" (McCormick 76).

On the scholarly side of the quarrel with Trilling and his gang, Ellison aligned himself also with the critical views of R. W. B. Lewis who, while calling Trilling "capable at once of more range and more exactness than almost any other critic in America today," nevertheless deemed *The Liberal Imagination* the voice of a "New Stoicism" built on an inchoate idea of reality that "evidently touches mind as well as matter" but still resists coherent formulation ("Lionel Trilling" 313–17). Reality so formlessly constructed was not a program for creative action but "a device for shoring up defenses" and sorely in need of the "doctrine of sustained tensions" and the "comic vocabulary" Kenneth Burke had developed in his *Attitudes toward History* (Lewis, "Lionel Trilling" 316). In *The American Adam* (1955), published between Trilling's and Chase's New Liberal postulations, Lewis framed his own neo-Socratic "dialogue" on innocence, tragedy, and the contending traditions for representing "reality" in American literature: a series of "great conversations" between an Emersonian "Party of Hope," which saw the infant American republic as a "new Adam" uncorrupted by the sins of the Old World past; a Hawthornesque "Party of Memory," distrustful of experience, which declared the emergence of the American Adam as dehumanized by its willful breach with that past; and a focal, Melvillean "Party of Irony," which simultaneously bolstered *and* undermined the Adamic conception by probing the "tragic" implications of the Adamic figure within the verifiable realities of the historical process (Lewis, *American Adam* 1–10). In an epilogue on "Adam as Hero in the Age of Containment," Lewis identified a current of debilitating and defensive skepticism in midcentury American thought that he linked to the wide influence of Lionel Trilling. At the same time, Lewis discerned the contemporary spiritual descendants of the party of irony to be the "truest and most fully engaged" American novelists of the postwar era: Ralph Ellison, J. D. Salinger, and Saul Bellow. Turning Trilling against himself, Lewis reminded readers that "fiction, Lionel Trilling has said, imitates the will in action, and of late the will has become oddly disempowered and reluctant to initiate action." By contrast, Lewis admonished, while the irony of Ellison, Bellow, and Salinger "is fertile and alive; the chilling skepticism of the mid-twentieth century represents one of the modes of death. The new hopelessness is, paradoxically, as simple-minded as innocence" (*American Adam* 196).

In its own gloss on the vagaries of hope, memory, and irony in America, C. L. R. James's *Mariners, Renegades, and Castaways* (1953) interpreted Herman Melville allegorically in order to frame the problem of Cold War containment as a crisis between authoritarianism and humanism rather than between an old and a new liberalism, as Lionel Trilling and Richard Chase would have it. James shared Ellison's and Richard Wright's attraction to popular culture as a locus of cultural critique, as well as their unapologetic attraction also to the cosmopolite icons of international modernist high culture. But the Trinidadian expatriate's dialectical preoccupation with a pre-Freudian psychology of totalitarianism and his more limited exposure to the intricacies of America's interethnic "quarrel" with the rulers of democracy deflected his view of Melville's party of irony away from the matrices of existential tragedy and hyperbolic humor that Ellison fixed on in the metaphysical tales of the White Whale, the doomed Spanish slaver, and the Black Guinea. With James Baldwin, for whom Melville seems to have held limited interest beyond the rhetoric of Father Mapple's sermon on Jonah, dialogue about the party of irony was better pursued with respect to Henry James, whose retinue of satirically rendered New World innocents furnished Baldwin with ample models for his own stable of anxiously American characters. For Anatole Broyard as well, the Melvillean ironic temper stood at great remove from his own hypermodern bohemian moods and modulated wit, so that Ellison's Melvillean ancestry communicated most pointedly with Broyard through the filters supplied by Trilling and Chase. With Nathan Scott, despite his priestly robes and erudite homiletics, a closer intellectual colloquy was possible for Ellison, in part because of Scott's theological interest in "Melville's quarrel with God" and in part because the canons of theological restraint were not so binding on Scott as to keep him from reproving his former teacher, in an initial review of Trilling's *The Middle of the Journey*, for employing "polemical tactics" on the religious question that were "not very far removed from those of Senator McCarthy" (Scott, "Lionel Trilling's Critique" 18).

Strangely enough, among the critical minds set in conversation here, the richest concord of sensibilities with Ellison's Melvillean spirit resided potentially with Richard Chase, whose venturesome 1949 critical study of the Melvillean corpus had gathered Freudian psychology, the myth and ritual theories of the Cambridge School, and the folklore analyses of Constance Rourke so treasured by Ellison into a stream of startling readings that revealed Melville more fully than ever before as a supremely "humorous writer, as well as a lyric and epic" one:

> In *Mardi* the humor is often uncomfortably hearty, jovial, and broad. In *Moby Dick* it is lyrical and heroic; it expresses itself in a subtly flowing stream of fantasy, alternately gay, grim, festive, erotic, regretful, and sad. In *The Confidence Man* it is spare, light-footed, buoyant, and savage. In many mythologies the Promethean culture-hero easily modulates into the comic demigod whom the anthropologists call "the trickster." This is true of the American mythology, both Indian and white. The Yankee peddler and the Crockett-like backwoods hero, who merge in the figure of Uncle Sam, are as much comic Prometheuses as the sly bear and rabbit magicians of the Indians." (Chase, *Herman Melville* 67)

Ellison's own literary goals and credo resonate here in Chase's capsule portrait of Melville's often unacknowledged comic vision. But Ellison had dismissed Chase namelessly in a single parenthesis of "Society, Morality and the Novel" as "one of Mr. Trilling's disciples [who] has deduced from it [the James catalogue of American negativities] that personality exists in the United States only in New England and in the South" (*GTT* 265), which presents an irony of another sort, worthy of its own discussion elsewhere.

For our purposes here, a sharp disjunction becomes clear between Chase's stylish, subtle, spirited, and scholarly study of Herman Melville—a study whose preface explicitly aligned itself with Trilling's political agenda for the New Liberalism—and the awkward, ill-advised, amateurish pseudo-dialogue Chase mounted as an imaginary roundtable on the state of American democracy and the liberal imagination. Perhaps, as one shrewd reviewer suggested, the method of *The Democratic Vista* was, consciously or unconsciously, a literary gimmick, a formulaic evasion of a subject too complex and confused to be rendered in bite-size literary form (Marty 948). If so, it offered a prime target for the kind of comic confrontation and dismissal that the Melvillean spirit had bequeathed to twentieth-century party of irony operatives such as Ellison and Saul Bellow. Bellow was one of those Jewish American writers that the austere and disaffiliated Lionel Trilling found too jocularly Jewish for comfort. But Bellow's jocularity helped make him a master of comic confrontation in the novel. As Ellison noted admiringly to Ishmael Reed in a comment about Bellow's prizewinning novel *Mr. Sammler's Planet* (1970), in one scene Bellow "has a Black pickpocket make the symbolic gesture of drawing his pecker out on the main character. The thing sets up all kinds of reverberation in the narrative. It becomes damn nigh metaphysical" (Graham and Singh 373). Bellow's hero, Mr. Sammler, is an elderly Jewish intellectual and survivor of the Holocaust who was left one-eyed and psychically wounded by his Nazi ordeal and who uses his intact eye to screen the outside world's insanities and his blind eye as an internal filter of events closer at hand. Mr. Sammler's confrontation with the black pickpocket opens up his whole *modus operandi* and sense of reality to new possibilities. Like the pasteboard surrogates for Lionel Trilling and his gang in Richard Chase's *The Democratic Vista*, Mr. Sammler is ripe for confrontation and a fall. And by the rules of Bellow's comic logic, the stilted New Liberal fantasy figures of Chase's Socratic pseudo-drama had earned a metaphysical comeuppance capable at least of exposing them to a higher reality, as Mr. Sammler is. But Ellison's final comment on Bellow's scenario revealed him to be an even harsher and more surreal taskmaster than his colleague in irony: "[I]f I had written the scene," he averred, "I would have tried to make it even more eloquent by having the pickpocket snatch it out and hit the hero over the head with it. I would have further physicalized the metaphysic—soma to psyche!" (Graham and Singh 373). Though he had spared Richard Chase such a measure of chastisement, in the quarreling quest for reality Ellison had long since embarked on and in the face of the obstacles put before him by the agencies of illiberal imagination, no understated metaphor could be fully eloquent or illuminating and none metaphysical enough.

With the retort to Lionel Trilling and his disciples conveying its own distinctive freight of metaphor and metaphysics, Ellison's second flight of essays, *Going to the Territory*, appeared in 1986 at the middle of a decade cultural historians quickly began to deride as having almost nothing intrinsic to distinguish it except, perhaps, the extent to which its political symbols and cultural obsessions were foraged from other periods (Bondi vii). It was the onset of the cyberculture age and the internet, a time when advancing computer technologies in data storage and manufacturing design made archiving, replicating, and simulating cultural artifacts and political symbols possible almost without limit. Cultural desires and political outlooks, too, could be appropriated wholesale from other eras. The old modernist impulse to "make it new" yielded easily to a *post*modern inclination to make it "retro," so that the arts and literature of the 1980s routinely referred to points backwards in time to make themselves fully understood. As the inescapable political personification of the decade, President Ronald Reagan, ex-actor turned conservative torchbearer, embodied a syndrome that yoked politics and culture to recirculated agendas: "an economic philosophy derived from the 1920s (or perhaps from the 1890s), a populist rhetoric borrowed from the 1930s, the can-do optimism of the 1940s, and an anti-communism straight out of the 1950s" (Bondi vii). No less retro, Reagan's political opponents attacked him "via the liberalism of the 1930s and 1940s or through the social radicalism of the 1960s and 1970s" (Bondi vii). The worlds of art, fashion, and graphic design resurrected older styles in shameless profusion: simulated 1930s Art Deco, 1940s Abstract Expressionism and film noir, 1950s commercial kitsch, and 1960s rock music and countercultural experimentalism held sway simultaneously. Throughout the decade Reagan's generational cohort, their sense of the "normal" and "natural" moored in the 1940s and 1950s, warred on one front with baby boomers who had rebelled against those same norms during the 1960s and 1970s. On another front, they battled a new hip-hop generation that surfaced during the 1980s from the black urban underground, armed with the gangster rhetoric of a threatening crossover musical symbiosis that now sported an MTV high visibility that was no longer the sociological hyperbole it had been for Ellison in the 1940s.

Now in his seventies and just three years Reagan's junior, Ellison had been awarded the National Medal of Honor at the president's hand the year before *Going to the Territory* appeared—the last in a series of public honors that had begun two decades earlier during the "new frontier" and "great society" administrations of John F. Kennedy and Lyndon Johnson. Ellison was still the unswerving New Deal Democrat who had once located himself to the political left of the Communist Party, and in his seventh decade he opposed the Reagan presidency: "Reagan," he told interviewer Walter Lowe in 1982, "is dismantling many of the same processes and structures that made it possible for me to go from sleeping on a park bench to becoming a writer" (Graham and Singh 385). Ellison brought an oppositional outlook also to the cultural and literary turns of 1980s retrospection. The public evasion of cultural memory in official American institutional life and the invisible force of repression and cultural amnesia at the level of individual experience continued as thematic concerns in his public statements as well as in the fragments of the unfinished manuscript novel he had been slowly releasing over the years. The shadowy presence "[b]etween the idea / and the reality / [b]etween the motion / and the act" that framed the prose pieces of his first essay collection back in 1964 remained immanent in the second. If Ronald Reagan's rise to power at the beginning of the 1980s highlighted for critical observers the ominous divide between "acting" and "being," it served in the arc of Ellison's conscious thought to echo ironically the tensions between "being" and "doing" that had preoccupied André Malraux, Jean-Paul Sartre, and Albert Camus during the ascendancy of existentialist debate in the 1930s and 1940s span of the Spanish Civil War and World War II.

Going to the Territory had its own moorings in that earlier era, and in its own way, too, was a work of collected retrospection—with its center of chronological reference primarily in the politically and culturally riven decade of the 1960s. Ellison's literary "ancestors" William Faulkner and Ernest Hemingway had died a quarter century before, at the outset of that decade, and the sixties had claimed Ellison "relatives" Richard Wright and Langston Hughes as well. Though his cross-racial ties with literary figures such as Saul Bellow and Robert Penn Warren persisted, Ellison had outlived nearly all the other personal icons of his formative years: most disconcertingly, his novelistic avatar, Malraux, had died in 1976. Among the cultural critics Ellison especially respected, Stanley Edgar Hyman, his amiable foil in *Shadow and Act*'s "Change the Joke and Slip the Yoke" had died in 1970. But Ellison's generational ties to other noteworthy allies and old sparring partners in the critical arena—Kenneth Burke and Irving Howe, for example—fared better. Burke remained productive intellectually and was an occasional correspondent. Howe was vigorous enough so that his "intellectual autobiography," *A Margin of Hope*—strangely silent somehow about the famous critical exchange recounted in Ellison's "The World and the Jug"—had appeared four years ahead of *Going to the Territory*, with a recantational retrospective on the half-century rise and decline of the old anti-Stalinist Left that had important points of contact with Ellison's own leftist ordeal. In addition, longtime Ellison friend and fellow Russophile Joseph Frank published *Dostoyevsky: The Stir of Liberation, 1860–1865*, the third of a planned five-volume study of the Russian genius, in lockstep with *Going to the Territory* in 1986.

Professionalized retrospection in the academy that was especially germane to longstanding Ellison interests also generated volumes that year of the collected letters of Dylan Thomas, Joseph Conrad, and William Butler Yeats; the collected poems of William Carlos Williams and the stories of Ellison acquaintance Wright Morris; major biographies of Theodore Dreiser, Vladimir Nabokov, Wallace Stevens, William James, and "the young Hemingway," as well as Arnold Rampersad's prizewinning first volume of the life of Langston Hughes—for which Ellison had been interviewed extensively. Also, the "Freedom Movement," as Ellison still preferred to call it, was now producing its own corpus of scholarship. David Garrow's *Bearing the Cross*, a major study of Martin Luther King, Jr., and the Southern Christian Leadership Conference, which mentioned Ellison briefly, was published in close conjunction with an intriguing multiauthored historical analysis called *Why the South Lost the Civil War*. In addition, Ellison's still intense preoccupation with the vagaries of American social and legal historiography found common cause, but interpretive slants distinct from his own, in the release that year, too, of old New Liberal Arthur Schlesinger's *The Cycles of American History* and two books—Michael Kammen's *Machine That Would Go of Itself: The Constitution in American Culture* and

Forrest McDonald's *Novus Ordo Seculorum: The Intellectual Origins of the Constitution*—engaged provocatively in what Kenneth Burke had decades earlier dubbed "the dialectic of constitutions."

During the years when Ellison had been hard at work on *Invisible Man*, Schlesinger's 1949 Cold War missive *The Vital Center* had labored in concert with Reinhold Niebuhr's *The Nature and Destiny of Man* (2 volumes, 1941 and 1943) and Lionel Trilling's *The Liberal Imagination* (1950) to fabricate the postwar New Liberal ideology that Ellison had had to confront soon thereafter, against the backdrop of the mid-1950s Eisenhower doctrine and the onrushing civil rights movement. *Invisible Man*'s riffing philosophy of "history as boomerang" offered the same rebuff to schematic theorizing such as Schlesinger's that it had in 1952. But thirty years later the presidential historian was nevertheless now propelling his unrefurbished liberal centrism into the intensifying 1980s debates over multiculturalism and cultural pluralism that Ellison found himself also repeatedly addressing—with a voice again opposing New Liberal pieties about the anarchic, balkanizing dangers of diversity. Back in the 1950s Ellison's retort in "Society, Morality, and the Novel" to Trilling's and Schlesinger's racially evasive brand of Cold War liberalism had attacked on two flanks: against the liberal imagination's elevation of the Jamesian novel of manners over the more raucous imaginative currents Ellison navigated, and against Trilling's forebodings that the "death of the novel" was once again at hand if the high road to the novel of manners became the road not taken. Three decades later those issues were being reformulated for the 1980s in the growing furor around New Journalism impresario Tom Wolfe's heavily hyped and racially charged "comic novel of manners," *The Bonfire of the Vanities*, which had been appearing in installments of *Rolling Stone* magazine as *Going to the Territory* headed toward its release date (Wolfe, "Stalking" 54).

Since the 1970s Wolfe had been championing the rise of novelized journalism as a media movement that "would wipe out the novel as literature's main event"; and in that movement's manifesto anthology, *The New Journalism* (1973), he touted "nonfiction novels" by Joan Didion, Truman Capote, Norman Mailer, and Hunter Thompson as cases in point (3–52). Wolfe's own *Radical Chic and Mau-Mauing the Flak Catchers* (1970) had already advanced the New Journalism standard into territory that novelists who were enlisted instead in the disquieting movement for Black Art had staked out for themselves (Wolfe, "Stalking" 46). Not unexpectedly, Wolfe's acerbic images of Black Panther "Mau Maus" on the make in Park Avenue penthouses inflamed the increasingly nationalistic black literary circles of the moment. Though by 1986 the New Journalism had not yet come close to wiping the novel out, Wolfe's heavily marketed serialization (it would appear in book form in 1987 and as a film in 1990) was not quite a capitulation. Wolfe had repatriated into his own novelistic debut the self-same fictional techniques of social realism he had earlier ruthlessly appropriated for journalistic nonfiction: scene-by-scene construction, kinetic dialogue with precise class and ethnic inflections, vivid sensory images, and a potpourri of "everyday gestures, habits, manners, customs, styles of furniture, clothing, decoration, styles of traveling, eating, keeping house, modes of behaving toward children, servants, superiors, inferiors, peers, plus the various looks, glances, poses, styles of walking and other symbolic details that might exist within a scene" (Kellman 113–14). Critics routinely agreed that as a novel of manifest postmodern angst, *The Bonfire of the Vanities* was, if not wholly original, nonetheless a tour de force *pastiche* of panoramic Balzacian social observation, Thackerayan satire on the vanities of high and low society, and Trollopian psychological penetration—with a winking echo of the conclusion to Gustave Flaubert's *Madame Bovary* as a closing flourish in its final paragraph. None of the reviewers, however, noted what would have been unmistakable in any parallel reading of *Invisible Man*, that Wolfe had premised his whole enterprise on the self-same narrative omen of modern urban turmoil with which Ellison had opened his own first novel back in 1952: an unseeing and potentially murderous nighttime racial encounter on the streets of the great metropolis sets a prototypic white man, who imagines himself to be the victim of a prospective mugging, against a young black man of blossoming intellect and great expectations whose common humanity remains unperceivable in the face of the white man's unreasoning fear.

In the 1950s Ellison's elliptical prologue had averted the incipient murder and turned the misperceived encounter into the first of a series of illuminating, tragicomic epiphanies on the anonymous young black man's spiraling way through a landscape of racial antagonism, distorted sexual fantasy, and Machiavellian political intrigue. Ellison ultimately carried him and the novel's readers beyond the realm of social realism into a surreal,

Dostoyevskian psychological underground. In the 1980s Wolfe spun his neojournalistic novel of manners toward an alternative, more socially mobile destination. Taking the white "victim" of the imagined mugging as *his* protagonist, Wolfe instead made the murder a grisly and prolonged reality—with a Mercedes as the unlikely murder weapon and the prototypic young black man the comatose *corpus delicti*. Moreover, he made his anointed white hero-victim—a fortyish Wall Street bond trader who imagines himself "prince of Park Avenue" and "Master of the Universe"—an unself-conscious vehicle, subsequently, for a caricaturing dissection of the "Laboratory of Human Relations" Wolfe uncovered in West Side dinner parties, Midtown law firms, City Hall courtrooms, and Harlem and South Bronx storefront churches. In this terrain the spectre of overt racial conflict had worked its way out of the paranoiac underworld of white supremacist pulp fiction to become the omnipresent subtext—and a prime marketing asset—of Wolfe's aspiring Big New Social Novel. In a prologue stream of consciousness that reverses, by analogy, Ellison's sermon on "the blackness of blackness" and the Invisible Man's psychic descent into the Dantesque inferno of slavery, Wolfe's opening mindscape has the mayor of New York deliver a fervid soliloquy while being routed from a Harlem stage by demonstrators who represent the minions of what has become a postmodern urban inferno: fantasizing about rich white condominium dwellers safely watching the scene on television, the mayor shouts, "Do you really think this is *your* city any longer? Open your eyes! . . . Do you think money will keep it yours? Come down from your swell co-ops, you general partners and merger lawyers! It's the Third World down there! Puerto Ricans, West Indians, Haitians, Dominicans, Cubans, Colombians, Hondurans, Koreans, Chinese, Thais, Vietnamese, Ecuadorians, Panamanians, Filipinos, Albanians, Senegalese, and Afro-Americans! Go visit the frontiers, you gutless wonders!" (*Bonfire* 7).

As a publishing house property well aware of the book trade's blockbuster complex, Wolfe was facing—as Ellison also would if the unbirthed novel *Going to the Territory* supplanted were finally to come to print—a literary marketplace dominated multifariously by Stephen King's factory of formula horror fiction; Ann Rice's vampire sequels; the espionage and military adventure fiction of Robert Ludlum, John Le Carré, and Tom Clancy; the courtroom thrillers of Scott Thurow; and the "glitz novels" of

Jackie Collins, Danielle Steele, and Sidney Sheldon. Moreover, to access the video dreamscape of the directionless but moneyed urban and suburban young, publishers were energetically promoting a literary "brat pack" of twenty-something hotshot "yuppie" novelists who had emerged in tandem with their counterparts among Hollywood actors, directors, and screen-writers—all evincing the 1980s obsession with status, drugs, shopping-mall self-gratification, unentangled sex, and hyperbolic celebrity (Bondi 80, 82). The *Village Voice* had dubbed this 1980s novelistic upsurge "socialite real-ism" in a retrospective pun on that Stalinist/Trotskyite bone of literary contention—revolutionary *Socialist* Realism—which Ellison had encoun-tered as a "highly regarded theory" in the 1930s and 1940s and which he had struggled to come to terms with at the time (Graham and Singh 8).

Four decades later, deliberating the political and moral functions of the novel remained one of the primary clusters of concern voiced in *Going to the Territory*. That issue's importance for writers in the 1980s had been signaled a few years earlier when the publication of novelist John Gardner's *On Moral Fiction* (1978) precipitated a deeply divided reaction in the liter-ary world. That reaction was captured in part in a Gardner-William Gass debate in the pages of the *New Republic* and in a front-page forum of the *New York Times Book Review* (Chavkin 172–82). It pitted loyal but belea-guered aficionados of the character-driven "traditional novel," whose "premises on art and morality" Gardner presumably endorsed, against those architects of postmodern literary gamesmanship such as Gass. The fascination of the latter cohort with the narcotic possibilities of "crystal-line" linguistic sculpture left them indisposed, Gardner charged, to the ancient artistic imperatives of "clear moral effect," "valid models for imita-tion," "eternal verities," and a "benevolent vision of the possible which can inspire and incite human beings toward virtue, toward life affirmation as opposed to destruction or indifference" (Gardner 3–17). Gardner's philippic relied heavily on the classical and medieval models established by Homer and Dante but especially on the more modern example of the nineteenth-century Russian novel and the views in particular of Leo Tolstoy's *Chto takoye iskusstvo?* (1898; *What Is Art?*). There, the Russian master's late-in-life turn to social reform and a version of Christian anarchism expressed itself in an aesthetic system which gave the novel essentially religious and ethical responsibilities in the renovation of a debilitated social order. As such, with evangelist Jerry Falwell's archconservative "moral majority" regularly making headlines through its Bible-Belt calls to fundamentalist redemption, Gardner opponents such as John Barth had no difficulty associating *On Moral Fiction* with "a shrill pitch to the right" (Morace 1081).

Ellison had been on the frontlines in analogous circumstances during the 1950s, first in a 1955 symposium called "*What's Wrong with the American Novel?*" and shortly thereafter in the anthology of writerly missives for Old Left social realist Granville Hicks's *The Living Novel*, a post-Stalinist Cold War–era response to the "death of the novel" agitations that had been spawned by Lionel Trilling and the workings of the liberal imagination. As already noted, "Society, Morality, and the Novel" was Ellison's contribution to Hicks's collection, and it comprises the most extended of three related ruminations in *Going to the Territory* on the fate and function of the form to which Ellison had dedicated his life. Ellison's essay—which we have already examined at length—revealed marked continuities with John Gardner's moralist agenda but not with Gardner's air of authoritarian prescription, his constrained sense of the novel's inherited classicist traditions, nor his derogation of writers such as Saul Bellow, Joseph Heller, or Kurt Vonnegut. For them, as for Ellison, irony, satire, and tragicomedy were crucial novelistic tools—tools not so much of moral instruction as of secular revelation and of what Kenneth Burke calls "perspective by incongruity."

Tom Wolfe's foray into the novelistic arena posed an even more direct confrontation with Ellison's conscious moral thought, though no explicit record of this has surfaced in Ellison's public pronouncements. For, when Wolfe followed up the plotline initiated in *Rolling Stone* with a nonfiction provocation two years later in *Harper's* called "Stalking the Billion-Footed Beast: A Literary Manifesto for the New Social Novel," he simultaneously resurrected Ellison's old antagonist Lionel Trilling as a major player in the 1980s literary psychodrama. And Wolfe pushed the old familiar issues of Russian Social(ist) Realism front and center as recycling novelistic concerns. When questioned about which novelists influenced him and his journalistic approach to novels the most, Wolfe counted Balzac as his greatest discovery; and in the course of touting Philip Roth as his favorite living writer, he referred obliquely to Ellison as one of the living writers of note whose reputation had been put in limbo by an un-Balzacian want of prolificity (Scura 64–65).

With respect to the place of journalistic methods in the creative process, Ellison had believed since the 1940s that "the work of literature differs basically from reportage not merely in its presentation of a pattern of events, nor in its concern with emotion (for a report might well be an account of highly emotional events), but in the deep personal necessity which cries full-throated in the work of art and which seeks transcendence in the form of ritual" (*S&A* 55). Although Ellison made no direct mention of the current controversies in his new collection, both matters reverberated in *Going to the Territory*, where "Society, Morality, and the Novel" (which had been denied its appropriate place in *Shadow and Act* in 1964 by editorial considerations [Graham and Singh 334]) was finally being anthologized under Ellison's own imprimatur and where Ellison's decades-long engagement with Russian literature was on display in several essays. Though few of his readers or critics were aware of it, Ellison had served at Bard College during the late 1950s and early 1960s as a professor of Russian literature. Where the Anglophone creative and scholarly command of Russian literary traditions was concerned, he had far greater expertise indeed than either John Gardner or Tom Wolfe.

Like Gardner, Wolfe buttressed his appeal for novelistic reform with the example of nineteenth-century Russian Realist fiction—Tolstoy's *Anna Karenina* and Nikolay Gogol's *Dead Souls*, in particular—though major French and English figures such as Balzac, Zola, and William Thackeray furnished shock-troop support for his neo–Social Realist polemic. But where Gardner used Russian exemplars to bemoan the *moral* decadence and evasiveness of contemporary American writing, Wolfe used the canonical Russian Realists instead to charge American novelists since the 1960s with massive failures of will and of epic ambition, as well as with the loss of a reportorial sense of mission on behalf of the "real world." That world, Wolfe believed, had been abandoned for an "avant-garde position out beyond realism" by a damnable flood tide of Absurdist novels, Magical Realist novels, novels of Radical Disjunction, neo-Fabulist novels, Minimalist novels (by "K-Mart Realists" who write "about real situations, but very tiny ones"), and Puppet-Master novels "in love with the theory that the novel is, first and foremost, a literary game, words on a page being manipulated by an author" (Wolfe, "Stalking" 49–50). The philosophical quandaries over what constitutes "reality" and how it is to be represented in words get short shrift in Wolfe's manifesto. They are remanded to the soothing paradigms of Newtonian science and to tidy journalistic metaphors for information gathering, on the one hand—which presume reality to be conscious, concrete, and collectible—and to metaphors of engineering technology, on the other, in which "the introduction of realism into literature in the eighteenth century . . . was like the introduction of electricity into engineering. It was not just another device" (Wolfe, "Stalking" 50).

Ultimately for Wolfe, constructing the New Social Novel was an adjunct of the New Journalism, that is, an enterprise of collecting, juxtaposing, and combining linguistically photographable fragments of social experience into a grand reportorial pastiche. "I'm weighing whether this should be fiction or nonfiction, because everything in it is going to be based on a journalistic reality. The question to me is a completely technical one," he admitted to an interviewer in 1974 during the early stages of work on the novel (Scura 67). Fourteen years later, when the book was finally released— to the thunderous acclaim of conservative critics—he remained certain that "the future lies in realism and not in magic realism or metafiction or any of the other nonrealistic fashions of the past twenty years" (Scura 272). Russian scholar Mikhail Epstein noted afterwards that Wolfe's manifesto "makes a stunning impression on a reader from the Soviet Union or Eastern Europe": he found it an eerily unself-conscious American double for the midcentury state-sponsored Socialist Realism in the Soviet Union—right down to the combinatory logic and technological metaphors—that Joseph Stalin and his chief ideologue, Andrei Zhdanov, had imposed in 1934 on the fledgling Writers Union of the USSR as a preamble for the subsequent proliferation of pre–World War II Popular Front initiatives in Europe and America (Epstein 147–60). In Stalin's and Zhdanov's vision of Communist efficiency, writers were most properly "engineers of the soul," duty-bound to the state not to squander their scientific or managerial talents by turning away from reality toward "deviant," avant-garde spheres of fantasy and subjectivity. During the proselytizing spread of literary Stalinism in the Depression-torn 1930s, Ellison had been following the close-at-hand lead of mentors Richard Wright and Langston Hughes and the transcontinental example of André Malraux—all enlisted in support of revolutionary socialist ideals but all wrestling with their own "deviant" artistic tendencies. Ellison had undergone his literary novitiate at *New Masses* under such a regimen, as administered by Communist Party front organizations and "fellow travelers." So he was more than a little familiar with the rhetoric of socialist/socialite realism and the possibilities and perils of reportorial pastiche that Tom Wolfe was hawking decades later in the 1980s.

Not just Wolfe's New Social Novel, but his program for literary reform, too, bespoke the ascendancy of pastiche and its frames of dislocated reference as accompaniments of 1980s neo-Realism. Two years before *Going to the Territory* appeared, Marxist literary theoretician Frederic Jameson published a now famous essay in *New Left Review* titled "Postmodernism, or The Cultural Logic of Late Capitalism" in which pastiche loomed large as the distinguishing stylistic feature of 1980s culture and retrospection (Jameson 53–92). In Jameson's view, the pervasiveness of pastiche in postmodern society signaled the failure of originality and the loss of genuine historical sensibility. The 1980s wholesale reworkings of older period styles had become detached from any substantive understanding of the past, so that, instead of texts and cultural artifacts marking the recovery of true historical consciousness, they represented at most only our shibboleths and stereotypes about the past, our mere *gestures* toward conventions about the past rather than knowledgeable reconsiderations of those conventions. The longing for history may have been real, but history proper had been remade in the manufactured images of late capitalism. So the simulated recreations of an imagined past now pervaded architecture, painting, film, advertising, social theory, religion, language, literature, and pop music: Disneyland and Las Vegas provided prime examples, and tourist shrines, mirroring Reaganite politics and economics. As Ellison was well aware, African American culture, now no longer insulated from "mainstream" developments and social debilitations by the legal or extralegal force of segregation, was heeding the Zeitgeist. And it was no longer invisible.

In 1982, the year Random House released a special thirtieth anniversary edition of *Invisible Man*, Ellison acknowledged in a *Playboy* interview that his novel's controlling metaphor for race relations in America no longer obtained. There was no way, he said, "given the history of the past 30 or 40 years, for it to be the same as it was then" (Graham and Singh 383). Americans, black and white or other, were much more aware now "that American culture is part African" and were presumably more at ease with that fact, to which he added the corroborating evidence that, while he was listening to Olivia Newton John on the radio that morning, she had sounded triumphantly "like a young Diana Ross" (Graham and Singh 383). Far more dramatic demonstrations of a postinvisibility cross-racial symbiosis were in the offing, however: first and foremost with the release that year by Michael Jackson, late of the Motown Jackson Five, of his album *Thriller*, from which six of nine cuts became hits on the way to making it the best-selling album of all time and making Jackson what *Time* magazine called a "one man rescue team for the record business" (Bondi 86). On video Jackson's perfectly choreographed and costumed pastiche of old-time spins, glides, hip rolls, and 1960s James Brown moonwalks reconfigured the industry's MTV visual style and strategy. The 40 million copies charged to Michaelmania enabled Jackson by 1986 to spin off $40 million to buy ATV music and the rights to some 250 songs written by John Lennon and Paul McCartney (Bondi 33, 86–87). The surreptitious, increasingly technologized vernacular hybridity that Ellison had proclaimed in *Shadow and Act* during the 1960s to be the main vector of American cultural innovation had, by the 1980s, outstripped his most sweeping prognostications. Coupled with the meteoric rise of *The Cosby Show* to the top of the TV ratings in the 1986–87 season and the simultaneous crossover explosion of rap music in the wake of Queens-based Run-D.M.C.'s platinum triumph with their album *Raisin' Hell*, black American culture's high visibility was no longer simply the self-contradiction it had seemed to be in the 1950s era of *Ozzie and Harriet* or *Leave It to Beaver*. But if *The Cosby Show* recapitulated the forms and formulas of the 1950s white family sitcom in the image of the black bourgeoisie and if the sampling, mixing, and scratching modalities of the hip-hop sound seemed to embody Jameson's deracinated rearrangement of a fragmented past into addictive simulations, then Ellison's modernist projection in *Invisible Man* of black street-corner hipsters as potentially "the bearers of something precious" (*IM* 333) had become, perhaps, one more source of postmodern mirage.

Perhaps understandably, Ellison's publisher did not market his new nonfiction collection as a postmodern happening of any sort or as a book with any particular pertinence to contemporary concerns, but rather as a long-awaited "companion volume" to the collection he had published two decades earlier. The prepublication blurbs, book-jacket text, and artwork for *Going to the Territory* bespoke the author's quiet dignity, cosmopolite associations, and mature *Vanity Fair* elegance—all of which were capsulized photographically in the back-cover image of Ellison seated nonchalantly in his study, one arm angled upward and akimbo, while attired in dark suit, tie, and breast-pocket handkerchief, beneath a mounted figurine of African sculpture. Now an elder statesman of African American letters and an apparently undaunted survivor of Black Arts internecine warfare, Ellison had earned the right, the iconography implied, to the poised retrospection the new collection embodied. The book's title, the jacket made clear, referenced explicitly the Ivy League academic symposium at Brown University— the 1979 Ralph Ellison Festival—for which Ellison's autobiographical address had provided a controlling theme: the movement of artistic spirit toward imaginative freedom. What readers would find between the covers of *Going to the Territory*, then, was a backward glance over familiar territory, a sign of continuity and a source of assurance about the old canon of humanist values that the elegant, brown-skinned author shared now, by popular consensus, with a many-hued audience of like-minded Americans.

A less nostalgic marketing concept might just as easily have focused, as this chapter does in part, on the nuanced discontinuities between *Shadow and Act* and its new companion that gave *Going to the Territory* alternative relevance: the absence this time of an orienting introduction to announce the author's vantage points in time and conceptual space, as well as personal development; the decisive way that the opener, "The Little Man at Chehaw Station," directs the initial locus of concern away now from the artist, the creative process, and the primacy of craft toward the imagined audience instead and the pragmatic social problem of cultural pluralism; the shifts in thematic emphasis and rhetorical strategy, for example, that are on display in "An Extravagance of Laughter," as made possible by racial realignments of the national political equation over three decades. The discontinuities included also the backstory of the 1970s and 1980s "culture wars" over institutionalized multiculturalism that an essay like "What America Would Be Like without Blacks" anticipates. They highlighted the lingering tensions over the divisive legacy of the Vietnam War and the age of Black Power that surfaces in "The Myth of the Flawed White Southerner" and "If the Twain Shall Meet." They implicated the unresolved quest for leadership in social policy and cultural redefinition that is broached in "What These Children Are Like." Noteworthy too as points of demarcation were the jurisprudential reorientation dramatized in "Perspective of Literature"; the more intimate perspective on the author himself—his underlying attitudes and emotional experiences, past and present—for which *Going to the Territory* provides flashes of intended and inadvertent revelation in "Portrait of Inman Page" and the title essay; the turn in general away from musicologically oriented cultural criticism toward the rhetorical or dramatistic—excepted only by "Homage to Duke Ellington on His Birthday"; and finally, the radically altered literary scene in which, by the implications of its own design, the new book would be received.

As has become clearer, too, in retrospect, literary realignments around gender, generational cohorts, and nationality in the black literary world had substantively reconfigured the contexts in which new creative or critical works by black writers would be addressed. By the mid-1980s the male-centered warrior ethos of the Black Arts Movement had been driven from frontline media coverage—though many of its most singular voices were only now reaching full maturity—in favor of a black feminist literary upsurge of oppositional "womanist" distinction. Moreover, after a decade and a half of intense proselytizing in poetry, drama, and short fiction, the aging streetwise apostles of Black Power and the Black Aesthetic now faced, in turn, an onrushing self-proclaimed "post-Black Power" generation of young suburban-bred, college-trained "cultural mulattoes," who began espousing a "*New* Black Aesthetic" rooted consciously in postmodern parody and pastiche and who made the Black Arts Movement itself a primary target. Moreover, on the international scene, the continuing global ferment from political decolonization on the African continent, which supplied much of the self-conscious *negritude* of Black Arts culture building, had been successfully converted by African artists themselves into an expanding orbit of imaginative self-exploration that finally asserted a commanding presence of its own in 1986 through Wole Soyinka's acceptance of the Nobel Prize for Literature. Ellison had been neither unaware of nor indifferent to such developments.[3] But their impact on him had remained largely unspoken in his own published observations, at the same time that his own work and reputation had become an unquiet but quizzical touchstone.

Toni Morrison, for instance, who had published four novels and was at work on her fifth, *Beloved*, when *Going to the Territory* appeared, had acknowledged *Invisible Man* long since as a work that influenced her

powerfully—as both a worthy example and a point of reaction. In the
1970s she had critiqued as authoritarian and inauthentic the Black Arts
Movement efforts to fabricate, *ex nihilo*, a revolutionary cosmology and
mythology for African American literature. In 1974 in *Black World* she had
announced plans for a multifaceted, multigenerational "Black Book" modeled instead on the collective recovery of ancestral memory and a communal reclamation project of rigorous folkloric archaeology closely akin
to what Ellison had sketched out in *Shadow and Act* (Morrison, "Behind"
87–89). Morrison fulfilled her vision for that work of communal recovery,
in part, by shepherding *The Black Book* promptly to publication that year.
But her growing conviction that major male voices in the black literary
canon kept women peripheral and out of memory fueled her other creative
contestations. The lack of central, affirming female presences in Ellison's
fiction became the juncture at which her own novelistic imperatives
diverged from what she saw of his. In a 1981 interview, she confessed that,
although preoccupied with books by great black novelists of the past, she
"always missed some intimacy, some direction, some voice. Ralph Ellison
and Richard Wright—all of whose books I admire enormously—I didn't
feel were telling *me* something. I thought they were saying something about
it or *us* that revealed something about *us* to *you* to others, to white people, to men" (Taylor-Guthrie 96). So for Morrison, as for other dissenting
members of the Black Arts generation, the body of Ellison's work, both his
fiction and his cultural criticism, became a visible high ground for testing,
differentiating, and defining each writer's own distinctive stances—though
Ellison's mastery of creative technique and aesthetic theory were rarely
challenged in the process. Morrison's first novel, *The Bluest Eye* (1970), had
in fact focused its revisionary feminist energies on key episodes of *Invisible
Man*—the famous Trueblood family incest episode most notably. Critics
would subsequently demonstrate, through comparisons with Morrison's
Breedlove family, that she had reimagined Ellison's episode on terms of her
own, giving her analogues to the silent female victims and their supporters
in Ellison's original scenario the central voices and controlling perspectives within her own novelistic recreation (Awkward 81–87; Duvall 242,
246–48).

Ishmael Reed made the pattern of testy symbiosis even more explicit,
more expansive, and more studied. A mantic postmodernist and master of

"Neo-Hoodoo" pastiche who became a formidable polemicist in his own right, he too had framed *his* first novel, *The Freelance Pallbearers* (1972), in part as a series of parodic riffs on *Invisible Man*. The scenes in Ellison's text of the grandfather's riddling deathbed admonitions, of the narrator's expulsion from college, of Jim Trueblood's wailing blues soliloquy, of the Invisible Man's recruitment into a treacherous cabal after giving a stirring speech—the stages of his painful discovery of his own invisibility—are all yoked into a chain of mocking Neo-Hoodoo recapitulation in Reed's initial effort to fabricate his own divergent fictional cosmology (Fox 40–41). A corollary chain of Ellisonian entanglement surfaced outside the images of fiction, in Reed's stormy reactions to Ellison's unapologetic public jabs against the technical deficiencies of the "obscenely second-rate" agitprop writing so often associated with the young Black Arts Movement. In a parodic self-interview Reed conducted with himself in 1974, he denounced Ellison's complaints as superficial and challenged writers of his own generation to do an interview with the older man "in which he is pressed to say exactly what he means about lack of craftsmanship, giving specifics, examples and suggestions—I mean . . . that way he would be performing a wise service to these young authors" (Dick and Singh 66–67). Reed would take up himself the challenge from his self-interview and, in the aforementioned company of Steve Cannon and Quincy Troupe in 1977, undertook one of the most revealing engagements with Ellison ever conducted. Ellison obliged willingly and expansively. When he was "pressed" about formative influences from his 1930s and 1940s immersion in radical politics and its tense mix of black and Jewish writers and rival ideologies, Ellison divulged more about the attendant complexities of developing an independent creative *vision* and a comprehensive cultural *perspective* than his interrogators could have anticipated (Graham and Singh 342–77).

This "service" to the younger generation helped Reed push one step farther. As Black Arts proselytizer Larry Neal had done a few years before in *Black World*'s 1970 special issue on Ellison, Reed consulted Harold Cruse's cautionary left-wing chronicle, *The Crisis of the Negro Intellectual* (1967), as a guide to the Stalinist-Trotskyite milieu Ellison had traversed. Reed turned next to Norman Podhoretz's memoir *Making It* (1967) and William Barrett's *The Truants* (1982), in which the modernist movement that championed Freudianism, Marxism, and Existentialism is demystified and dissected from within, to understand the New Liberal and neoconservative strains of Cold War anticommunism adopted by the ex-Stalinist New York Jewish circles Ellison moved among during the postwar incubation of *Invisible Man*. In an interview a few months before Reed released his seventh novel, *Reckless Eyeballing*—it too published in company with *Going to the Territory* in 1986—Reed worked out an interpretive stance on Ellisonian modernism that affirmed *Invisible Man* as "a fine book" but one whose modernist values had appealed (without authorial premeditation) to the impure motives of *Partisan Review* and *Commentary* "aesthetic traditionalists." In Reed's view, they had promoted Ellison's novel all the way to the National Book Award because, behind closed doors, "they like[d] the anti-Stalinism, the impotent first person, the incest, and the satire of Rastafarianism" (Dick 246). Acknowledging *Invisible Man* as a worthy winner nonetheless, Reed took issue with Ellison primarily because his satire of the Rastas was strategically "misdirected": though Ellison joked about the Rastafarian movement, that movement was nevertheless worldwide, still growing, and had outlived modernism—so the joke was more properly on modernism's Freudian, Marxist, and existentialist champions. Nevertheless, in *Reckless Eyeballing*, where Reed parodies black wannabe art and relationships caught up in the murderous hyperbole of feminist excess, he worked carefully beneath the surface of his tale to dramatize a reading of the Jewish-black symbiosis under political crisis that aligned itself with the readings Ellison and then Cruse had pioneered. Although reviewers of *Reckless Eyeballing* would focus almost exclusively on the book's *roman à clef* provocations regarding Alice Walker and Ntozake Shange (who provide readily decipherable targets of caricature), for Reed himself the womanists had been secondary targets in a novel that was "basically about the parallelism between the Jewish and Afro-American experiences": their analogous roles as scapegoats in Nazi Germany and Jim Crow America, the parallel sexualization of the "racial" threat in Nazi and white supremacist ideologies, the genocidal propensities latent in both host societies (Dick 254).

Like Ishmael Reed, Charles Johnson began his multidimensioned career as novelist, screenwriter, cartoonist, historian, and philosopher under the aegis of Black Arts working principles—especially those proclaimed by Ellison's still antipathetic antagonist from *Shadow and Act*, Amiri Baraka. But Johnson's deep attraction also to Edmund Husserl's phenomenology, to Zen Buddhist meditation, and to fabulistic experiment drew him away from the constraining environs of Baraka's programmatic Black Aesthetic toward less encumbered terrain. A student of John Gardner at Southern Illinois University, Johnson had produced his first novel, an allegorized *bildungsroman* titled *Faith and the Good Thing* (1974), which critics immediately saw as a regendered counterpart to *Invisible Man*. By 1980 Johnson had published in *Obsidian*, one of the few surviving Black Arts literary journals, a manifesto calling for a new "philosophical Black fiction—art that *interrogates* experience" ("Philosophy"). Ostensibly, such fiction would pursue "a fresh encounter with Black life," an encounter that would be stripped of constraining formulas and racial presuppositions and for which Ellison's *Invisible Man*, Richard Wright's *The Outsider*, and Cyrus Colter's *The Hippodrome* were almost the only methodological models. Among Husserl's philosophical disciples, Johnson singled out especially the German phenomenologist and philosophical anthropologist Max Scheler as a hermeneutic guide. Scheler had been an idealistic "Personalist," in addition—a tradition whose American transcendentalist practitioners included Walt Whitman and Bronson Alcott—and he had been particularly concerned with the *modes* by which the questing human consciousness differentiates between truth and falsity, the possible and the impossible. In the fictive world Ellison had created, which was "without boundaries, . . . a vast seething, hot world of fluidity," Johnson saw the closest approach yet in black writing to that particular mode of revealing ultimate truths— the "saying that is showing"—which Scheler calls "alethia" (C. Johnson, "Philosophy" 57). Johnson had published his own alethian masterwork, *Oxherding Tale*, in 1982, a genre-bursting, metafictional, cross-cultural fusion of Zen parable, phenomenological comedy, and nineteenth-century slave narrative. Moreover, to the corpus of texts linked genealogically to Ellison that clustered around *Going to the Territory* in 1986, Johnson added a vanguard collection of eight gnomic fables, *The Sorcerer's Apprentice: Tales and Conjurations*, which reconfigured science fiction, horror story, Oriental enigma, Kantian transcendentalism, conjure-lore mysticism, and DuBoisian double-consciousness into a stream of startling and witty fictive meditations on enduring philosophical issues. When Johnson became, in 1993, the first black male after Ellison to win the National Book Award, he devoted his acceptance speech largely to lauding Ellison's creative and critical vision as the model upon which his own ontological adventure in the prize-winning *Middle Passage* was based.

With so many ties to the works of other writers clustered about it on publication, *Going to the Territory* should hardly have been considered in isolation—as if it were engaged in conversation only with its companion-ate predecessor. Yet that was precisely what happened in the hands of most evaluators. By comparison with the reception of *Shadow and Act* in 1964, the new book was even more widely reviewed—on both sides of the literary color line. The dozens of notices in newspapers and periodicals across the country routinely acknowledged many of the thematic continuities between the two volumes. Reviewers noted almost universally Ellison's unifying emphasis on the primacy and moral responsibility of art and the artist in a still evolving democratic society. They reiterated his continuing insistence on the irrepressibility and underground vitality of black vernacular culture and its suprapolitical shaping force on the development of a genuine cultural pluralism in American society—regardless of ongoing policy disputes among the political directorate about how best to accommodate or countermand it. Many reviewers paid close attention also to what seemed more apparent now as an anti-Manichaean strain in Ellison's broader vision: his both/and, rather than either/or, perspective on cultural, moral, and political issues such as segregation and integration and its alliance in his social philosophy with an implicit valuation of "mulatto" hybridity over the static notions of racial or artistic purity that he derided as "blood magic" and "blood thinking." Radiating from the title essay outward, Ellison's affirmation of ancient Greek concepts championed by Heraclitus—that "geography is fate" and that the essence of human experience is not stability and order but flux and constant change—regularly caught reviewers' eyes also, together with the way Ellison insistently linked these notions to the possibilities and limitations of individual choice while using his own autobiographical meditations as prima facie evidence. At yet another level of abstraction, scholarly reviewers in particular paid attention to Ellison's unabating "humanist" commitment to literary means of perceiving and expressing experience over against the statistical and morphological workings of the "sociological imagination."

But despite these consensual understandings about Ellison's second nonfiction assemblage, intriguing contrasts in fact also emerged, particularly in the altered racial dynamics of literary response. Where *Shadow and Act* had gone largely unnoticed in the black press and in the commentary of major African American literary figures, *Going to the Territory* garnered wide attention now from both vectors of the black literary world. But whereas *Shadow and Act* had characteristically undergone an exacting scrutiny of its author's political militancy in the few instances when the black press had in fact taken notice, black reviewers of the new book focused primarily on Ellison's cultural and aesthetic concerns, his cross-generational appeal, and his legacy for the future. Although *Shadow and Act* had been entertained by liberal white reviewers—Irving Howe, Robert Penn Warren, and Norman Podhoretz the highest placed among them—as a welcome respite from the "more hysterical proclamations" coming from the pens of 1960s black incendiaries, white reviewers of *Going to the Territory* seemed more inclined now than their black counterparts to interrogate Ellison's known political affiliations, or alleged lack thereof, in order to measure his active engagement in the continuing cause of freedom. But then, too, Ellison's white reviewers now appeared to have greater conscious stakes in African American culture generally than their predecessors had a generation earlier.

Despite whatever literary realignments had taken place, the most revealing commentaries on *Going to the Territory*, from both sides of a blurring color line, seemed less interested in striking poses than in striking up a conversation with the book's author on his chosen topics of perennial, peculiarly American interest. In the interest again of expanding the contextual sphere of these conversations and giving Ellison's Burkean allegiances "dramatistic play," we can see their revelations working strategically both ways. Louis Menand, reviewing the book in the *New Republic*, for instance, prefaced his remarks with an expansive effort to put Ellison's writings as a whole in multiple contexts and "lines of filiation." He did so first by putting Ellison's social philosophy about the problem of the one-and-the-many decidedly at odds with two forms of idealization: "the progressive's idealization of America, based on a vision of self-subsistent subcultures cohabiting in Platonic bliss" and "the reactionary's idealization based on a myth of ethnic purity" (Menand, "Literature" 37). With rare judiciousness Menand located Ellison's view of the relative autonomy or interdependence of African American literary culture on an historical continuum that stretches from Sterling Brown and Arthur P. Davis in the 1940s to Albert Murray in the 1960s, Robert Stepto and Henry Louis Gates in the 1970s, and Werner Sollors more recently. He balanced Ellison's cultural standing and public influence between his extraordinary access to powerful cultural institutions, on the one hand, and his adopted persona as an austere and solitary icon on the other.

If Menand proceeded to assign Ellison at one pass to the sociable intellectual traditions of American pragmatism and at another to a reclusive world of self-referencing "parables of possibility" akin to William Wordsworth's, it was in part because the reviewer's own intellectual orientations asserted themselves. The role of T. S. Eliot's *The Waste Land* as a key object of discovery in Ellison's literary novitiate, which was reiterated in *Going to the Territory*, converged readily enough with Menand's preoccupations in his own *Discovering Modernism: T. S. Eliot and His Context*, the book he published just a few months after—though Menand's stern reading there of Eliot as an opportunistic nineteenth-century Victorian in twentieth-century dress jars with Ellison's own vernacularized version of Eliot as partly a whiteface minstrel man performing "that Shakespeherian Rag." Menand saw Ellison's ideas about the function of the novel in American democracy as a latter day version of Matthew Arnold's optimistic faith in culture as a bulwark against anarchy and conservative reaction. And he interpreted the constitutional theory of America that Ellison ratified at several turns in *Going to the Territory* as a counterpart to the theory broached in E. L. Doctorow's essay "A Citizen Reads the Constitution," which serves as a coda for the anthology of anti-Reaganite scholarly assaults on "the jurisprudence of original intent" that Menand was then coediting in response to Ronald Reagan's roiling 1987 nomination of "strict constructionist" Robert Bork to the U. S. Supreme Court (Menand, *America in Theory* 281–97). The reviewer's conversation with Ellison, in other words, implicated wider circles of exchange and engagement, which remained pertinent, if unspoken, in the review.

Similarly, Robert Farnsworth's review of *Going to the Territory* in the *Kansas City Star* implicated a broader and more engaging dialogue than the conversation at hand made explicit. Two years earlier, Farnsworth had published a 1984 biography of Melvin Tolson, the extraordinary Texas and Oklahoma poet-professor and Harlem chronicler whom Ellison had first encountered back in the Southwest in 1931 and later as an "adulatory" Marxist and fellow Harlem radical in the 1940s (Jackson, *Ralph Ellison* 77, 317). Their Harlem exchanges had taken place while Tolson's abstract Communist enthusiasms were at an apex, and Ellison's and Richard Wright's in stages of activist disillusion. Farnsworth's review portrayed the Ellison of the 1980s less like Menand's optimistic purveyor of autobiographical parables than as an embattled polemicist, one whose collected missives readers should regard not as scattered notes or rationalizations but as "an extended explanation of the cultural position of the author of *Invisible Man*" (Farnsworth, "Ralph Ellison Still Working" 8). Ellison had a *position* to elaborate, Farnsworth asserted, "a substantial, thoroughly considered critical base for his novel," which, he insisted, *Going to the Territory* consistently defends, whether Ellison employed warm personal anecdotes, such as those about pianist-professor Hazel Harrison in "The Little Man at Chehaw Station," or edgy psychohistorical excavations, such as that in "An Extravagance of Laughter," the extended meditation linking the rituals of lynching and of American theatrical comedy that he composed expressly for the new book. Farnsworth's image of Ellison as combative partisan reflected in part the view of Ellison through Tolson's eyes, which Farnsworth had quoted at length in his biography.

The relationship between the two writers had been breached, sadly, a few months before Tolson's death in 1966 at an American Academy of Arts and Letters reception honoring the renowned poet, where he felt himself slighted in some unspoken way by Ellison. Tolson had afterward sketched some ambivalent personal notes about the occasion, which expressed both his resentment over what he saw as an ideological wall grown up between them *and* his acid critique of Ellison's literary politics and personal loyalties:

> The Brotherhood in *I. M.* is defeatist. . . . I knew Ellison when he was a
> Communist and have been to his flat. . . . Both of us were in the radical movement
> years ago. He and I understood Negro society as no other writers do. I can read
> between the lines. He can't get involved in the Negro movement. The ideological
> battle is the most bitter and devastating battle there is. Ex-Communist turns
> on Communist. Ellison knows that I know; but he knows I cannot be bought.
> I haven't changed; he has. . . . He is an individualist. I am a social writer. Ellison
> claims he is a descendant of Emerson. He says the Negro endures; I say he

advances. He and I have debated long. I don't want to write an Alger story of a Negro who succeeded. I have a social approach to man's problems. (Farnsworth, *Melvin B. Tolson* 299)

Though Farnsworth did not pause over Tolson's bizarre allusion to *Invisible Man* as "an Alger story of a Negro who succeeded," he had otherwise documented the matter with scrupulous scholarship in the Tolson biography: he took careful notice there of the sincere letter of condolence Ellison had written Tolson's widow after his death and the absence therein of any indication that Ellison was ever aware of Tolson's unvoiced anger. But the scholarly assessment, in Farnsworth's authorial voice, let his vexed subject cast the final verdict: that, unlike Tolson, Ellison had not kept faith with his radical past (Farnsworth, *Melvin B. Tolson* 300). Following suit, Farnsworth's review of *Going to the Territory*, straining for detachment, treated Ellison's book in decidedly neutral tones—as cool, calculating, self-protective polemicism.

With no such biographical entanglements, Eric Lott's review, the last in the glance here outside African American literary circles, set *Going to the Territory* in yet another sphere of context and filiation—at the juncture of New Left and hip-hop generation rumination, where the Tolson backstory still held anecdotal sway and where the conversations with literary texts, old and new, took place in a "fresh" vernacular idiom Ellison surely understood but just as surely did not speak. The title for Lott's review, "Home-Boy Ralph E. Stakes Out His Turf," signaled the new subcultural locus, and the reviewer's opening salvo looked back into the "stone cold" eye with which Harlem Writers Guild headman John O. Killens had "trashed *Invisible Man* on its appearance in 1952 because, with its fantastic collection of Toms, pimps, perverts and robotic communists, it did not live up to the demands of respectable socialist realism" (Lott, "Home-Boy"). Lott outflanked this particular audience's conventional leftist notions, however, with the challenging consideration that, "problem is, Ellison's a cusp figure, a writer who came of age between the 'revolutionary' '30s and the 'formalist' '40s, and his writings betray certain contradictions generated in part by that history." Lott theorized that Ellison had not shifted from one commitment to another, as Killen and Tolson and countless partisans on the left had long maintained, so much as "absorb both and transcend them, moving beyond the white-inspired dualisms of protest, yet grounding his ideas of art in the rituals and myths of an often oppressive society." Ellison's aesthetics may have veered "skyward of sociology or politics," but art and culture had remained for him "profoundly social expressions of the human realities, including race, in which they're embedded." Ellison wore the unavoidable contradictions, Lott surmised, in various creative and critical masks that enabled everyone to have their own Ellison. But despite his "e-pluribus ruminations" and constant invocations of the holy American text, the Constitution, facile attempts to dismiss Ellison as an "assimilationist" could not stand.

From such a perspective, *Going to the Territory* became a defensible sally in Ellison's ongoing definitional efforts to keep a cutting edge on his "improbably optimistic assessments of the fluidity and 'randomness' of American life." Ellison's "mythological" version of America as a "culture-of-cultures," fusing minority contributions into a miscegenated whole through the "unconscious logic of the democratic process" and "vernacular revolt," had important elements of truth, Lott conceded, but remained "a dangerous kind of idealism" in the face of resurgent racism on college campuses and urban street corners. Lott proceeded to track some of the apparent fissures in Ellison's mythos to the disjunctions between his more programmatic statements about macrocultural processes, on the one hand, and the intricate, overriding analyses he offered, on the other, of concrete cultural circumstances entangled in "the pressures, obstacles and limits stemming from American race relations." On balance, the interpretive advantage seemed clearly on Ellison's side, as in those essays from *Going to the Territory*, such as "What These Children Are Like," where he first explodes sociological misnomers such as "cultural deprivation" as imposed blindly on resource-strapped black urban communities and then targets in reverse the experiential impoverishment of materially privileged suburban cultures habituated to psychotherapy and social insulation. Ultimately, Lott housed Ellison with W. E. B. DuBois as a social thinker and unrelenting apostle of African American resilience. In the wake of this exchange with Ellison, Lott turned his analytical attention to the upsurge of "socialite realism" in the hip-hop fiction of Trey Ellis and the New Black Aestheticians and subsequently to the dialectics of "love and theft" in the rituals of blackface minstrelsy among white, male, working-class audiences. He affixed himself unapologetically to Ellison's lines of filiation and declared Ellison's vernacular theorizing to be as indispensable to his own working scholarship as he concluded *Going to the Territory* was "to anybody's theory of American culture" (Lott, "Hip-Hop" 691–92).

Taken together, these representative engagements with Ellison's conscious thought by Louis Menand, Richard Farnsworth, and Eric Lott marked a clear advance over the stances of white reviewers who had confronted *Shadow and Act* in the 1960s. They were less transfixed by the impasses in "race relations" at the moment and more able to focus their attentions on what Ellison thought about the enduring dynamics of the nation's whole cultural pattern and trajectory or his assumptions about the comprehensive shaping force of African American cultural creativity and the surreptitious power of cross-racial symbiosis. Ellison's vernacular theories and his deflation of the reigning sociological postulation of hegemonic "Anglo-conformity" were no longer to be dismissed as "hyperbolic" and "absurd," as they had been by several white critics confronting *Shadow and Act*. Ellison's particular brand of "melting-pottery" might still be regarded skeptically, as idealist mythologizing, by left-leaning critics like Lott. But now the conceptual underpinnings were assumptions to be modified, not disregarded.

For African American reviewers of *Going to the Territory*, the stakes of the conversation with Ellison differed dramatically. Where black writers and scholars had been almost "invisible" in the response to *Shadow and Act*, a decided reversal had taken place that now gave high visibility to black literary notables as arbiters of Ellison's literary achievements. Among the commentators assigned to gauge Ellison's new book, Julius Lester reviewed it for the *Boston Globe*, David Bradley for the *Los Angeles Times*, John Edgar Wideman for the *New York Times*, Leon Forrest for the *Chicago Tribune*, and Cyrus Colter for the *Chicago Sun-Times*. Collectively, they lent credence to claims made at the outset of the decade by historian John Hope Franklin about a new generational synthesis. In his foreword for Michael Harper and Robert Stepto's decade-defining anthology *Chant of Saints: A Gathering of Afro-American Literature, Art, and Scholarship* (1979), Franklin asserted that the nation was now at the cutting edge of "the most productive period in the history of Afro-American literature and culture" (x). *Chant of Saints*, he thought, would eventually be recognized as probably the most significant of all the successors to Alain Locke's Harlem Renaissance anthology, *The New Negro*. Indeed, *Chant* had modeled and marketed itself as such, in marked contrast to LeRoi Jones's and Larry Neal's Black Arts Movement anthology, *Black Fire* (1967), a decade earlier. In the pages of Harper and Stepto's "epic and familial poem," Franklin had glimpsed a world "not of street scholars and gypsy artists but of college and university-based professionals—to an extent not possible in any previous period of Afro-American history" (qtd. in J. Wright, "Chimed Chants" 218). They had not yet, and were not likely to become, a black leisure class of scholars and literati devoted exclusively to the arts, the pure love of learning, and the corollary influence of public opinion—the class whose absence sociologist Kelly Miller had bemoaned in *The New Negro*. But the "air of security, if not solidarity and self-esteem, if not chauvinism" that Franklin saw in their work signaled the death of the defensive posture and the move toward grandeur in African American art that those prophesying a black "New Land" foresaw at the beginning of the 1970s (Foreword ix–xi). Devoid of the rebellious optimism and mani-festo mood that energized the insurgencies of the 1920s and the 1960s alike but armed with a tough-minded skepticism, with a more flexibly Africa-conscious cultural nationalism distilled from two decades of black intellec-tual ferment and with the whole array of postmodern critical and creative techniques, they now comprised what Ishmael Reed called "an invasion of creative gangsters"—and they were making off with the prizes: Pulitzer Prizes, National Book Awards, National Endowment for the Humanities fellowships, distinguished artist chairs, poet laureateships.

Though none of the womanist icons Reed satirized in *Reckless Eyeballing* surfaced among the reviewers of *Going to the Territory*, the con-tingent of Julius Lester, David Bradley, John Wideman, Leon Forrest, and Cyrus Colter represented important facets of the new literary dispensa-tion. As if to suggest that the "priest-governed" leadership tradition that DuBois once decried might now be rechanneling its energies into secular-ized inspiration, three of them—Lester, Bradley, and Forrest—were either sons of black ministers or "highly churched." But each of these three lit-erary careers betray aspects of a widening reaction against ancestral black religious orthodoxies that was evident in Ellison's work as well. The reso-lute secularity behind Ellison's widespread deployments of the rhetoric of religion suggests some common ground of reaction, particularly within this threesome of his reviewers: in Lester's iconoclastic journey from civil rights Christian activism to religious experimentation and then Jewish conversion at midlife (A. Johnson, "Julius Lester" 138–41); in Bradley's turn away from his family's multigenerational tradition of ministerial vocation toward insistently secular concerns (Metzger); and in Forrest's deflection away from Baptist and Catholic parental affiliations to extended literary service with the Nation of Islam (Andrews, Foster, and Harris 293). But more pertinent to Ellison's frames of reference, all five had become literary professionals in whose lives public political activism, like religion, was subordinated to the specific demands of that literary profession. All, to one degree or another, had found institutional bases in colleges or universities. Several had won major literary prizes—Bradley, Lester, Wideman. Four of them publicly acknowledged Ellison as a significant literary influence. And one, Cyrus Colter, a generational peer of Ellison, shared his Russophile enthusiasms. But what may have mattered most in framing these reviewing exchanges was a shared dedication to constructing—on a scale without precedent in black literary life—panoramic, pangenerational fictions of African American historical experience in the form of novelistic trilogies, topical series, Faulknerian regional sagas, folklore cycles, and the like. The kind of epic ambition Tom Wolfe found wanting in so many other contemporary American novelists bloomed here in profusion. And for most of these writers the precedents Ellison set had been germinal.

Not for Julius Lester, however: he opened his review of *Going to the Territory* by citing Ellison as a puzzling anomaly in literary life, both because no other American had acquired so "great a reputation on such a small body of work" and because, despite being admitted to the "hallowed realm" of literary greats, "he has had no influence on the writers, black or white, of succeeding generations" (Lester, "Quiet Power" A13). Lester quickly backed away from this categorical canard by admitting James Alan McPherson as an exception. But the puzzle remained. *Invisible Man* was indeed, he concurred, "one of the most masterfully crafted novels of 20th century American literature." Yet—and here he spoke clearly for himself— "most black male writers, at least, have sought to continue the literary tradition of Richard Wright, James Baldwin, and Amiri Baraka." Evidencing no earlier contact with Ellison's critical ideas, Lester's encounter with *Going to the Territory* became apparently a voyage of discovery on which, he wrote, "cool," "elegant" essays free of angry introspection "sparkle with intelligence"; and "the subtlety of Ellison's mind is a joy to experience"

("Quiet Power" A13). The Ellison that Lester discovered so belatedly differed not only from other black intellectuals but from his white counterparts, too, "in his refusal to be an ideologue." Ellison was not a radical or a liberal or a conservative either, Lester concluded, but—if he was to be categorized at all—"much more the man-of-letters, who believes in the primacy of literature and, in particular, the novel." However, in a time when, from his own perspective, the Enlightenment traditions of liberal and socialist humanism alike were being exploded and deconstructed, Lester found the unapologetic humanist faith of "Society, Morality and the Novel" a "startling statement to be presented with." Startling, but not compelling: that the novel was to Ellison "the most articulate art form for defining ourselves and for asserting our humanity," as well as "our most rational form for dealing with the irrational" (*GTT* 246), showed a confidence and passion Lester could only envy, since to him this was "a tender truth" rooted in "an unreality that does not want to take into account" the harder facts that "Americans do not read novels" and that more of them "were influenced by the movie *E. T.* than have ever read any single novel."

Surprisingly, Lester found Ellison's pluralist cultural theories of America not only compelling but persuasive to boot, "particularly when describing the cultural and linguistic influence of black on whites, and whites on blacks, as well as the cross-influence of American's ethnic strains" ("Quiet Power" A13). The "metamorphosis of cultural forms" Ellison apotheosized in his title essay, "Going to the Territory," and the idea in "Perspective of Literature" of the Constitution as "the still-vital covenant by which Americans of diverse backgrounds, religions, races, and interests are bound" had "remarkable freshness" for Lester—and apparently no residue of "tender" unreality. Ellison's direct links in these respects to Lester's own intellectual enterprises and issues were apparent, if as yet unexcavated. Ellison's "masterfully crafted" fiction demonstrated to Lester, as it had to so many other African American writers, how the deep reservoir of black oral traditions could be transformed by modernist methods and reclaimed for contemporary audiences. In *Invisible Man* Ellison had worked this modernist "metamorphosis of cultural forms" on the Brer Rabbit fables and "Jack" tales of black oral tradition and then outlined his working compositional principles in *Shadow and Act*. In the course of his own development as a writer, Julius Lester had turned from the 1960s apocalyptics of his *Look Out, Whitey! Black Power's Gon' Get Your Mama* (1968) and

Revolutionary Notes (1969) to creating cycles of "retold" history and folklore for children, wherein he could "just straight, tell a story, and have it received as narrative without any literary garbage" or hysterics (A. Johnson, "Julius Lester" 140). Starting with *Black Folktales* (1969) and *The Knee-High Man and Other Tales* (1972), he had begun reclaiming from the distorted versions generated by devotees of the Southern "Plantation Tradition" the genuine spiritual legacies of black folk wisdom and resistance. His own modernist reclamations of black folk narratives culminated in a four-volume cycle of "retold" *Tales of Uncle Remus*, the first of which, *The Adventures of Brer Rabbit* (1987), he was shepherding to publication during his reviewing encounter with *Going to the Territory*, a book now whose guiding "clarity and moral perspicacity" ultimately led him to wonder "if black male writers have not made a mistake" in looking away from Ellison's intellectual reservoir of "cool, quiet power" (Lester, "Quiet Power" A14).

Like Julius Lester, David Bradley opened his conversation with Ellison by framing the author of *Invisible Man* as "a bit of a problem" and by highlighting the seeming incongruity between Ellison's "less than prolific output" and his prodigious literary status (Bradley 1). Ellison's career, Bradley suggested, is comparable not so much to those of voluminous contemporaries such as Norman Mailer and James Baldwin, as to that of Tillie Olsen, who published a first chapter of her masterly Depression-era novel *Yonnondio*, in 1934, and then disappeared for three decades before resurfacing with a collection of short fiction and the completed novel. Since Ellison surfaced first with masterwork already in hand, the analogy seems unwarranted, save for Bradley's joint implication that *Going to the Territory* serves as the marker for a disappearing act. The conceptual dynamics Bradley encountered between its covers, however, forced him to reconsider his disappointed expectations and to confront Ellison's new nonfiction on its own terms—except that it was not *really* new, he protested, save for just two of the sixteen pieces. What Bradley discovered in the cumulative trajectory of those sixteen pieces to quiet his demurrals, however, was the powerfully unifying theme of American pluralism, not as mere description or idealist apologia, but as a pragmatic tool of discovery and deflation that, despite Ellison's advancing age, was still directed more to dialectics than to nostalgia: "*Going to the Territory* is *not* memoir," Bradley recognized, "and even the most nostalgic of these recollections is pointed to punch holes in some cherished theory of race in America" (14). Ellison's opening salvo,

"The Little Man at Chehaw Station," provided Bradley a crux of heuristic illumination and a scene he found reminiscent of *Invisible Man*'s underground logic: four "foul-mouthed black workingmen" arguing in "a small, rank-smelling lamp-lit room" in the basement of Lincoln Center about the subtleties of operatic performance. Here, the resonance with Bradley's own literary explorations—unmentioned in the review—becomes clearer. A summa cum laude scholar at the University of Pennsylvania, he had completed his graduate degree on an exchange scholarship at the University of London. As the son of a mother devoted to researching local history and genealogy and a father who was an AME minister and church historian, Bradley had rejected his father's hierocratic views of history for history-making secular fiction told instead "from the bottom up."

Bradley's first novel, *South Street* (1975), had focused on the working-class world of a Philadelphia street-corner bar, a world he rendered as "Shakespearean comedy. Low comedy, low characters, lots of bawdy jokes, Falstaffian people, whores, the whole business"—but stripped of stereotype by the eyes of an empathetic narrator (Metzger 26). His second novel, *The Chaneysville Incident* (1982), won praises as "the best novel about the black experience in America since Ellison's *Invisible Man*," partly because it performed its own fictional riffs on familiar Ellisonian motifs: a deathbed scene between an uninitiated protagonist and a knowing elder whose revelations spur an inadvertent plunge into underground history, the protagonist's confrontation with an ancestral legacy of camouflaged guerrilla warfare and subversion, psychosexual entanglements across the color line that link ambivalent love and alienation to the repressed and fragmented history of slavery, evocative allusions to the slave narrative tradition itself, and the modulated appropriation of self-reflexive Jamesian narration and Faulknerian vernacular styles. Though Bradley thought of himself as "an old-fashioned writer" in terms of his attraction to Victorian models and his elevation of plot and character over abstract ideas, he had worked out a decidedly modernist synthesis that invited comparison with Ellison's. Bradley was apparently at ease with the association. Rather than seeing the Ellison of *Going to the Territory* as cool, remote, and polemical, he emphasized the "hilariously sarcastic style," which surfaced so often in Ellison's essays, as the signature of an inviting personality that was "witty, literate, endearingly modest, delightfully puckish" (14).

Like David Bradley, John Wideman opened his encounter with *Going to the Territory* in a lament and closed it with an encomium. It was not the missing new novel, however, that initially disappointed him so much as the slim portion of previously unpublished critical thinking and the new book's "disquieting resemblance" to *Shadow and Act*. Wideman was thoroughly familiar with the earlier volume and framed his comments around relationships between the two ("What Is Afro?" 14). A Phi Beta Kappa graduate of the University of Pennsylvania and the first African American Rhodes Scholar since Alain Locke, he had studied literature at Oxford; published his first novel, *A Glance Away*, in 1967 during the height of Black Arts ascendancy; and then forged an academic career in which "slave narratives, folklore, and the novels of Richard Wright and Ralph Ellison have been most important to me" (O'Brien 215, 216). Through *Shadow and Act*'s interviews on the art of fiction, Wideman had discovered that he shared with Ellison the life-altering experience of having been introduced to T. S. Eliot's *The Waste Land* at a formative age. As with Ellison, the hermeneutic struggle to understand "the whole texture of the poem, its tonal qualities, the effects of the movement from vernacular to high literary speech, the echoes of foreign languages" left a permanent imprint on Wideman that was evident in the Eliotic mood and style of *A Glance Away* and in an African American narrator admittedly akin to Eliot's J. Alfred Prufrock (O'Brien 216). At another turn, Ellison's immersion in the visual arts and surrealistic literary experiment had corollaries in Wideman's development as well: Wideman's third novel, *The Lynchers* (1973), experimented surrealistically with the use of a Hieronymus Bosch painting as a controlling metaphor and structural device. And soon after, with Ellison's imagery of the jazzman's "true academy" as an allusive backdrop, Wideman had gone "woodshedding" for eight years to "find" himself and "a new language to talk about [his] experience" before reentering the literary jam session with the *Homewood Books* (1992)—*Hiding Place* (1981), *Sent for You Yesterday* (1983), and *Damballah* (1981) (Andrews, Foster, and Harris 775). These were works of genealogical reclamation and memory reborn, made explicitly so with "begat charts" as opening devices and with a manifestly Ellisonian sense of celebratory purpose: "The three books offer a continuous investigation, from many angles, not so much of a physical location, Homewood, the actual African-American community in Pittsburgh where

I was raised, but of a culture, a way of seeing and being seen. *Homewood* is an idea, a reflection of how its inhabitants act and think. The books, if successful, should mirror the characters' inner lives, their sense of themselves as spiritual beings in a world where boundaries are not defined by racial stereotypes and sociological statistics" (Wideman, *Homewood Books* vii–viii).

For Wideman, "what captures the reader of *Going to the Territory*, then, is not novelty, not outrageous theories and claims, but the subtle jazzlike changes Mr. Ellison rings against the steady backbeat of his abiding concerns as artist and critic" ("What Is Afro?" 14). After two decades of imaginative exchange, Ellison's voice seemed to him an "assured, calm, wise" instrument with a "relaxed, intimate tone" full of the "quiet power and authority"—echoing Lester's perception—derived from having "lived more than 30 years with his classic, *Invisible Man*, towering over his shoulder." Wideman then pointed readers of the *New York Times* to two crucial things about the new collection: Ellison's own emphasis on the importance of "peripheral vision" as an interpretive tool, and Wideman's external view of Ellison himself as "a connoisseur of irony and dissonance." Regarding the first of these, Ellison's longstanding interest in perceptual optics and cognitive psychology made him acutely aware of how the human mind processes its environment and of the "priming effect" in which items seen at the periphery of vision—and not consciously processed—are identified faster and more accurately only when the perceiving subject focuses on them. In "Remembering Richard Wright," the jazzlike changes Ellison now rang against the backbeat of his famous review of *Black Boy* in *Shadow and Act* were at least quadruple: Ellison opened by rereading Wright now in light of the venerable Heraclitean maxim that "geography is fate." And Ellison revisited his own imaginative encounter with *The Waste Land* by filtering it through the "scenes, ideas, and experience" of the Tuskegee milieu. From a new vantage point four decades later, he reconsidered Wright's *Black Boy* as a forerunner of the "new" nonfiction novel being touted by Tom Wolfe and company. And Ellison redefined Wright's significance as a literary phenomenon by setting him this time not against Hemingway, Steinbeck, Malraux, or Thomas Mann but against Jack Johnson's legendary engagements with a succession of "Great White Hopes"—concluding that, in

Wright's redoubtable literary skill and élan, "we had for the first time a Negro American writer as randy, as courageous, and as irrepressible as Jack Johnson" (*GTT* 215). The underground lesson Ellison offered his readers this time, and that Wideman quoted in assent, was to "keep a sharp eye on what's happening in the unintellectualized areas of our experience. Our peripheral vision had better be damned good. Because while baseball, basketball and football players cannot really tell us how to write our books, they do demonstrate where much of the significant action is taking place" (*GTT* 215–16). Wideman had been an extraordinary athlete himself, having made "All-Ivy" and the Big Five Basketball Hall of Fame. But at the same time he had found himself riven by the racial self-denial his athletic success had once seemed to demand. The Homewood native son's own trajectory as athlete, scholar, and woodshedding novelist had reversed the processes of inner division, allowing him, too, alongside Wright and Ellison, to "assume a boxer's stance." So the surreal image that Ellison retrospectively unveiled of a confidently black literary intellectual fused with the gold-toothed heavyweight champion "race man" became an ideal marker, in the boisterous 1980s, of Ellison's enduring connoisseurship in irony and dissonance.

Leon Forrest brought a more intimate, less measured prior acquaintance with Ellison to his review of *Going to the Territory*—as might be expected, since Ellison had been a longtime literary hero and personal mentor to Forrest and had helped shepherd his first novel, *There Is a Tree More Ancient Than Eden*, to publication under Toni Morrison's editorship in 1973. Ellison had written a foreword for the book, lauding Forrest for his "furiously eloquent prose," his "tortured, history-wracked, anguished, Hound-of-Heaven-pursued, Ham-and-Oedipus-cursed, Blake-visioned, apocalypse-prone projection of the human predicament." Forrest's novel marked the beginning of a career, Ellison continued, "of a novelist in the grand manner; one who is unashamed to be serious, philosophical—even religious" or to "pit his talents against the achievements of the great masters of the form." Ellison made a veiled reference here to the current debates about the state and future prospects of the American novel that Tom Wolfe's insurgency on behalf of the nonfiction novel was aggravating that same year through his release of *The New Journalism*. Ellison then dropped the veil and used the occasion to offer his own calm intervention in the broader literary quarrel:

> It is my opinion that Leon Forrest demonstrates in his first published work a knowledge that has been resisted by some of the most talented of American novelists: that it is a cowardly waste of time for the writer to rail against the chaotic and surreal nature of American society as outrivaling the form-creating powers of fiction. For rather than confining his efforts to projecting a neat, minor slice of life, he seems to assume that, whether we like it or not, the day-to-day, here-and-now life of American society is the only life we have to live, and that, as such, it is the writer's challenge and his task. Therefore, Forrest has given his considerable energies and talents to the discovery of the literary means and angles of vision necessary to reduce this confounding, pluralistic society of ours to eloquent form. That he has done so with such a large measure of success in his first novel provides us not only with a source of delight but with one of profound instruction. (Ellison, Foreword)

Novelists of high ambition and panoramic sweep like Leon Forrest, in other words, were the answer to what ailed the American novel, not the timid slice-of-lifers *or* the New Journalists. The year before, in an interview conversation Forrest arranged for the Nation of Islam newspaper *Muhammed Speaks*, Ellison had railed against the cliché-ridden fictions about African American life, by both white and black writers, that flip-flop "from Sambo to Nat Turner" and thereby leave out "most of us"—along with the possibility of achieving the "resonance" that accompanies more complex literary visions (Graham and Singh 216). On another note, in response to Forrest's query about what ideally constitutes "the writer's kind of mind," Ellison supplied an answer that revealed the personal as well as the prototypical:

> I suspect it is the type of mind, [that] while not losing sight of the factual nature of reality, is obsessed with extracting those characters, nuances, and rhetoric which, as he re-combines them in terms of literary forms, . . . convey what he considers most important in life. . . . The life of the imagination leads him to combine those images he has extracted from reality. The writer trains the imagination by reading imaginative writers, reading biography and autobiography of certain writers' lives and what they have to say about their own work. (Graham and Singh 217)

What Forrest already understood to be a "highly associative" sensibility Ellison made more concrete by comparing its dynamics to "the image of blowing on a flame." Then, when Forrest borrowed Ellison's own terms to frame another writerly question about "what is the process, the *metamorphosis* that goes into re-making a speech or sermon into art," Ellison confided that "it is a blending of forms: church, congregation and drama. It is involved with re-birth and transcendence . . . with themes of consciousness of characters" (Graham and Singh 220).

Over the decade following the interview with Ellison, Forrest wrote two more novels, *The Bloodworth Orphans* (1977) and *Two Wings to Veil My Face* (1984), completing the Forest County trilogy that he modeled expressly on Faulkner's Yoknapatawpha County family sagas and Joyce's Dublin cycle and that he infused with jazz-blues-gospel and sermonic stylizations inspired by *Invisible Man*. In 1979 Forrest participated in the Ralph Ellison Festival organized by Michael Harper and contributed a critical essay, "Luminosity from the Lower Frequencies," that traced the influences of Lord Raglan's "myth of the birth of the hero" and Dostoyevsky's device of characterological "doublings" on Ellison's novel. Unsurprisingly, Forrest's review of *Going to the Territory* reflected a rich intimacy with Ellison's world, distilled in comments about what Forrest considered to be two major new mountings of Ellison's ideas: "The Little Man at Chehaw Station" and "An Extravagance of Laughter." In the first of these, Forrest suggested, Ellison had finally given a name to the underground figure he had long employed in his fiction and essays as "a knowing, troubling witness to our riddled democracy": "Connoisseur, critic, trickster, the little man is also a day-coach, cabin-class traveler. . . . Being quintessentially American, he enjoys the joke, the confounding of hierarchical expectations, fostered by his mask: that cultural incongruity through which he, like Brer Rabbit, is able to convert even the most decorous of audiences into his own briar patch and temper the chilliest of classics to his own vernacular taste" (qtd. in Forrest, "America's 'Little Man'"). Ellison had multiplied the little man into the group of black workingmen arguing over operatic finesse, whom Forrest aptly recognized as witnessing "cousins" to the Chehaw Station stalwart, along with the refined Miss Hazel Harrison, to whom the essay was dedicated. Like "An Extravagance of Laughter," the essay about the little man was a spiral of humor and "stunning insight" that Ellison had embodied with Twain's and Whitman's concerns for democracy and its failures—concerns that Forrest, like Ellison, insisted were "an *imperative* theme for an American author."

From an angle of vision left intriguingly vague, Forrest bracketed "An Extravagance of Laughter" alongside Virginia Woolf's *A Room of One's Own*—a juxtaposition that, on reflection, resonates suggestively. Himself a writer "from the American Negro briar patch," as Ellison's foreword explicitly remarked, Forrest had apparently turned his briar patch perspective to comparative advantage. He may have grounded the distaff side of his analogy in Woolf's outspoken dissatisfaction with the methods and male-centered outlook of the triumvirate of novelists—H. G. Wells, Arnold Bennett, and John Galsworthy—who dominated the British literary public in the early decades of the twentieth century: a clear analogue for Ellison's war on entrenched racial cliché and stereotype in canonical American letters. Or he may have referenced Woolf's quest for imaginative autonomy: her emancipatory spatial metaphor of "a room of one's own" could be associated tropologically with Ellison's "territory ahead of the rest." He may have found Woolf's idealizing concept of androgyny as a path to unity and harmony—over rigid separation into "male" and "female" qualities—to be an apt corollary for Ellison's concept of cultural pluralism and the vernacular sensibility as vital ingredients of a whole and healthy democracy. Or he may have discovered in Woolf's attraction to the tragic sense of life in the great nineteenth-century Russian writers—Tolstoy, Dostoyevsky, and Anton Chekhov—an attraction Ellison also shared to such richly articulated but foreign visions of the experiencing self caught in violently uncertain circumstances, visions that resonated more deeply with her own apprehensions than the fictions of what passed for reality in the society she inhabited.

Cyrus Colter, last of the reviewers of *Going to the Territory* to be considered here, shared this "transnational" apprehension with Ellison more completely than did any of the others. A lawyer by training, whose literary career began at the advanced age of fifty, Colter was old enough to have participated peripherally in the Chicago Renaissance that brought Richard Wright, Frank Marshall Davis, Theodore Ward, Arna Bontemps, and Margaret Walker together in the South Side Writers Group in 1936. Influenced, on one hand, by the Chicago School of Sociology theories of environmental determinism and, on the other hand, by the liberatory visions he discovered in the novels of Herman Melville and James Joyce, Colter was entranced by a whole corpus of major Russian writers—Aleksandr Pushkin, Gogol, Dostoyevsky, Ivan Turgenev, Chekhov, and Tolstoy. Their portraits of a rapidly changing, once feudal society across a wide spectrum of social classes, vocations, and spiritual states led him to decry the often monoschematic black American literary focus on the poor and to aspire instead to become a storyteller "who would write—not only about the ghetto dweller—but about the black middle class and the black intelligentsia" (Stamatel 51). Colter's attraction also to the French existentialist philosophies and fictions of Sartre and Camus impelled his earliest short-story collection, *The Beach Umbrella* (1970), toward a distinctive synthesis of determinist-existentialist themes about the human condition. He explored those themes in a series of Chekhovian vignettes about black characters whose grimmest realities are comprised not so much of racism as of materialist and metaphysical angst. Though at first "awed by Ellison's *Invisible Man* and Baldwin's *Go Tell It on the Mountain*" (Colter, "Fought" 874), Colter undertook a series of novels, *The Rivers of Eros* (1972), *The Hippodrome* (1973), and *Night Studies* (1980), that oscillated ambitiously between the modes of Greek tragedy, existentialist nightmare, and epic quest.

The second of these was the novel that Charles Johnson classed alongside *Invisible Man* and Wright's *The Outsider* as examples of phenomenologically "fresh" encounters with African American experience. *The Hippodrome* developed a plot premise closer to the violent surrealism of the hallucinatory sequences in *Invisible Man* than to Wright's more naturalistic framework: in its opening scene, Jackson Yaegar, a writer on religious themes, has murdered his wife and his wife's white lover and is on the run with his wife's severed head in a brown bag. Simultaneously offered refuge and held captive in the Hippodrome—a ghetto circus where a troupe of blacks stage sexual theater for white audiences—Colter's perpetrator becomes a victim himself, caught in the spotlight of orchestrated race rituals akin to those in Ellison's phantasmagoric Battle Royal—and steeped similarly in existentialist import. With framing epigraphs from Richard Wright's Dostoyevskian parable *The Man Who Lived Underground*, from

Sartre's revulsive existentialist masterwork, *Nausea*, and from Jean Genet's inverse theology of criminal saintliness in *Miracle of the Rose*, Colter experimented with a logic of negative morality as pristine as its parallels in Wright's existential antiheroes and Ellison's personified master of chaos, Bliss Proteus Rinehart. Intriguingly, what Colter chose to emphasize when he turned his attentions to Ellison's *Going to the Territory* was Ellison's "great care, precision and deliberation—his 'cool'—together with the marvelous embroidery of the apt and learned allusions" that informed Ellison's homages to Wright, Duke Ellington, and Romare Bearden, as well as the masterful dialectics in "The Myth of the Flawed White Southerner" and "Society, Morality, and the Novel" (Colter, "Ralph Ellison Again Visible").

Colter's attention to the textual embroidery and modulations of genre and style in Ellison's expository prose highlights what may have been an association in his mind with the twentieth-century school of Russian "ornamental" writers he and Ellison both admired. More pointedly, Colter pronounced "An Extravagance of Laughter" to be a genre-blurring "tour de force," as much "story" as expository prose. Colter's extended commentary highlighted the raucous but steely way Ellison retrospectively treated his encounter with the 1936 theatrical version of Erskine Caldwell's *Tobacco Road*. Ellison's essay embedded, Colter averred, a "highly novelistic" treatment of bizarre scenes too implausible to succeed as nonfiction but "wonderful" when rendered fictively. Colter had long considered Ellison a master of vernacular style, whose "treatment of the black folkloristic tradition has no equal" (Colter, "Fought" 861). His closing comments in "Ralph Ellison Again Visible, Still Vibrant" detailed how Ellison deployed the comic folk myth of the "laughing barrels"—apocryphal vessels of containment that black folks were supposed to laugh *into* instead of laughing directly *at* the follies of their white "superiors"—as an essayistic special effect. Counting himself among Ellison's admirers who would have preferred another novel to the volume of nonfiction, Colter brushed aside the explanation given him by one of Ellison's unnamed friends that the great man's "inordinately high standards" had forced him, in effect, to give up fiction. James Baldwin, after all, had not given up fiction after his "fiery, eloquent, inspired" first novel, *Go Tell It on the Mountain*, set a standard Baldwin had "never again reached." Baldwin, Colter declared, had continued doggedly to still write novels "almost as if it were an obligation." So why had Ellison not continued? He speculated that "maybe Ellison consciously or unconsciously is having it both ways—camouflaged interior monologue, fiction in the guise of non-fiction, novelettes masquerading as essay-memoirs." Maybe he had "an ace up his sleeve." These and other telltale signs that Ellison had not given up fiction were apparent in *Going to the Territory*, Colter concluded, in this gathering of "vintage, yet somehow 'new' Ellison" that was "dramatic, novelistic and sustained, with not a dull page in it."

Epilogue

Epilogue

THE LAST GESTALT:
ELLISON'S UNFINISHED BUSINESS

Cyrus Colter's speculations about the unfinished novel Ralph Ellison's admirers had so long awaited struck what was by then a far too familiar chord. In excerpts of an interview with reporter Brent Staples, published alongside John Wideman's assessment of *Going to the Territory*, Ellison deflected questions about his novelistic disappearing act back to 1967, to the squallish, ice-glazed November day when he and Fanny Ellison stood helplessly in the high winds outside their 200–year-old summer home in the Berkshires and watched it voraciously burn (Staples). They had just managed to get their Labrador retriever out, he recalled, but could not rescue the massy chunk of his uncompleted novel. "Until the recent stir about my new book of essays," he insisted then in 1986, the novel had "been coming very well." But when asked exactly when it would be done, he could only say, "I don't know." Was it like the first one? "It's quite different ... a broader canvas. Though I think it will have some of the wildness of *Invisible Man*." Would it be a multivolume affair—since the 1982 manuscript was rumored to be nearly twenty inches thick? "No, it's not; I know that's gotten around, though." Did it bother him that people always asked about it? "I don't feel particularly uncomfortable with it. I know I have become something of a joke on this subject. One of the things I've tried to do is not let the publicity surrounding a book get out of hand. When I was writing *Invisible Man*, no one was hanging around saying 'when, when.' I have made my peace with my slow pace of creation" (Staples).

The peace he made was a troubled one at best, as his own comments through the years made clear. In an interview with John Hersey a decade earlier—the most probing of all his exchanges about the intricacies of his own creative processes—when asked about how he generated the psychic energy to take on a massive work and sustain it, he responded: "Psychic energy? I don't know, I think of myself as kind of lazy. And yet, I do find that working slowly, which is the only way I seem able to work—although I write fast much of the time—the problem is one of being able to receive from my work that sense of tension, that sense of high purpose being realized, that keeps me going. This is a crazy idea that I don't understand—none of the Freudian explanations seem adequate" (Graham and Singh 279). He framed his own explanations instead in the language of Gestalt theory, which he had long since employed to help organize the psychological patterns of his fiction. Unlike the conventional Freudians, Gestalt theorists focused on the present, the "here and now," rather than the past. They had turned away from the older reductive process of tracing symptoms of personality disorder and dysfunction back to origins in the conflicts of infantile sexuality. They put a premium instead on developing awareness and personal responsibility out of a holistic, noninterpretative approach to the operations of mind and body as experienced in the immediate moment. And they had taken Freud's psychoanalytic concept of repetition-compulsion and reconfigured it as "unfinished business": The client feels compelled to repeat in daily life everything he cannot bring to a satisfactory conclusion; so in therapy, he struggles to bring his unfinished business—the splits, polarities, inadequacies, voids—into awareness by divining and acting out the meaning of his pertinent contemporary behaviors (Gregory 291–92). By the time of the tumultuous 1960s, advocates of the Gestalt approach such as Fritz Perls and Paul Goodman had integrated the psychoanalytic, existential, and phenomenological approaches Ellison had absorbed years earlier into a new theoretical and therapeutic synthesis particularly attractive to creative artists. Freud's *Interpretation of Dreams* had been a key critical tool in Ellison's intellectual development, and the Gestaltists, too, made dreams and dreaming a central feature of their therapeutic process. But it was the client's *own* "dreamwork" of nonjudgmentally retrieving and replaying the

content of his dreams and memories and fantasies, not the *analyst's* interpretations, that mattered, a practice Ellison cultivated by religiously keeping
his early mornings free "in case the night before had generated something
that could be put to good use":

> I never know quite what has gone on in my subconscious in the night. I dream
> vividly, and all kinds of things happen; by morning they have fallen below the
> threshold again. But I like to feel that whatever takes place becomes active in
> some way in what I do at the typewriter. In other words, I believe that a human
> being's life is of a whole, and that he lives the full twenty-four hours. And if he is
> a writer or an artist, what happens during the night feeds back, in some way, into
> what he does consciously during the day—that is, when he is doing that which is
> self-achieving, so to speak. Part of the pleasure of writing, as well as the pain, is
> involved in pouring into that thing which is being created all of what he cannot
> understand and cannot say and cannot deal with, or cannot even admit, in any
> other way. The artifact is a completion of personality. (Graham and Singh 280)

Much more than Freud's theories about the relationships between
jokes, wit, and the unconscious—which Ellison had put to "good use" in
powerful essays such as "Twentieth Century Fiction and the Black Mask of
Humanity" or "Change the Joke and Slip the Yoke" Gestalt concepts recognized the psychological force of aesthetic phenomena such as "form" and
"shape," "figure" and "ground." On these terms the classical and vernacular
tunes he had played in his youth, the modernist poetry and sculptures he
had experimented with in the course of discovering his writerly vocation,
and his life-altering first novel itself, were all psychic *Gestalten*—projective
patterns or perceptual constructs whose full significance emerged only
when heard or seen against the background noise or the skein of associated
events. Ellison confrere Anatole Broyard had consulted Max Wertheimer,
the renowned Gestalt psychiatrist, to address Broyard's agonizing inability to complete the contracted, rumor-laden novel that was supposed to
become his own career-making magnum opus (Gates, *Thirteen* 198–99).
Wertheimer knew very well, and wrote extensively, that creativity was a
more complex phenomenon than the "brick-and-mortar" process of
merely *associating* old ideas in new ways. Creative thinking depended on
the formation and alteration of holistic *Gestalten*, whose elements were far
more intricately linked than mere "association" comprehended. As André

Malraux's psychology of art made clear, the masterworks of the visual arts were made up of myriad elements, all of which were interrelated such that the wholes somehow became something much greater than the sums of their associated parts. As Ellison also knew, from direct experience, creative musicians did not engender their creations by writing single notes or clusters of notes on paper in the hope of producing original associations. Instead, they typically conjured up from the deep well of their semiconscious imaginings some inchoate idea of a finished structure or design and then worked backward to complete or expand the idea in disciplined, polished, final form. As Kenneth Burke's concept of the "representative anecdote" suggested, artists might likewise begin by intuiting some microcosm of the whole structure and then rearranging its parts or "charting" its larger pattern, as Ellison had with *Invisible Man.* As if in a repeat illustration, the genesis of his new novel, Ellison recognized,

> started with the idea of an old man being so outraged by his life that he goes poking around in the cellar to find a forgotten coffin, which he had bought years before to insure against his possible ruin. He discovers that he has lived so long that the coffin is full of termites, and that even the things he had stored in the coffin have fallen apart. Somehow, this said something to my imagination and got me started. You can see that it could go in *any* direction. But then it led to the other idea, which I wrote first, of a little boy being placed in a coffin, in a ritual of death and transcendence, celebrated by a Negro evangelist who was unsure whether he was simply exploiting the circus sideshow shock set off by the sight of a child rising up out of a coffin, or had hit upon an inspired way of presenting the sacred drama of the resurrection. In my mind all of this is tied up in some way with the significance of being a Negro in America and at the same time with the problem of our democratic faith as a whole. Anyway, as a product of the imagination, it's like a big sponge, maybe, or a waterbed, with a lot of needles sticking in it at various points. You don't know what is being touched, where the needles are going to end up once you get them threaded and penetrated, but somehow I kept trying to tie those threads together and the needle points pressing home without letting whatever lies in the center leak out. (Graham and Singh 277–78)

Ellison confessed at the same time his

> uncertainty about some of the things I'm doing, and especially when I'm using more than one main voice, and with a time scheme that is much more

fragmented than in *Invisible Man*. There I was using a more tidy dramatic form. *This* novel is dramatic within its incidents, but it moves back and forth in time. In such a case I guess an act of faith is necessary, a faith that if what you are writing is of social and artistic importance and its diverse parts are presented vividly in the light of its overall conception, and if you *render* the story rather than just tell it, then the reader will go along. That's a lot of ifs.

The hydraulic metaphors he now employed to describe the workings of his creative imagination were more constrained and vulnerable than those he had used during the artistic struggle to complete *Invisible Man*. Thirty years before, in his address to the 1945 Conference of Psychologists and Writers, just a few months before he had that famous moment of inspiration in a barnyard in Vermont, he had linked the dark, unknown potential of the revolutionary imagination to cosmogonic powers able, if given a chance, to "toss a fistful of mud into the sky and create a 'shining star'" (*S&A* 49). Similarly, in the new introduction he wrote for the Thirtieth Anniversary Edition of *Invisible Man* in 1982, he recalled imagining the organizational and stylistic achievement he had attained with that first flight as "a star-burst of metamorphosis" (*IM* ix). If he had indeed now made peace with the slow pace of his creation, and if the chaotic intractability of his steadily massing manuscript kept him from imagining himself any longer as a star-bound bringer of light advancing on chaos and the dark, he had nonetheless sustained the victory of conscious thought and the will to endure in the face of oncoming defeat. When Ellison's dream-work finally ended in the spring of 1994, with his business still unfinished, that transcendental victory, not the book-shaped hellhound on his trail, would become, on his own terms, the last Gestalt.

Notes

CHAPTER 1

1. Lawrence Jackson's biography of Ellison's first four decades, through the appearance of *Invisible Man* in 1952, has provided the major advance in our understanding of Ellison's "emergence" as an artist and social thinker. Besides clarifying and consolidating the biographical details scattered through Ellison's essays and interviews over the years, Jackson retrieves Ellison from the often isolating frameworks in which critics routinely place him; and Jackson reveals the rich network of communal and personal relationships that distinguish Ellison's perspectives on African American culture from those of friend and mentor Richard Wright. Jackson's work emphasizes also the extent to which Ellison's creative achievement in *Invisible Man* is grounded, on the one hand, in the critical and theoretical labors of his years in the Stalinist-Trotskyite radical Left and, on the other, in inclinations evident early on toward heretical or iconoclastic stances toward political and artistic orthodoxies alike. Jackson is the first scholar to tease out the signal European influence of André Malraux on Ellison's literary thought; and though the biography does not pursue the array of pivotal nineteenth- and twentieth-century Russian influences—beyond Dostoyevsky—on Ellison's intellectual career, it does develop a broader view of Ellison's literary cosmopolitanism than any previously available. As in David Levering Lewis's two-volume biography of W. E. B. DuBois, Jackson opts to let his endnote citations serve also as a substitute bibliography, which may frustrate scholarly researchers. But the research is detailed there copiously and accessibly and constitutes a great aid for other scholars who may dispute Jackson's emphases and interpretations at various points but will remain indebted nonetheless to his groundbreaking industriousness.

2. Robert Bone's essay "Ralph Ellison and the Uses of the Imagination," which appeared first in *TriQuarterly* in 1966 and then later that year in Herbert Hill's collection *Anger and Beyond*, is the earliest expansive effort to employ *Shadow and Act* systematically as an interpretive key to *Invisible Man* and to Ellison's intellectual outlook. Bone attempts to discover the "foundations of Ellison's aesthetic" in the blues and jazz worlds of Louis Armstrong, Charlie

239

Parker, Jimmy Rushing, and Bessie Smith; and he traces Ellison's affinity for the nineteenth-century American transcendentalists to his novelistic commitment to revitalizing the picaresque tradition of Renaissance Spain. Bone explains Ellison's return to picaresque traditions as an ethnic strategy common also to Jewish American writers such as Saul Bellow, who took up a genre largely abandoned by white Anglo-Saxon Americans after *Huckleberry Finn*, Bone argues, as an index of belated Jewish access, also, to "the basic conditions of bourgeois existence." Bone focuses also on the rituals of masking and naming in Ellison's literary aesthetic, linking them philosophically to Emerson's transcendentalist reification of the Poet as "Namer" or "Language-Maker." But Bone's reading of Ellison as literary intellectual remained firmly circumscribed by the boundaries of American national consciousness, so that the more cosmopolitan universe of Ellison's "ancestral" ties to French, Russian, German, Italian, and other transatlantic literatures remained largely unplumbed.

3. Berndt Ostendorf's essay "Ralph Ellison: Anthropology, Modernism, and Jazz," originally published in Robert O'Meally's collection *New Essays on Invisible Man* (1988) has much in common with the approach taken in this book. Professor Ostendorf's emphasis on Ellison as a *bricoleur* of language, as an *experimental* rather than systematic thinker, and as one who favors dynamic over static conceptual paradigms, all reinforce the interpretations outlined in 1980 in my "Dedicated Dreamer, Consecrated Acts: Shadowing Ellison" for the *Carleton Miscellany* special Ellison issue. My own approach to Ellison's intellectual world, however, has a more developmental and intertextual focus; and where Ostendorf proposes three "encompassing frames"—the ritual theories of symbolic anthropology, a revisionary modernist *episteme*, and the jazz idiom—for interpreting Ellison's work and opinions, my own quartet of strategic Ellisonian "impulses" is rooted in a decidedly Burkean interpretive scheme aligned intentionally with Ellison's rhetorical terminologies and "conscious thought." Accordingly, where Ostendorf interprets Ellison's political outlook by describing him as a "slipped Marxist" *analogous* to Leszek Kolakowski, I emphasize Ellison's explicit intertextual alignments with the antimaterialist dialectics of André Malraux; and where Ostendorf produces a reading of Ellison's "trickster" forms of humanism again through analogy with Kolakowski's neo-Marxian concept of conjoined "priest" and "jester" functions, my own approach emphasizes instead Ellison's direct and frequently voiced indebtedness to the tragic and tragicomic protoexistentialism of Miguel de Unamuno.

4. Maryemma Graham and Amritjit Singh's edited collection of interviews, *Conversations with Ralph Ellison* (1995), compiles nearly all of the public exchanges Ellison sanctioned for printed release. Their perceptive introduction warns readers that "most of us tend to think of Ellison as aloof in style and manner, the embodiment of his own metaphor, a kind of 'invisible man' of recent American literature. This may indeed have been the public Ellison, a man

overshadowed by his own reputation, chuckling with friends to deflect their questions about his second novel, and reluctant to claim most of what we have often wanted to attribute to him. But the interviews . . . evoke a very different Ellison indeed. We find in them a man of tremendous vitality, alert and sensitive, well-read and argumentative, a man determined to fight for his point of view" (xi).

CHAPTER 2

1. See David Grossvogel, *The Blasphemers: The Theatre of Brecht, Ionesco, Genet*; Arnold Hincliffe, *The Absurd*; Lionel Trilling's discussion of "anticulture" in *Beyond Culture*; and Gerald Graff, *Literature against Itself*.

2. See Alfred McClung Lee and Norman D. Humphrey, *Race Riot*, and *Report of the National Advisory Commission on Civil Disorders*. On the history of lynching as a literary race ritual, see Trudier Harris, *Exorcising Blackness*.

3. A variety of critics have discussed the historical dimensions of *Invisible Man*. See, for example, Richard Kostelanetz, "The Politics of Ellison's Booker: *Invisible Man* as Symbolic History"; Edward Margolies, "History as Blues: Ralph Ellison's *Invisible Man*" in his *Native Sons* (127–48); and Russell Fischer, "Invisible Man as History."

4. In their appended notes and documentation, Drake and Cayton acknowledged using Myrdal's criteria for the "ideal study" of a black community to judge their own work—finding themselves ultimately disagreeing with Myrdal's structuralist disregard of distinctive black "class" formations and the ethos of various black subgroups (Drake and Cayton 788–89).

5. *Black Bourgeoisie* created tremendous controversy in black communities because of its focus on the psychopathology of black social marginality and on the derelictions of the black middle class—themes Drake and Cayton had largely suppressed.

6. By the time of Frazier's 1962 reissue of his study, the emergence of the civil rights movement and its new leadership cadre made it clear that such a phenomenon was inexplicable in the terms *Black Bourgeoisie* had originally offered. Frazier admitted as much, but offered no full reassessment. Drake and Cayton, in fact, had provided the more clear-sighted and prophetic reading back in 1945.

7. The consolidation of this new science appeared at the end of the decade in Alvin Gouldner's *Studies in Leadership: Leadership and Democratic Action* (1950).

8. Ellison's introduction to the thirtieth anniversary edition of *Invisible Man* demystifies the genesis of the novel, if not its "representative anecdote," by consolidating various facets of the novel's creative origins—the military associations in particular—that had been recounted only in scattered pieces over the years.

9. The continuing critical debates over *Invisible Man*'s problematic resolutions and denouement have had nothing so much in common as a fulsome detachment

from the concrete intellectual and cultural history of black literary radicals during the 1940s. Carl Milton Hughes's 1953 pioneering study, *The Negro Novelist: A Discussion of the Writings of American Negro Novelists, 1940–1950*, remains the only broad survey. No more comprehensive study has yet appeared.

10. The inability of Anglo-American postwar "consensus" historians to account for the emergence of the civil rights movement and its successor, Black Power, though partly anatomized in recent years, has yet to be contrasted explicitly with the comparative prescience of postwar African American historians, who indeed shared many progressivist assumptions about the nature of the postwar world but who could consent not at all to Daniel Bell's presumptively representative dictum that "for the radical intellectual who had articulated the revolutionary impulses of the past century and a half, there was now an end to chiliastic hopes, to millenarianism, to apocalyptic thinking—and to ideology" (393). For representative views about black historical contexts during the postwar years, see Samuel Du Bois Cook, "A Tragic Conception of Negro History," and William B. Hixson, Jr., "The Negro Revolution and the Intellectuals," both in *Understanding Negro History*, edited by Dwight Hoover (Chicago: Quadrangle, 1968).

11. See, for example, Ellison's oblique but readily deciphered allusions to Malcolm X in his interview with Ishmael Reed and companions, "The Essential Ellison," 149–50.

12. For an aptly focused explication of this recurring motif in its initial setting in *Invisible Man*, see Houston Baker, "To Move Without Moving."

CHAPTER 3

1. Kenneth Warren's essay, "Chaos Not Quite Controlled: Ellison's Uncompleted Transit to *Juneteenth*," in Ross Posnock's *Cambridge Companion to Ralph Ellison*, brings Edmund Wilson into a more surreal conjunction with Ellison through a richly suggestive reading of Ellison's dream-vision essay "Tell It Like It Is, Baby," drafted in Rome in 1956 during Ellison's tenure there at the American Academy but left unpublished until 1965, at the height of Civil Rights and Black Power insurgency. Wilson's *Patriotic Gore* (1962) brought the Civil War–era politics of slavery and the Lincoln assassination into close association in Ellison's mind with the politics and political murders of the later era and with the evolving tangle of concerns in the manuscript novel from which *Juneteenth* was extracted. Reworking myth-ritual theory again into his renderings of modern events, Ellison evoked the Hamlet and Orestes tales of rising and dying kings as a framework that seems clearly linked to the assassination mythos that envelops Senator Sunraider in *Juneteenth*. Warren's essay reads Edmund Wilson's appearance alongside Abraham Lincoln in Ellison's dream reverie as part of a symbolic logic of modern tragedy that Ellison struggled unavailingly to control.

2. Though he spent only his last two decades in the United States, Whitehead has come to be regarded more as an American than a British philosopher and

as exerting a major influence on analytic philosophy, modernist theology, educational philosophy, and social science in America. The cosmology and metaphysics of *Science and the Modern World* and *Process and Reality* (1929), written at Harvard, are acknowledged as having had the greatest impact on American thought; but the influence of these works on American literary life has been explored only glancingly. For a brief resume of Whitehead's significance in America, see Daniel Wilson's entry on Whitehead in *A Companion to American Thought* edited by Richard W. Fox and James T. Kloppenberg (1995). For a broader purview, see Victor Lowe's interpretive study *Understanding Whitehead* (1962) and his two-volume compendium, *Alfred North Whitehead: The Man and His Work* (1985, 1990).

3. Ellison's notes for the chapter on the "Black Edison" outline sections on "Invention of the 'Third Rail' by Granville T. Woods," "Matzeliger and McCoy Inventions," "Louis Howard Latimer, etc.," and a "Summary about negro inventors."

CHAPTER 4

1. In *Mariners, Renegades and Castaways: The Story of Herman Melville and the World We Live In*, published in 1953, James had written that "my ultimate aim, and my book on Melville is merely a preparation for it, is to write a study of American civilization" (quoted by Anna Grimshaw and Keith Hart as the epigraph for James's posthumously released *American Civilization* [1993]).

2. Compare Baldwin's essay "Uses of the Blues," collected in *The Price of the Ticket* (1985), with Ellison's "Richard Wright's Blues," in *Shadow and Act*, and Wright's foreword to Paul Oliver's *Blues Fell This Morning* (1960).

3. In his interview with Ishmael Reed, Quincy Troupe, and Steve Cannon, Ellison responded to their queries about his assessments of emerging African writers by saying that, for him, writers like Chinua Achebe "raised the question of what, precisely, is an 'African' writer? He strikes me as a Western writer—just as certain writers from former French colonies, such as Cesaire, Senghor, and Ouologuem who are French writer-intellectuals, no matter what they tell you about negritude. I think that Amos Tutuola, who wrote *The Palm-Wine Drinkard*, is far more 'African' than any of the others" (Graham and Singh 375–76).

Bibliography

Adams, Robert M. "Masks and Delays: Edmund Wilson as Critic." *Sewanee Review* 56 (Spring 1948): 272–86.

Anderson, Jervis. "Profiles (Ralph Ellison): Going to the Territory." *New Yorker* 22 Nov. 1976: 55+.

Andrews, William, Frances Smith Foster, and Trudier Harris, eds. *The Oxford Companion to African American Literature.* New York: Oxford University Press, 1997.

Auerbach, Erich. *Mimesis: The Representation of Reality in Western Art.* 1953. Princeton: Princeton University Press, 1974.

Awkward, Michael. *Inspiriting Influences: Tradition, Revision, and Afro-American Women's Novels.* New York: Columbia University Press, 1989.

Baguley, David. "Emile Zola." *The Johns Hopkins Guide to Literary Theory and Criticism.* Ed. Michael Groden and Martin Kreiswirth. Baltimore: Johns Hopkins University Press, 1994. 749–50.

Baker, Houston. *Blues, Ideology, and Afro-American Literature: A Vernacular Theory.* Chicago: University of Chicago Press, 1984.

———. "To Move without Moving: An Analysis of Creativity and Commerce in Ralph Ellison's Trueblood Episode." *PMLA* 98 (Oct. 1983): 828–45.

Baldwin, James. *The Fire Next Time.* New York: Dial, 1963.

———. *Go Tell It on the Mountain.* New York: Knopf, 1953.

———. *Nobody Knows My Name.* New York: Dial, 1961.

———. *Notes of a Native Son.* Boston: Beacon, 1955.

Barrett, William. *The Truants: Adventures among the Intellectuals.* Garden City: Anchor-Doubleday, 1982.

Batchelor, R. E. *Unamuno Novelist: A European Perspective.* Oxford: Dolphin, 1972.

Bell, Daniel. *The End of Ideology: On the Exhaustion of Political Ideas in the Fifties.* Glencoe: Free, 1960.

Benston, Kimberly, ed. *Speaking for You: The Vision of Ralph Ellison.* Washington: Howard University Press, 1987.

Bims, Hamilton. "A Search for God in Contemporary Literature: Nathan Scott Seeks Prophecy in Modern Literature." *Ebony* Apr. 1975: 44–52.

245

Blanchot, Maurice. "Time, Art, and the Museum." *Malraux: A Collection of Critical Essays.* Ed. R. W. B. Lewis. Englewood Cliffs: Prentice-Hall, 1964. 147–60.

Bondi, Victor, ed. *American Decades, 1980–1989.* Detroit: Gale, 1996.

Bone, Robert. "Ralph Ellison and the Uses of the Imagination." *Anger and Beyond.* Ed. Herbert Hill. New York: Harper and Row, 1966. 86–111.

Borklund, Elmer. *Contemporary Literary Critics.* New York: St. Martin's, 1977.

Bradley, David. "Two Works: Once upon a Time in Black and White America." *Los Angeles Times* 8 Aug. 1986, Book Reviews sec.: 1+.

"Bradley, David (Henry), Jr." *Contemporary Authors: New Revision Series.* Detroit: Gale, 1999. 63–66.

Brawley, Benjamin. *The Negro Genius.* New York: Dodd, Mead, 1937.

Brown, Sterling. *Negro Poetry and Drama and The Negro in American Fiction.* Washington: Associates in Negro Folk Education, 1937.

Broyard, Anatole. *Aroused by Books.* New York: Random House, 1974.

———. "Books: Lionel Trilling Encores." *New York Times* 26 Oct. 1979: C28.

———. "Books of the Times: *E. M. Forster.* By Lionel Trilling." *New York Times* 2 Apr. 1980: C26.

———. "Four by Trilling." *New York Times* 10 June 1978: 17.

———. *Intoxicated by My Illness: And Other Writings on Life and Death.* Ed. Alexandra Broyard. New York: Potter, 1992.

———. *Kafka Was the Rage: A Greenwich Village Memoir.* New York: Southern Books, 1993.

———. *Men, Women and Other Anticlimaxes.* New York: Methuen, 1980.

———. "A Portrait of the Hipster." *Partisan Review* June 1948: 721–27.

———. "Portrait of the Inauthentic Negro: How Prejudice Distorts the Victim's Personality." *Commentary* 10 (July–Dec. 1950): 56–64.

Bunche, Ralph. "The Programs of Organizations Devoted to the Improvement of the Status of the American Negro." *Journal of Negro Education* July 1939: 539–50.

Burke, Kenneth. *Attitudes toward History.* 2nd ed. Los Altos: Hermes Publications, 1959.

———. *Permanence and Change: An Anatomy of Purpose.* 1935. Los Altos: Hermes Publications, 1954.

———. *The Philosophy of Literary Form.* 1941. 2nd ed. Baton Rouge: Louisiana State University Press, 1967.

Callahan, John. *In the African-American Grain: The Pursuit of Voice in Twentieth-Century Black Fiction.* Chicago: University of Illinois Press, 1988.

Casillo, Robert. "Lewis Mumford." *Dictionary of Literary Biography.* Vol. 63. Detroit: Gale, 1988: 184–200.

Chase, Richard. *The American Novel and Its Tradition.* Garden City: Anchor-Doubleday, 1957.

———. *The Democratic Vista: A Dialogue on Life and Letters in Contemporary America.* Garden City: Doubleday, 1958.

———. *Herman Melville: A Critical Study*. New York: Macmillan, 1949.

Chavkin, Allen, ed. *Conversations with John Gardner*. Jackson: University Press of Mississippi, 1990.

Colter, Cyrus. *The Hippodrome*. 1973. Evanston: Northwestern University Press, 1994.

———. "Fought for It and Paid Taxes Too: Four Interviews with Cyrus Colter." With Gilton Gregory Cross, Fred Shafer, Charles Johnson, and Reginald Gibbons. *Callaloo* 14.4 (1991): 855–97.

———. "Ralph Ellison Again Visible, Still Vibrant." *Chicago Sun-Times* 10 Aug. 1986: C9.

"Colter, Cyrus." *Contemporary Authors: New Revision Series*. Detroit: Gale, 1998. 103–05.

Conley, John. "They Shall Have Music." *Atlantic* Feb. 1961: 100–03.

Covo, Jacqueline. *The Blinking Eye: Ralph Waldo Ellison and His American, French, German, and Italian Critics, 1952–1971*. Metuchen: Scarecrow, 1974.

Cox, Oliver. "Leadership among Negroes in the United States." *Studies in Leadership: Leadership and Democratic Action*. Ed. Alvin Gouldner. New York: Russell and Russell, 1965. 228–71.

Davis, Arthur P. "Intellectual Estrangement." *Phylon* 14.3 (1952): 335–37.

De Courcel, Martine, ed. *Malraux: Life and Work*. New York: Harcourt Brace Jovanovich, 1976.

De Lissovoy, Peter. "The Visible Ellison." *Nation* 9 Nov. 1964: 334–36.

Del Rio, Angel. Introduction. *Three Exemplary Novels*. By Miguel de Unamuno. New York: Grove, 1956. 11–35.

Dick, Bruce, and Amritjit Singh, eds. *Conversations with Ishmael Reed*. Jackson: University Press of Mississippi, 1995.

Dobson, Melissa. "Broyard, Anatole Paul." *The Scribner Encyclopedia of American Lives*. New York: Scribner's, 1998.

Drake, St. Clair, and Horace Cayton. *Black Metropolis: A Study of Negro Life in a Northern City*. 1945. New York: Harcourt, Brace, 1970.

DuBois, W. E. B. *Black Reconstruction in America: An Essay toward a History of the Part Which Black Folk Played in the Attempt to Reconstruct Democracy in America, 1860–1900*. 1935. Cleveland: Meridian, 1964.

———. *The Gift of Black Folk*. 1924. New York: Washington Square, 1970.

———. "The Nature of Intellectual Freedom." *W. E. B. Du Bois Speaks: Speeches and Addresses, 1920–1963*. Ed. Philip Foner. New York: Pathfinder, 1970. 232–34.

———. "The Revelation of St. Orgne the Damned." *W. E. B. Du Bois Speaks: Speeches and Addresses, 1920–1963*. Ed. Philip Foner. New York: Pathfinder, 1970. 100–23.

Duvall, John N. "Naming Invisible Authority: Toni Morrison's Covert Letter to Ralph Ellison." *Studies in American Fiction* 25.2 (Autumn 1997): 241–53.

Ellison, Ralph. "The Alain Locke Symposium." *Harvard Advocate* 107 (Spring 1974): 19–28.

———. "Big White Fog." *New Masses* 12 Nov. 1940: 22–23.

———. Blurb. *Hue and Cry.* By James A. McPherson. Boston: Atlantic Monthly, 1969.

———. *The Collected Essays of Ralph Ellison.* Ed. John F. Callahan. New York: Modern Library, 1995.

———. "Editorial Comment." *Negro Quarterly* 1 (Winter–Spring 1943): 295–302.

———. "The Essential Ellison." Interview. *Y'Bird Magazine* 1 (Autumn 1977): 126–59.

———. Foreword. *There Is a Tree More Ancient Than Eden.* By Leon Forrest. New York: Random House, 1973. N. pag.

———. *Going to the Territory.* New York: Random House, 1986. Cited as *GTT.*

———. "The Great Migration." *New Masses* 2 Dec. 1941: 23–24.

———. "Indivisible Man." Interview. *Atlantic Monthly* December 1970: 45–60.

———. "An Interview with Ralph Ellison." *The Black American Writer I.* Ed. C. W. E. Bigsby. Baltimore: Penguin Books, 1969. 153–68.

———. "Invisible Man." *Horizon* Oct. 1947: 104–18.

———. *Invisible Man.* Thirtieth Anniversary Edition. New York: Random House, 1982. Cited as *IM.* This edition contains the complete version of the author's indispensable new preface. The publication page lists the years 1947 (when the first chapter appeared in the English magazine *Horizon*), 1948 (when that chapter appeared in America in '48 Magazine of the Year), and 1952 (when the entire novel first appeared) as copyright dates and February 1972 as the first issue date of the Vintage paperback edition. The 1982 issue date of the Thirtieth Anniversary Edition was somehow omitted, which has created bibliographic confusion.

———. Notes for "Negroes of New York," ts. Ralph Ellison Papers. Library of Congress.

———. "On Initiation Rites and Power: Ralph Ellison Speaks at West Point." *Contemporary Literature* 15 (1974): 165–86.

———. "Ralph Ellison: Twenty Years After." Interview. 1971. *Studies in American Fiction* 1 (1973): 1–23.

———. "Richard Wright and Recent Negro Fiction." *Direction* 4 (Summer 1941): 12–13.

———. *Shadow and Act.* 1966. New York: Random House, 1964. Cited as *S&A.* This is the authorized first paperback reprint of the 1964 hardcover edition.

———. "Stormy Weather." *New Masses* 24 Sept. 1940: 20–21.

———. "Study and Experience." Interview. *Massachusetts Review* 18 (Autumn 1977): 417–35.

———. "Transition." *Negro Quarterly* 1 (Spring 1942): 87–92.

Ellison, Ralph, and Albert Murray. *Trading Twelves: The Selected Letters of Ralph Ellison and Albert Murray.* Ed. Murray and John F. Callahan. New York: Vintage Books, 2001. Cited as *TT.*

Epstein, Mikhail. "Tom Wolfe and Social(ist) Realism." *Common Knowledge* 1.2 (1992): 147–60.

Fabre, Michel. *The Unfinished Quest of Richard Wright*. New York: Morrow, 1973.

Farnsworth, Robert M. *Melvin B. Tolson, 1898–1966: Plain Talk and Poetic Prophecy*. Columbia: University of Missouri Press, 1984.

———. "Ralph Ellison Still Working to Reveal His 'Invisible Man.'" *Kansas City Star* 7 Sept. 1986: 1D+.

Fischer, Russell. "*Invisible Man* as History." *CLA Journal* 17 (Mar. 1974): 338–67.

Fitzgerald, F. Scott. *The Great Gatsby*. New York: Scribner's, 1925.

Forrest, Leon. "America's 'Little Man' Comes Out of Hiding in *Going to the Territory*." *Chicago Tribune* 10 Aug. 1986, sec. 14: 11.

———. "Luminosity from the Lower Frequencies." Harper and Wright 82–97.

———. *Relocations of the Spirit*. Wakefield: Asphodel/Moyer Bell, 1994.

Fox, Robert Elliot. *Conscientious Sorcerers: The Black Postmodernist Fiction of LeRoi Jones / Amiri Baraka, Ishmael Reed, and Samuel R. Delany*. New York: Greenwood, 1987.

Franklin, John Hope. Foreword. *Chant of Saints: A Gathering of Afro-American Literature, Art, and Scholarship*. Ed. Michael S. Harper and Robert B. Stepto. Chicago: University of Illinois Press, 1979. ix–xi.

———. *From Slavery to Freedom*. New York: Knopf, 1947.

Frazier, E. Franklin. *Black Bourgeoisie: The Rise of a New Middle Class in the United States*. 2nd ed. New York: Macmillan, 1962.

Fuller, Hoyt. "Books Noted." *Negro Digest* Aug. 1965: 51–52.

Gardner, John. *On Moral Fiction*. New York: Basic Books, 1978.

Gates, Henry Louis, Jr. *The Signifying Monkey: A Theory of Afro-American Literary Criticism*. New York: Oxford University Press, 1988.

———. *Thirteen Ways of Looking at a Black Man*. New York: Random House, 1997.

Gayle, Addison. *The Way of the New World: The Black Novel in America*. Garden City: Anchor, 1975.

Gerhart, Mary, and Anthony C. Yu, eds. *Morphologies of Faith: Essays in Religion and Culture in Honor of Nathan A. Scott, Jr.* Atlanta: Scholars, 1990.

Goldberger, Avriel. *Visions of a New Hero: The Heroic Life according to André Malraux and Earlier Advocates of Human Grandeur*. Paris: Minard, 1965.

Gouldner, Alvin, ed. *Studies in Leadership: Leadership and Democratic Action*. 1950. New York: Russell and Russell, 1965.

Graff, Gerald. *Literature against Itself*. Chicago: University of Chicago Press, 1979.

Graham, Maryemma, and Amritjit Singh. *Conversations with Ralph Ellison*. Jackson: University Press of Mississippi, 1995.

Greenlee, James W. *Malraux's Heroes and History*. DeKalb: Northern Illinois University Press, 1975.

Gregory, Richard, ed. *The Oxford Companion to the Mind*. New York: Oxford University Press, 1987.

Grossvogel, David. *The Blasphemers: The Theatre of Brecht, Ionesco, Genet*. Ithaca: Cornell University Press, 1966.

Harper, Michael S., and John S. Wright, eds. *A Ralph Ellison Festival*. Spec. issue of *Carleton Miscellany* 18.3 (1980): 3–242.

Harper, Michael S., and Robert B. Stepto, eds. *Chant of Saints: A Gathering of Afro-American Literature, Art, and Scholarship*. Chicago: University of Illinois Press, 1979.

Harris, Max. "The Sacramental World of Nathan A. Scott, Jr." *Religious Studies Review* 20 (Apr. 1994): 121–24.

Harris, Trudier. *Exorcising Blackness: Historical and Literary Lynching and Burning Rituals*. Bloomington: University of Indiana Press, 1984.

Harris-Lopez, Trudier. *South of Tradition: Essays on African American Literature*. Athens, GA: University of Georgia Press, 2002.

Hemingway, Ernest. "A Clean, Well-Lighted Place." *The Fifth Column and the First Forty-Nine Stories*. New York: Scribner's, 1939. 477–81.

Hicks, Granville. "The Grounds for Dissent." *New York Times Book Review* Jan. 1956: 7.

———, ed. *The Living Novel: A Symposium*. New York: Macmillan, 1957.

———. "The Shortcomings of Liberalism." *New Leader* 33 (19 Aug. 1950): 22–24.

Hincliffe, Arnold. *The Absurd*. New York: Barnes and Noble, 1969.

Hoover, Dwight, ed. *Understanding Negro History*. Chicago: Quadrangle, 1968.

Horvath, Violet M. *André Malraux: The Human Adventure*. New York: New York University Press, 1969.

Hughes, Carl Milton. *The Negro Novelist: A Discussion of the Writings of American Negro Novelists, 1940–1950*. New York: Citadel, 1953.

Hughes, Langston. "The Need for Heroes." *Crisis* June 1941: 185+.

Hyman, Stanley Edgar. *The Armed Vision*. Rev. ed. New York: Random House, 1955.

Isaacs, Harold. *The New World of Negro Americans*. London: Phoenix House, 1963.

Jackson, Lawrence. *Ralph Ellison: Emergence of Genius*. New York: Wiley, 2002.

James, Henry. *The Bostonians*. Introd. Lionel Trilling. London: Lehmann, 1952.

Jameson, Frederic. *Postmodernism, Or, The Cultural Logic of Late Capitalism*. London: Verso, 1991.

Jarrett, Keith. Foreword. *The Complete Guide to High-End Audio*. By Robert Harley. 2nd ed. Albuquerque: Acapella Publishing, 1998. xvii–xviii.

Jenkins, Cecil. *André Malraux*. New York: Twayne Publishers, 1972.

Johnson, Abby, and Ronald Johnson. *Propaganda and Aesthetics: The Literary Politics of Afro-American Magazines in the Twentieth Century*. Amherst: University of Massachusetts Press, 1979.

Johnson, Anne Janette. "John Edgar Wideman." *Contemporary Black Biography*. Vol. 5. Detroit: Gale, 1994. 277–81.

———. "Julius Lester." *Contemporary Black Biography*. Vol. 9. Detroit: Gale, 1995. 138–41.

Johnson, Charles. *Being and Race: Black Writing Since 1970*. Bloomington: Indiana University Press, 1988.

———. *Faith and the Good Thing.* New York: Viking, 1974.

———. Introduction to John Gardner. *On Writers and Writing.* Ed. Stewart O'Nan. New York: Addison-Wesley, 1994. vii–xxi.

———. "Philosophy and Black Fiction." *Obsidian* 6 (Spring–Summer 1980): 55–61.

———. "The Singular Vision of Ralph Ellison." *Turning the Wheel: Essays on Buddhism and Writing.* New York: Scribner's, 2003. 105–11.

———. *The Sorcerer's Apprentice.* New York: Atheneum, 1986.

Jones, LeRoi, and Larry Neal, eds. *Black Fire: An Anthology of Afro-American Writing.* New York: Morrow, 1968.

Judy, Ronald A. T., and Jonathan Arac, eds. *Ralph Ellison: The Next Fifty Years.* Spec. issue of *Boundary 2* 30.2 (2003). Durham: Duke University Press, 2003.

Karl, Frederick. *The Adversary Literature: The English Novel in the Eighteenth Century.* New York: Farrar, Straus and Giroux, 1974.

Kellman, Steven G. "The Bonfire of the Vanities." *Magill's Literary Annual, 1988.* Ed. Frank N. Magill. Pasadena: Salem, 1988. 112–15.

Koch, Adrienne. Rev. of *The Hero in History: A Study in Limitation and Possibility,* by Sidney Hook. *Weekly Book Review* 6 June 1943: 16.

Kostelanetz, Richard. "The Politics of Ellison's Booker: *Invisible Man* as Symbolic History." *The Black Novelist.* Ed. Robert Hemenway. Columbus: Merrill, 1970. 5–26.

———. "Ralph Ellison: Novelist as Brown-Skinned Aristocrat." *Shenandoah* 20 (Summer 1969): 56–77.

Krupnick, Mark. *Lionel Trilling and the Fate of Cultural Criticism.* Evanston: Northwestern University Press, 1986.

Lee, Alfred McClung, and Norman D. Humphrey. *Race Riot.* New York: Dryden, 1943.

Lester, Julius. *The Long Journey Home: Stories from Black History.* New York: Dial, 1972.

———. *Look Out, Whitey! Black Power's Gon' Get Your Mama.* New York: Dial, 1968.

———. *Lovesong: Becoming a Jew.* New York: Holt, Rinehart and Winston, 1988.

———. "The Quiet Power of Ralph Ellison." *Boston Sunday Globe* 13 July 1986: A13+.

———. *Search for the New Land: History as Subjective Experience.* New York: Dial, 1969.

———. *The Tales of Uncle Remus.* Illustrated by Jerry Pinckney. 3 vols. New York: Dial, 1987–90.

Levin, Harry. *The Power of Blackness: Hawthorne, Poe, Melville.* New York: Knopf, 1958.

Levine, Lawrence. *Black Culture and Black Consciousness: Afro-American Folk Thought from Slavery to Freedom.* New York: Oxford University Press, 1975.

Lewis, R. W. B. *The American Adam: Innocence, Tragedy, and Tradition in the Nineteenth Century.* Chicago: University of Chicago Press, 1955.

———. "The Ceremonial Imagination of Ralph Ellison." Harper and Wright 34–38.

———. "Ellison's Essays." *New York Review of Books* 28 Jan. 1965: 19–20.

———. "Lionel Trilling and the New Stoicism." *Hudson Review* 3.2 (Summer 1950): 313–17.

Locke, Alain. "Cultural Relativism and Ideological Peace." *Approaches to World Peace*. Ed. Lyman Bryson, Louis Finkelstein, and Robert M. MacIver. New York: Conference on Science, Philosophy, and Religion, 1944. 609–18.

———. "Freedom through Art: A Review of Negro Art, 1870–1938." *Crisis* July 1938: 227–29.

———. "Negro Contributions to America." *World Tomorrow* June 1929: 255–57.

———. "The Negro in American Culture." *Black Voices*. Ed. Abraham Chapman. New York: New American Library, 1968. 523–38.

———. "The Negro Poets of the United States." *Anthology of Magazine Verse for 1926 and Yearbook of American Poetry*. Ed. William Stanley Braithwaite. Boston: Brimmer, 1926. 143–51.

———. "The Negro's Contribution to American Culture." *Journal of Negro Education* July 1939: 521–29.

———, ed. *The New Negro: An Interpretation*. 1925. New York: Atheneum, 1970.

———. "Pluralism and Ideological Peace." *Freedom and Experience: Essays Presented to Horace Kallen*. Ed. Sidney Hook and Milton Konvitz. Ithaca: Cornell University Press, 1947. 63–69.

———. "Pluralism and Intellectual Democracy." *Second Symposium*. Ed. Lyman Bryson, Louis Finkelstein, and Robert M. MacIver. New York: Conference on Science, Philosophy, and Religion, 1942. 196–209.

Lott, Eric. "Hip-Hop Fiction." *Nation* 19 Dec. 1988: 691–92.

———. "Home-Boy Ralph E. Stakes Out His Turf." *In These Times* 29 Apr.–5 May 1987: 20.

———. *Love and Theft: Blackface Minstrelsy and the American Working Class*. New York: Oxford University Press, 1993.

Maguire, Roberta S. *Conversations with Albert Murray*. Jackson: University Press of Mississippi, 1997.

Malraux, André. *Days of Wrath*. Trans. Haakon M. Chevalier. New York: Random House, 1936. Trans. of *Le Temps du mépris*. Paris: Gallimard, 1935.

———. *Man's Fate*. Trans. Haakon M. Chevalier. New York: Smith and Haas, 1934. Trans. of *La Condition humaine*. Paris: Gallimard, 1933.

———. *Man's Hope*. Trans. Stuart Gilbert and Alastair Macdonald. New York: Random House, 1938. Trans. of *L'Espoir*. Paris: Gallimard, 1937.

———. *The Voices of Silence*. Bollingen Series 24. Princeton: Princeton University Press, 1978. Revision of *The Psychology of Art*. 3 vols. Trans. Stuart Gilbert. New York: Pantheon, 1949–51. Trans. of *La Psychologie de l'art*. 3 vols. Geneva: Skira, 1947–50.

Margolies, Edward. *Native Sons: A Critical Study of Twentieth Century Negro American Authors*. Philadelphia: Lippincott, 1968.

Marty, M. E. Rev. of *The Democratic Vista*, by Richard Chase. *Christian Century* 20 Aug. 1958: 948+.

McCormick, John. *Catastrophe and Imagination: An Interpretation of the Recent English and American Novel*. London: Longmans, Green, 1957.

McSweeney, Kerry. *Invisible Man: Race and Identity*. Boston: Twayne Publishers, 1988.

McWillliams, Jim, ed. *Passing the Three Gates: Interviews with Charles Johnson*. Seattle: University of Washington Press, 2004.

Menand, Louis. *Discovering Modernism: T. S. Eliot and His Context*. New York: Oxford University Press, 1987.

———. "Edmund Wilson." *The Johns Hopkins Guide to Literary Theory and Criticism*. Ed. Michael Groden and Martin Kreiswirth. Baltimore: Johns Hopkins University Press, 1994. 734–35.

———. "Literature and Liberation: *Going to the Territory*, by Ralph Ellison." *New Republic* 4 Aug. 1986: 37–40.

Menand, Louis, Leslie Berlowitz, and Denis Donoghue, eds. *America in Theory*. New York: Oxford University Press, 1988.

Metzger, Sheri Elaine. "David Henry Bradley, Jr." *Contemporary Black Biography*. Vol. 39. Detroit: Thomson-Gale, 2003. 25–28.

Mills, C. Wright. Rev. of *The Hero in History*, by Sidney Hook. *New Republic* 21 June 1943: 834.

Morrison, Toni. "Behind the Making of *The Black Book*." *Black World* Feb. 1974: 86–90.

Morace, Robert A. "On Moral Fiction." *Masterplots II: Nonfiction Series*. Vol. 3. Ed. Frank Magill. Englewood Cliffs: Salem, 1989. 1077–81.

Moses, Wilson. "The Rising Tide of Color." *The Golden Age of Black Nationalism*. Hamden: Archon, 1978. 251–71.

Mumford, Lewis. *Sketches from Life: The Autobiography of Lewis Mumford; The Early Years*. New York: Dial, 1982.

———. "Utopia, the City, and the Machine." *Interpretations and Forecasts, 1922–1972: Studies in Literature, Biography, Technics, and Contemporary Society*. New York: Harcourt Brace Jovanovich, 1975. 241–58.

Murray, Albert. *The Blue Devils of Nada*. New York: Pantheon Books, 1996.

———. *From the Briarpatch File: On Context, Procedure, and American Identity*. New York: Pantheon Books, 2001.

———. *The Hero and the Blues*. New York: Random House, 1973.

———. *The Omni-Americans: New Perspectives on Black Experience and American Culture*. New York: Dutton, 1970.

———. *South to a Very Old Place*. New York: McGraw-Hill, 1971.

Myrdal, Gunnar. *An American Dilemma*. New York: Harper and Row, 1944.

Nadel, Alan. *Invisible Criticism: Ralph Ellison and the American Canon*. Iowa City: University of Iowa Press, 1988.

Neal, Larry. "Afterword: And Shine Swam On." *Black Fire: An Anthology of Afro-American Writing*. Ed. LeRoi Jones and Larry Neal. New York: Morrow, 1968. 637–56.

———. "The Black Writer's Role: Ralph Ellison." *Liberator* Jan. 1966. 9–11.

———. "Ellison's Zoot Suit." *Ralph Ellison: A Collection of Critical Essays*. Ed. John Hersey. Englewood Cliffs: Prentice-Hall, 1974. 58–79.

Nelson, Emmanuel S., ed. *Contemporary African American Novelists: A Bio–Bibliographical Critical Sourcebook*. Westport: Greenwood, 1999.

Newson, Gillian. "David Sarser: A True Recording Idol." *Who's Who in the Roxio Discussion List Community*. 26 Oct. 2001. <http://roxio.com>.

Nye, David. *Electrifying America: Social Meanings of New Technology*. Cambridge: MIT Press, 1990.

O'Brien, John, ed. *Interviews with Black Writers*. New York: Liveright, 1973.

O'Meally, Robert G. *The Craft of Ralph Ellison*. Cambridge: Harvard University Press, 1980.

———, ed. *Living with Music: Ralph Ellison's Jazz Writings*. New York: Modern Library, 2001.

———, ed. *New Essays on Invisible Man*. Cambridge: Cambridge University Press, 1988.

———. "The Rules of Magic: Hemingway as Ellison's 'Ancestor.'" *Southern Review* 21 (1985): 751–69.

Ostendorf, Berndt. "Ralph Waldo Ellison: Anthropology, Modernism, and Jazz." O'Meally 95–121.

Ottley, Roi, and William Weatherby, eds. *The Negro in New York: An Informal Social History, 1626–1940*. New York: Praeger Publishers, 1969.

Pinsker, Sanford. "Lionel Trilling." *The Oxford Encyclopedia of American Literature*. Ed. Jay Parini. New York: Oxford University Press, 2004. 208–12.

Podhoretz, Norman. *Making It*. New York: Random House, 1967.

———. "The Melting Pot Blues." *New York Herald Tribune* 25 Oct. 1964: 1+.

Porter, Horace. *Jazz Country: Ralph Ellison in America*. Iowa City: University of Iowa Press, 2001.

Posnock, Ross. *Color and Culture: Black Writers and the Making of the Modern Intellectual*. Cambridge: Harvard University Press, 1998.

Rampersad, Arnold. *The Life of Langston Hughes*. 2 vols. New York: Oxford University Press, 1986–88.

Rourke, Constance. *American Humor*. 1931. New York: Doubleday, 1953.

———. *The Roots of American Culture*. Ed. Van Wyck Brooks. New York: Harcourt, Brace and World, 1942.

Scott, Nathan A., Jr. *The Broken Center: Studies in the Theological Horizon of Modern Literature*. New Haven: Yale University Press, 1966.

———. "The Dark and Haunted Tower of Richard Wright." *Graduate Comment* 7 (1964): 93–99.

———. "Ellison's Vision of Communitas." Harper and Wright 41–50.

———. "Judgment Marked by a Cellar: The American Negro Writer and the Dialectic of Despair." *University of Denver Quarterly* 2.2 (1967): 5–35. Rpt. in *Cavalcade: Negro American Writing from 1760 to the Present*. Ed. Arthur P. Davis and Saunders Redding. Boston: Houghton Mifflin, 1971. 820–42.

———. "Lionel Trilling's Critique of the Liberal Mind." *Christianity and Society* 16.2 (Spring 1951): 9–18.

———. *Mirrors of Man in Existentialism.* New York: Collins (World Publishing), 1978.

———. *The Poetry of Civic Virtue: Eliot, Malraux, Auden.* Philadelphia: Fortress, 1976.

———. *Rehearsals of Discomposure: Alienation and Reconciliation in Modern Literature.* New York: Columbia University Press, 1952.

———. *Three American Moralists: Mailer, Bellow, Trilling.* London: University of Notre Dame Press, 1973.

"Scott, Nathan A., Jr." *Contemporary Authors: New Revision Series.* Detroit: Gale, 1981.

"Scott, Nathan Alexander, Jr." *Encyclopedia of African American Religions.* Eds. Larry G. Murphy, et al. New York: Garland Publishing, 1993.

Scura, Dorothy M., ed. *Conversations with Tom Wolfe.* Jackson: University Press of Mississippi, 1990.

Segal, Julius. "A Psychologist Views Audiophilia." *High Fidelity: The Magazine for Music Listeners* Sept. 1955: 50.

Sprinkle, Melvin. "A High Efficiency Triode Amplifier." *Radio and Television News* May 1950: 55+.

Stamatel, Janet P. "Cyrus J. Colter." *Contemporary Black Biography.* Vol. 36. Detroit: Thomson-Gale, 2003. 50–53.

Staples, Brent. "In His Own Good Time." *New York Times Book Review* 3 Aug. 1986: 14.

Stepto, Robert B. *From behind the Veil: A Study of Afro-American Narrative.* Chicago: University of Illinois Press, 1979.

———. "Literacy and Hibernation: Ralph Ellison's Invisible Man." Harper and Wright 112–41.

Sundquist, Eric, ed. *Cultural Contexts for Ralph Ellison's Invisible Man.* Boston: St. Martin's, 1995.

Taylor-Guthrie, Danille, ed. *Conversations with Toni Morrison.* Jackson: University Press of Mississippi, 1994.

Trilling, Lionel. *Beyond Culture.* New York: Viking, 1965.

———. Introduction. *The Bostonians.* By Henry James. London: Lehmann, 1952. vii–xv.

———. *The Liberal Imagination: Essays on Literature and Society.* New York: Harcourt Brace Jovanovich, 1950.

———. *The Middle of the Journey.* 1947. New York: New York Review of Books, 2002.

"Trilling, Lionel." *American National Biography.* New York: Oxford University Press, 1999.

Unamuno, Miguel de. *The Agony of Christianity and Essays on Faith.* Trans. Anthony Kerrigan. Princeton: Princeton University Press, 1974.

———. *Novela/Nivola.* Trans. Anthony Kerrigan. Princeton: Princeton University Press, 1976.

———. *The Tragic Sense of Life in Men and Nations.* Trans. Anthony Kerrigan. Princeton: Princeton University Press, 1972.

United States. Kernan Commission. *Report of the National Advisory Commission on Civil Disorders.* New York: Bantam Books, 1968.

Walling, William. "Art and Protest: Ralph Ellison's *Invisible Man* Twenty Years After." *Phylon* 34 (1973): 120–34.

Warren, Kenneth. "Chaos Not Quite Controlled: Ellison's Uncompleted Transit to *Juneteenth." The Cambridge Companion to Ralph Ellison.* Ed. Ross Posnock. New York: Cambridge University Press, 2005. 188–200.

———. *So Black and Blue: Ralph Ellison and the Occasion of Criticism.* Chicago: University of Chicago Press, 2003.

Warren, Robert Penn. "The Unity of Experience." *Commentary* May 1965: 91–96.

Watts, Jerry Gafio. *Heroism and the Black Intellectual: Ralph Ellison, Politics, and Afro-American Intellectual Life.* Chapel Hill: University of North Carolina Press, 1994.

Weisbord, Robert. "Black America and the Italian-Ethiopian Crisis." *Ebony Kinship.* Westport: Greenwood, 1973. 89–114.

Weixlmann, Joe, and John O'Banion. "A Checklist of Ellison Criticism, 1972–1978." *Black American Literature Forum* 12 (Summer 1978): 51–55.

Wellek, René. *A History of Modern Criticism, 1750–1950.* Vol. 6. New Haven: Yale University Press, 1986.

———. "Philosophy and Post War American Criticism." *Concepts of Criticism.* New Haven: Yale University Press. 316–43.

West, Cornel. "Lionel Trilling: Godfather of Neo-Conservatism." *New Politics* ns 1.1 (Summer 1986): 233–42.

Whitehead, Alfred North. *Science and the Modern World.* 1926. London: Free Association Books, 1985.

Whittemore, Reed. "Beating That Boy Again." *New Republic* 14 Nov. 1964: 25–26.

Wideman, John. *The Homewood Books: Hiding Place, Sent for You Yesterday, Damballah.* 1981–85. Pittsburgh: University of Pittsburgh Press, 1992.

———. "What Is Afro? What Is American?" *New York Times Book Review* 3 Aug. 1986: 14–15.

"Wideman, John Edgar." *Contemporary Authors: New Revision Series.* Detroit: Gale, 1998: 415–20.

Wilson, Edmund. *Axel's Castle: A Study in the Imaginative Literature of 1870–1930.* 1931. New York: Scribner's, 1953.

Wolfe, Tom. *The Bonfire of the Vanities.* New York: Farrar, Straus and Giroux, 1987.

———. "The New Journalism." *The New Journalism.* Ed. Wolfe and E. W. Johnson. New York: Harper and Row, 1974. 3–52.

———. "Stalking the Billion-Footed Beast: A Literary Manifesto for the New Social Novel." *Harper's* Nov. 1989: 45–56.

Wright, John S. "Chimed Chants from Dark and Dutiful Dyelis: A Review Essay." Harper and Wright 215–30.

———. "The Conscious Hero and the Rites of Man: Ellison's War." O'Meally 157–86.

———. "Dedicated Dreamer, Consecrated Acts: Shadowing Ellison." Harper and Wright 142–99.

———. "Jack-the-Bear Dreaming: Ellison's Spiritual Technologies." Judy and Arac 175–94.

———. "To the Battle Royal: Ralph Ellison and the Quest for Black Leadership in Postwar America." *Recasting America: Culture and Politics in the Age of Cold War.* Ed. Lary May. Chicago: University of Chicago Press, 1988. 246–66.

Wright, Richard. "Blueprint for Negro Literature." *Amistad* 2. Ed. John A. Williams and Charles Harris. New York: Random House, 1971. 3–20. Rpt. of "Blueprint for Negro Writing." *New Challenge* 1 (Fall 1937).

———. "How Bigger Was Born." Afterword. *Native Son.* By Wright. New York: Library of America, 1991. 853–81.

Index